A COMPILATION OF WORKS LISTED IN GRANGER'S INDEX TO POETRY 1904-1978

A COMPILATION OF WORKS LISTED IN GRANGER'S INDEX TO POETRY 1904-1978

A cumulative and complete listing by Granger Symbol, Title, and Author of over 1500 works analyzed and indexed in *Granger's Index to Poetry* from the First Edition of 1904 to the Edition of 1978.

Prepared by
The Editorial Board
Granger Book Co., Inc.

GRANGER BOOK CO., INC.
GREAT NECK, NEW YORK

Copyright © Granger Book Co., Inc. 1980
All rights reserved

Library of Congress Cataloging in Publication Data

Main entry uder title:

A compilation of works listed in Granger's Index to
  poetry, 1904–1978.

     1. Poetry–Bibliography. 2. English poetry–
Bibliography. 3. Recitations–Bibliography. 4. Granger, Edith. Index to poetry and recitations.
I. Granger Book Co. II. Title.
Z7156.A1C64   [PN1111]   016.80881   80-65559
ISBN 0-89609-201-1

CONTENTS

Preface vii

Introduction ix

Granger Symbol List
    Direction for Use 1
    List of Works 3

Title List
    Directions for Use 121
    List of Works 121

Author List
    Directions for Use 161
    List of Works 161

PREFACE

This work is intended to provide a complete and cumulative list of all the works which have been analyzed in all of the editions of *Granger's Index to Poetry*.

It does not, however, pretend to be more. It is not in itself an index and does not in any way supplant *Granger's* or abate its usefulness. Indeed, it is hoped that this volume, by accurately and completely bringing together in one source for the first time material contained in eleven editions and supplements of *Granger's*, will further enhance that indispensable reference.

Granger Book Co., Inc., the publisher of this work, does not publish *Granger's Index to Poetry* and has no affiliation with it. Granger Book Co. primarily publishes reprint editions of works which are listed in *Granger's*.

INTRODUCTION

Granger's Index to Poetry and Recitations was first published in 1904 by the A. C. McClurg Co. as a guide to anthologized verse and prose recitations. Subsequently, it has gone through six additional editions and five intervening supplements for a total of eleven volumes to date (through the 1978 Edition covering 1970-1977 which has replaced what would have been the Supplement for the period 1970-1975).

The first three editions and the first supplement were published by McClurg. Columbia University Press, the present publisher, assumed full editorial and publishing responsibilities in 1945 with the Supplement 1938-1944.

The volumes published by McClurg and the 1945 Supplement included prose selections. Recitations, and all prose selections, were dropped in the Fourth Edition which caused "and Recitations" to be omitted from the title.

Granger's Index to Poetry has become a standard reference tool for academic and public libraries. By enabling the reader to locate and identify poems and selections from poems that have been published in anthologies, it provides an indispensable reference service. Its reference utility and reliability have been further strengthened by the academic and professional excellence brought to it by the Editorial Staff of the Columbia University Press.

Granger's, however, is not cumulative, so that many works included in earlier editions are omitted in later ones. The general rule employed *ab initio* for the continued inclusion of a work is its in-print status; works are eliminated from subsequent editions when they have gone out-of-print or are not likely to be found in the average small library.

While the non-cumulative feature is consistent with *Granger's* original purpose to provide an index to the most accessible anthologies in small libraries, it may not fully serve the larger needs of other libraries. Sheehy *(Guide to Reference Books,* 9th ed.) recommends that "most libraries will find it advantageous to keep all (editions)."

INTRODUCTION x

The retention or acquisition of earlier editions has heretofore been the sole means of providing a complete access to all the works listed in all editions of *Granger's*.[1] Such accumulation of earlier volumes, however, has been difficult because each edition generally goes out-of-print at the time of publication of the succeeding edition.[2] Furthermore, as there are inconsistencies between editions, errors and inaccuracies in the early editions, and voluminous duplication of material among editions, the collection of all editions of *Granger's* does not satisfactorily alleviate the difficulties caused by the continual revision of *Granger's Index to Poetry*.

It is believed, therefore, that there is a need and application for a single source listing of all the works which have been indexed and analyzed in all editions and supplements of *Granger's* to date. Such a volume, by listing each work separately, by Granger Symbol, title, and author, and identifying the particular edition of *Granger's* wherein the work can be located, will enhance access to the great resource of *Granger's Index to Poetry*.

In addition, this listing can be utilized as a checklist of a library's *Granger* collection and in the selection of anthologies for purchase.

Arrangement

This volume lists the works which have been listed in *Granger's* in three ways: (1) by Granger Symbol, (2) by Title, and (3) by Author.

(1) Granger Symbol. This is the principal list in which the most complete information for each work is provided. Works are listed alphabetically by Granger Symbol (the brief alphabetical code assigned to identifying each work indexed in *Granger's)*. This conforms to the scheme of *Granger's*, wherein the complete title of a work and all its relevant publishing information are con-

---

[1] The New York Public Library, however, has attempted an alternative solution by gathering, in separate volumes, photographically reproduced copies of the Key to Symbols sections of particular editions of *Granger's*. Such volumes for 1918-1929 and 1940-1953 are maintained (and are annotated with NYPL location of the works indexed); similar volumes for other periods apparently have not been undertaken.

[2] The editors of Columbia University Press themselves had difficulty in locating copies of the Third Edition in preparing the Fourth; librarians who provided copies were gratefully acknowledged in the Preface.

tained in the Key to Symbols section, and the symbols are listed after the appropriate entries in the Title and First Line Indexes.

Reference to this list has been made from (i) the Title List (including variant titles) and (ii) the Author List.

(2) Title. Each work is listed alphabetically by its title as it appears on the title page. The title entry gives the work's Granger Symbol facilitating access to the principal list. Variant titles are also shown.

(3) Author. All works are listed alphabetically by author. Co-authors are also listed. The author entry provides: (i) main title and (ii) Granger Symbol.

A COMPILATION OF WORKS LISTED IN GRANGER'S INDEX TO POETRY 1904-1978

GRANGER SYMBOL LIST

Directions for Use: The Granger Symbol List is the principal list in which the most complete information is given for each work.

Works are listed alphabetically by Granger Symbol (the brief alphabetical code assigned to and identifying each work indexed in *Granger's)*. The Granger Symbol appears in the left column preceding each entry. Space is left after each symbol for the insertion of library call numbers.

When a symbol has been assigned to different works in two or more editions of *Granger's*, the second usage is indicated by an asterisk. When the symbol for a particular work has been changed from one edition of *Granger's* to another, the last form used is employed here as the primary symbol, and the earlier form is cross-referenced.

Every symbol created by every edition of *Granger's* is listed separately, whether duplicated or replaced, with cross-reference to the main symbol.

Title. The title given for each work is the title as listed in *Granger's* Key to Symbols (except where erroneous and incomplete titles have been corrected); variant titles are also given. Subtitles are not provided except when necessary to distinguish similarly titled works.

Reference to other editions of a work which are also indexed is made.

Author. The author's name given is the name which appears on the title page of the work. When this name is pseudonymous, the author's full legal name (when known) is provided.

Publication. The date of original publication is provided in parenthesis following the author's name. Other editions of the work assigned the same symbol in other editions of *Granger's* are also shown with publication dates. Publisher names are not given except where necessary to identify a work.

Editions of Granger's. The particular edition(s) of *Granger's* wherein a work is indexed is provided in the last line of each entry in the form of an alpha-numeric code. The letters and numbers represent particular editions and supplements of *Granger's:*

Code	Edition
1	First (1904)
2	Second (1918)
A	Supplement 1918-1928 (1929)
3	Third (1940)
B	Supplement 1938-1944 (1945)
4	Fourth (1953)
C	Supplement 1951-1955 (1957)
5	Fifth (1962)
D	Supplement 1960-1965 (1967)
6	Sixth (1973)
E	1970-1977 Edition (1978)

Where a different symbol for the same work was used in an earlier edition of *Granger's* the former symbol and the relevant edition are referred to in brackets following the code.

Example

MAPA [1]   MODERN AMERICAN POETS. [2] Conrad Aiken, ed. [3] (1927) [4] Enlarged edition of 1963 has title TWENTIETH-CENTURY AMERICAN POETRY, see TwAmPo[5] 6-5-4-3-A [6]   [MAP in A] [7]

(1) **MAPA** is the work's Granger Symbol;
(2) MODERN AMERICAN POETS is the main title;
(3) Conrad Aiken is the editor of the work;
(4) 1927 was the date of original publication;
(5) A later edition, in 1963, with a variant title, TWENTIETH-CENTURY AMERICAN POETRY, is also indexed in *Granger's;* full information regarding the later edition can be found in the main entry at the Granger Symbol identifying it, **TwAmPo**;
(6) MODERN AMERICAN POETS has been indexed in the

Sixth, Fifth, Fourth, & Third Editions of *Granger's* and in the Supplement 1919-1928;

(7) This work was originally assigned the symbol **MAP** in the Supplement 1919-1928 before being changed to its present form in the Third Edition.

AA *PS 586 .S7*	AMERICAN ANTHOLOGY, AN, 1787-1900. Edmond Clarence Stedman, ed. (1900) 6-5-4-3-2-1
AAS *1900a O*	ANCHOR ANTHOLOGY OF SIXTEENTH-CENTURY VERSE, THE. Richard S. Sylvester, ed. (1974) E
AATT *O*	ADAM AMONG THE TELEVISION TREES. Virginia R. Mollenkott, ed. (1974) E
AB 1-2 *O*	AUTHORS' BIRTHDAYS: TWENTY-FIVE PROGRAMS FOR CELEBRATING AUTHORS' BIRTHDAYS, Vols. I-II. Alice M. Kellogg, comp. (1896) 2
ABF *O*	AMERICAN BALLADS AND FOLK SONGS. John A. Lomax & Alan Lomax, comps. (1934) 6-5-4-3
ABS *PS 593 .L9 P7*	AMERICAN BALLADS AND SONGS. Louise Pound, ed. (1922) 5-4-3
ABVC *O*	ANOTHER BOOK OF VERSES FOR CHILDREN. Edward Verrall Lucas, ed. (1907) 3-2
ACP *PR 1195 .C4 L4*	ANTHOLOGY OF CATHOLIC POETS, AN. Shane Leslie, ed. (1925; rev. ed., 1953) 6-5-C-4-3-A
ACV *O*	ANTHOLOGY OF COMMONWEALTH VERSE, AN. Margaret J. O'Donnell, ed. (1963) 6-D
AD *O*	ARBOR DAY MANUAL. Charles Rufus Skinner, ed. (1890) 2-1
AD *	See **AOAH**
ADAH *O*	ARBOR DAY (Our American Holidays Series). Robert Haven Schauffler, ed. (1909)

ADP 4

    5-4-3-2 [OAA in 2]

ADP ARBOR DAY IN POETRY. Carnegie Library School Association, comp. (1926)
    A

ADP * ARBOR DAY PROGRAM, No. 1. FOR MIXED GRADES. Alice M. Kellogg. (1896). For ARBOR DAY PROGRAM, No. 2, see **NAE**
    3-2

ADPR ARBOR DAY IN THE PRIMARY ROOM. Susie M. Best (et al). (1907)
    3-2

AE ADVANCED ELOCUTION. Mrs. J. W. Shoemaker [Rachel W. (Hinkle) Shoemaker]. (1896)
    3-2-1

AE * ANALYTICAL ELOCUTION. James Edward Murdock. (1884)
    1

AEP-D ANTHOLOGY OF ENGLISH POETRY, AN: DRYDEN TO BLAKE. Kathleen Campbell, comp. (1930)
    4-3

AEP-W ANTHOLOGY OF ENGLISH POETRY, AN: WYATT TO DRYDEN. Kathleen Campbell, comp. (1930)
    4-3

AEV ANTHOLOGY OF ENGLISH VERSE, AN. John Drinkwater, ed. (1924)
    5-4-3-A

AFP ANTHOLOGY OF FRENCH POETRY. Henry Carrington, tr. (1900)
    4-3-2

AFV AMERICAN FAMILIAR VERSE, VERS DE SOCIETE. Brander Matthews, ed. (1904)
811.08 M43
    2

AGP ANTHOLOGY OF GERMAN POETRY THROUGH THE 19th CENTURY. Alexander Gode & Frederick Ungar, eds. (1964)
831.08 G538a
    D

AH 1-2 AMERICAN HISTORY BY AMERICAN POETS, Vols. I-II. Mrs. Nellie (Urner) Wallington, ed. (1911)
    2

AI AMERICAN IDEA, THE. Joseph B. Gilder, comp. (1902)
1

AIW AS I WALKED OUT ONE EVENING. Helen Plotz, comp. (1976)
E

AKE ALL KINDS OF EVERYTHING. Louis Dudek, ed. (1973)
Al. Coll.
P823 D8A4
E

AL AMERICAN LYRICS. Edith Rickert & Jessie Parton, comps. (1912)
811.08
B42
2

AlBD ALL THE BEST DOG POEMS. Edwin Burtis, comp. (1946)
5-4

AlDL ALL DAY LONG. Pamela Whitlock, comp. (1954)
5

ALG ALL IN A LIFETIME. Edgar A. Guest. (1938)
3

ALV ANTHOLOGY OF LIGHT VERSE, AN. Louis Kronenberger, ed. (1935)
6-5-4-3

AMA AMERICAN POETRY 1927; a miscellany. Louis Untermeyer, ed. (1927). For editions of 1922 & 1925, see **AP-2, AP-5**
A

AmD AMERICAN DECADE. Tom Boggs, ed. (1943)
4

AmePo AMERICAN POETS, THE, 1800-1900. Edwin H. Cady, ed. (1966)
6

AmFN AMERICA FOREVER NEW. Sarah Brewton & John E. Brewton, comps. (1968)
6

AmFP AMERICAN FOLK POETRY. Duncan Emrich, ed. (1974)
PS 477
.E5
E

AmLP AMERICAN LYRIC POEMS. Elder Olson, ed. (1964)
6-D

AMMV AMERICAN MYSTICAL VERSE. Irene Hunter,

AmNP   6

                            comp. (1925)
                            A
AmNP   AMERICAN NEGRO POETRY. Arna Bontemps,
PS 591   ed. (1963)
.N4B58   6-D
AmP   AMERICAN POETRY (American Literary Forms).
O   Karl Shapiro, ed. (1960)
                    6-5
AmP *   See APL
AmPA   AMERICAN POETRY ANTHOLOGY, THE.
PS 614   Daniel Halpern, ed. (1975)
.A612   E
AmPC   AMERICAN POEMS. Jascha Kessler, ed. (1964)
PS 614 .K45 6-D
AmPo   AMERICAN POETRY (Living Masterpieces of
O   American Literature, Vol. IV). Randall Stewart
                    & Dorothy Bethurum, eds. (1954)
                    5-C
AmPP   AMERICAN POETRY AND PROSE. Norman
O   Foerster, ed. (3d ed., 1947; 4th ed., 1957;
                    5th ed., 1970)
                    6-5-4
AmSS   AMERICAN SEA SONGS AND CHANTEYS.
O   Frank Shay, ed. (1948). Edition of 1924 had
                    title IRON MEN AND WOODEN SHIPS
                    6-5-4
AmSS *   AMERICAN STAR SPEAKER, THE, AND
                    MODEL ELOCUTIONIST. Charles Walter
O   Brown, comp. (1902)
                    2
AMV-1   ANTHOLOGY OF MAGAZINE VERSE FOR
O   1913. William Stanley Braithwaite, ed. (1913)
                    2
AMV-2   ANTHOLOGY OF MAGAZINE VERSE FOR
PS 614   1914. William Stanley Braithwaite, ed. (1914)
.A678   2
AMV-3   ANTHOLOGY OF MAGAZINE VERSE FOR
Same   1915. William Stanley Braithwaite, ed. (1915)
                    2
AMV-4   ANTHOLOGY OF MAGAZINE VERSE FOR
Same   1916. William Stanley Braithwaite, ed. (1916)
                    2

(1914-1929)

AMV-24 *PS 614 .A678*	ANTHOLOGY OF MAGAZINE VERSE FOR 1924. William Stanley Braithwaite, ed. (1924) A
AMV-25 *same*	ANTHOLOGY OF MAGAZINE VERSE FOR 1925. William Stanley Braithwaite, ed. (1925) A
AMV-26 *same*	ANTHOLOGY OF MAGAZINE VERSE FOR 1926. William Stanley Braithwaite, ed. (1926) A
AMV-35 *O*	ANTHOLOGY OF MAGAZINE VERSE FOR 1935, AND YEARBOOK OF AMERICAN POETRY. Alan F. Pater, comp. (1936) 3
AMV-36 *O*	ANTHOLOGY OF MAGAZINE VERSE FOR 1936, AND YEARBOOK OF AMERICAN POETRY. Alan F. Pater, comp. (1937) 3
AMV-37 *O*	ANTHOLOGY OF MAGAZINE VERSE FOR 1937, AND YEARBOOK OF AMERICAN POETRY. Alan F. Pater, comp. (1938). For edition of 1942, see AnMaVe 3
AmVN *O*	AMERICAN VERSE OF THE NINETEENTH CENTURY. Richard Gray, ed. (1973) E
AmVo *O*	AMERICAN VOICE; an anthology of current American poetry. (1942) Harbinger House B
AmWr *O*	AMERICAN WRITING, 1943. Alan Swallow, ed. (1944) B
AnAmPo *PS 586 .K7 1941*	ANTHOLOGY OF AMERICAN POETRY, AN. Alfred Kreymborg, ed. (1935; 2d rev. ed., 1941). Edition of 1930 had title LYRIC AMERICA, see LA 6-5-4-B
AnAnS 1-2	ANCHOR ANTHOLOGY OF SEVENTEENTH CENTURY VERSE, THE, Vol. I. Louis L. Martz, ed., Vol. II, Richard S. Sylvester, ed. (1969) 6

AnCaPo

AnCaPo	ANTHOLOGY OF CANADIAN POETRY. Ralph Gustafson, comp. (1942) 4-B
AnCL 868.08 F54a	ANTHOLOGY OF CONTEMPORARY LATIN-AMERICAN POETRY. Dudley Fitts, ed. (Rev. & enl. ed., 1947) 5-4
AnCV	ANTHOLOGY OF CONTEMPORARY VERSE, AN. Margaret J. O'Donnell, comp. (1953) C
AnEC	ANCIENT ENGLISH CAROLS, MCCCC TO MDCC. Edith Rickert, ed. (1928) 5-4
AnEnPo	ANTHOLOGY FOR THE ENJOYMENT OF POETRY. Max Eastman, ed. (1939) 6-5-4-B
AnFE	ANTHOLOGY OF FAMOUS ENGLISH AND AMERICAN POETRY, AN. William Rose Benét & Conrad Aiken, eds. (1945) 6-5-4
AnFP	ANTHOLOGY OF FRENCH POETRY FROM NERVAL TO VALERY IN ENGLISH TRANSLATION, AN. Angel Flores, ed. (1958) 5
AnGP PT 1160 .E5 F55 1965	ANTHOLOGY OF GERMAN POETRY FROM HOLDERLIN TO RILKE IN ENGLISH TRANSLATION, AN. Angel Flores, ed. (1960) 5
AnIA	ANTHOLOGY OF ITALIAN AND ITALO-AMERICAN POETRY. Rodolfo Pucelli, ed. & tr. (1955) C
AnIL	ANTHOLOGY OF IRISH LITERATURE, AN. David H. Greene, ed. (1954) 6-5-C
AnIV PR 8851 .C47 1948	ANTHOLOGY OF IRISH VERSE, AN. Padraic Colum, ed. (1922; rev. ed., 1948) 6-5-4-A [CIV in A]
ANL	ANTHOLOGY OF AMERICAN NEGRO LITERATURE. V. P. Calverton, ed. (1929) 4-3
AnMaVe	ANTHOLOGY OF MAGAZINE VERSE FOR

	1938–1942, AND YEARBOOK OF AMERICAN POETRY. Alan F. Pater, ed. (1942). For earlier editions, see **AMV-35** et seq. B
AnML	ANTHOLOGY OF MEDIEVAL LYRICS, AN. Angel Flores, ed. (1962) D
AnMo	ANCIENTS AND MODERNS: AN ANTHOLOGY OF POETRY. Stewart A. Baker, ed. (1971) E
AnMoPo	ANTHOLOGY OF MODERN POETRY. John Wain, ed. (1963) D
AnMP	ANTHOLOGY OF MEXICAN POETRY. Octavio Paz, comp. (1958) 5
AnNE	ANTHOLOGY OF NEW ENGLAND POETS, AN. Louis Untermeyer, ed. (1948) 6-5-4
AnNoLy	ANTHOLOGY OF NORWEGIAN LYRICS. Charles Wharton Stork, ed. & tr. (1942) 5-4-B
AnNZ	ANTHOLOGY OF NEW ZEALAND VERSE, AN. Robert Chapman & Jonathan Bennett, comps. (1956) 6-5
AnOE	ANTHOLOGY OF OLD ENGLISH POETRY, AN. Charles W. Kennedy, tr. (1960) 6-5
AnRP	ANTHOLOGY OF RECENT POETRY, AN. L. D'O. Walters, comp. (Enl. ed., 1932) 4
AnSL	ANTHOLOGY OF SWEDISH LYRICS, FROM 1750 to 1925. Charles Wharton Stork, ed. & tr. (1930) 5-4
AnSP	ANTHOLOGY OF SPANISH POETRY FROM GARCILASCO TO GARCIA LORCA, AN, IN ENGLISH AND SPANISH ORIGINALS. Angel Flores, ed. (1961) D
AnSpL 1-2	ANTHOLOGY OF SPANISH LITERATURE IN

ANTL

860.8
R31a

  ENGLISH TRANSLATION, AN, Vols. I-II. Seymour Resnick & Jeanne Pasmantier, eds. (1958)
  5

ANTL
 D
  AMERICAN IS NOT ALL TRAFFIC LIGHTS: POEMS OF THE MIDWEST. Alice Fleming, comp. (1976)
  E

ANYP
PS
613
.P3
  ANTHOLOGY OF NEW YORK POETS, AN. Ron Padgett & David Shapiro, eds. (1970)
  6

AOAH
 O
  ARMISTICE DAY (Our American Holiday Series). A. P. Sanford & Robert Haven Schauffler, eds. (1927)
  5-4-3-A [AD in A]

AP
 6
  AMERICAN POEMS (1625-1892). Walter C. Bronson, ed. (1912)
  3-2 [APM in 2]

AP *
 6
  AMERICAN POEMS. Horace Scudder, ed. (1880)
  2-1

AP **
 O
  AMERICAN POETRY. Gay Wilson Allen, Walter B. Rideout, & James K. Robinson, eds. (1965)
  6-D

AP-2
 O
  AMERICAN POETRY, 1922; a miscellany. Louis Untermeyer, ed. (1922). For edition of 1927, see **AMA**
  A

AP-5
 O
  AMERICAN POETRY, 1925; a miscellany. Louis Untermeyer, ed. (1925). For edition of 1927, see **AMA**
  A

APA
 O
  AMERICAN POETRY, 1671-1928. Conrad Aiken, ed. (1929) Revised edition of 1944 has title A COMPREHENSIVE ANTHOLOGY OF AMERICAN POETRY, see **CoAnAm**
  6-5-4-3

APAP   See **APP**

APB
 O
  AMERICAN POETRY. Percy H. Boynton, ed. (1918)
  3-A [BAP in A]

APD
 O
  AMERICAN POETRY. Alban Bertram DeMille, ed. (1923)
  3

APL	AMERICAN POEMS (1776–1922). Augustus White Long, comp. (1922) 3-2 [AmP in 2]
APM	See AP
APP	ATLANTIC PROSE AND POETRY. Charles Swain Thomas & H. G. Paul, eds. (1919) 3-A [APAP in A]
APPV	AMERICAN PATRIOTIC PROSE AND VERSE. Ruth Francis (Davis) Stevens & David H. Stevens, eds. (1917) 2
APr	AMERICAN PROSE. Horace E. Scudder, ed. (1880) 1
APW	AMERICAN POETRY FROM THE BEGINNING TO WHITMAN. Louis Untermeyer, ed. (1931) 5-4-3
ArRePo	ART OF READING POETRY, THE. Earl Daniels, ed. (1941) B
ArmLP	ARMENIAN LEGENDS AND POEMS. Zabelle C. Boyajian, comp. (1916; 1959) 5
AS	AMERICAN SONGBAG, THE. Carl Sandburg, comp. (1927) 6-5-4-3
ASD	ALL SORTS OF DIALOGUES. Clara J. [Fort] Denton, comp. (1898) 1
ASL	GOLDEN TREASURY OF AMERICAN SONGS AND LYRICS. Frederic Lawrence Knowles, ed. (1898) 2-1
ASR-1	APPROVED SELECTIONS FOR READING AND MEMORIZING: 1st YEAR. Melvin Hix, comp. (Rev. ed., 1908) 2
ASR-2	APPROVED SELECTIONS FOR READING AND MEMORIZING: 2d YEAR. Melvin Hix, comp. (Rev. ed., 1908) 2
AsYW	AS YOU WERE. Alexander Woollcott, ed. (1943) 4

AtBAP 12

AtBAP
821.08
Si 8a
ATLANTIC BOOK OF BRITISH AND AMERICAN POETRY, THE. Edith Sitwell, ed. (1958)
6-5

ATP
O
APPROACHES TO POETRY. Walter Blair & W. K. Chandler, eds. (1935; 2d ed., 1953)
6-5-C-4-3

AV
b
ANSWERING VOICE, THE. Sara Teasdale, comp. (1917; 1926; new ed., 1928)
5-4-3-A [TAV in A]

AVP
O
ANTHOLOGY OF VICTORIAN POETRY. Sir M. E. Grant Duff, ed. (1902)
1

AWB
811.08
Eg3
AMERICAN WAR BALLADS AND LYRICS, Vols. I-II. George Cary Eggleston, ed. (1889)
2-1

AWH
O
POETRY OF AMERICAN WIT AND HUMOR, THE. R. L. Paget, pseud. [i.e., Frederic Lawrence Knowles], ed. (1899)
2-1

AWP
808.1
V28
ANTHOLOGY OF WORLD POETRY, AN. Mark Van Doren, ed. (Rev. & enl. ed., 1936)
6-5-4-3

BAB
O
BALLADS OF AMERICAN BRAVERY. Clinton Scollard, ed. (1900)
2-1

BaBo
PR
1181
.L4
BALLAD BOOK, THE. MacEdward Leach, ed. (1955)
6-5-C

BALP
BLACK AMERICAN LITERATURE: POETRY. Darwin T. Turner, ed. (1969)
6

BaMNE
M
1629
.F58
B3
BALLADS MIGRANT IN NEW ENGLAND. Helen Hartness Flanders & Marguerite Olney, comps. (1953)
C

BANP
O
BOOK OF AMERICAN NEGRO POETRY, THE. James Weldon Johnson, ed. (1922; rev. ed., 1931)
6-5-4-3-A [BNP in A]

BAP
O
BOOK OF AMERICAN POETRY, THE. Edwin Markham, comp. (1934)
5-4-3

BAP * See APB
BaS O BALLADS AND SONGS; collected by the Missouri

Folk-Lore Society. H. M. Belden, ed. (1940)
4

BaSoIn BALLADS AND SONGS OF INDIANA. Paul G. Brewster, ed. (1940)
4-B

BaSoSo BALLADS AND SONGS OF SOUTHERN MICHIGAN. Emelyn Elizabeth Gardner & Geraldine Jencks Chickering, eds. (1939)
4-B

BAV BOOK OF AMERICAN VERSE, A. Alfred C. Ward, ed. (1935)
5-4-3

BB BALLAD BOOK, A. Katharine Lee Bates, ed. (1890)
3

BB * BALLAD BOOK, THE. William Allingham, ed. (1864)
2-1

BBB BOOK OF BRITISH BALLADS, A. Reginald Brimley Johnson, comp. (1912)
2

BBGG BEASTLY BOYS AND GHASTLY GIRLS, William Cole, ed. (1964)
6-D

BBGO BEING BORN AND GROWING OLDER. Bruce Vance, ed. (1971)
E

BBV BOOK OF BABY VERSE, THE. Joseph Morris, pseud. [i.e., Joseph Morris Bachelor] & St. Clair Adams, comps. (1923)
A

BBV * BOY'S BOOK OF VERSE, THE. Helen Dean Fish, comp. (1923; rev. ed., 1951)
6-5-C-4-3-A

BC BARTON'S COMIC RECITATIONS. Jerome Barton, ed. (1871)
1

BCEP BOOK OF CLASSIC ENGLISH POETRY, THE, 600–1830. Edwin Markham, comp. (1934). See **PYM**
5-4-3

BDD BURDETT'S DUTCH DIALECT RECITATIONS AND HUMOROUS READINGS. James S. Burdett, comp. (1884)
1

BE   14

BE   BUGLE ECHOES. Francis F. Browne, ed. (1886)
973.791 B81   2
BEL   BOOK OF ENGLISH LITERATURE, A. Frank-
                 lyn Bliss Snyder & Robert Grant Martin, eds.
                 (3d ed., 1933)
                 6-5-4-3
BeLS   BEST LOVED STORY POEMS. Walter E. Thwing,
                 ed. (1941)
                 6-5-4
BeMe   BEST OF MODERN EUROPEAN LITERATURE,
                 THE, 1920-1940. Klaus Mann & Hermann Kes-
                 ten, eds. (1945). Edition of 1943 had title
                 HEART OF EUROPE
                 4
BEN   BOOK OF THE EARTH (Book II of THE TORCH
                 BEARERS). Alfred Noyes. (1925)
                 3
BePJ   BEAUTIFUL POEMS ON JESUS. Basil Miller,
                 comp. (1948)
                 6-5-4
BeR   BEECHER'S RECITATIONS AND READINGS. E.
                 F. Smith, ed. (1874)
                 1
BeR *   BEFORE THE ROMANTICS. Geoffrey Grigson,
                 ed. (1946)
                 5-4
BESB   BEST ENGLISH AND SCOTTISH BALLADS. Ed-
                 ward Anden Bryant, comp. (1911)
                 2
BEV   See LEAP
BF   BLACK FIRE. LeRoi Jones & Larry Neal, eds.
                 (1968)
                 6
BFP   BOOK OF FIRESIDE POEMS, A. William R.
                 Bowlin, ed. (1937)
                 4-3
BFSS   BALLADS AND FOLK SONGS OF THE SOUTH-
                 WEST. Ethel Moore & Chauncey O. Moore,
                 comps. (1964)
                 6-D
BFV   BOOK OF FRIENDLY VERSE, THE. Joseph
                 Morris, pseud. [i.e., Joseph Morris Bachelor]
                 & St. Clair Adams, eds. (1924)
                 3-A

BFV *	See BFVR
BFVR	BOOK OF FAMOUS VERSE, A. Agnes Repplier, comp. (1892)
	3-2-1 [BFV in 2 & 1]
BGV	BOOK OF GEORGIAN VERSE, THE. William Stanley Braithwaite, comp. (1909)
	2
BHP	BOOK OF HUMOROUS POEMS, A. George A. Teter, ed. (1931)
	3
BHV	BOOK OF HEROIC VERSE, A. Arthur Burrell, comp. (1920)
	5-4-3-2
BiCB	BIRTHDAY CANDLES BURNING BRIGHT. Sara Brewton & John E. Brewton, eds. (1960)
	6-D
BIL	BECAUSE I LOVE YOU. Anna E. Mack, comp. (1894)
	2-1
BIP	BOOK OF IRISH POETRY, THE. Alfred Perceval Graves, ed. (1907?)
	2
BIrV	BOOK OF IRISH VERSE, THE. John Montague, ed. (1974). Same as THE FABER BOOK OF IRISH VERSE
	E
BIS	BUCK IN THE SNOW. Edna St. Vincent Millay. (1928)
	3
BiS	BIRD SONGS. Gwendolyn Reed, comp. (1969)
	6
BJC	BOOK OF JOYOUS CHILDREN, THE. James Whitcomb Riley. (1902)
	1
BLA	BIRD-LOVERS' ANTHOLOGY, THE. Clinton Scollard & Jessie B. Rittenhouse, comps. (1930)
	5-4-3
BLF	BALLADS FOR LITTLE FOLKS. Alice Cary & Phoebe Cary. Ed. by Mary Clemmer Ames. (1874)
	1
BlG	BLUE AND THE GRAY, THE. Claudius Meade Capps, comp. (1943)
	5-4

BLP	BEACON LIGHTS OF PATRIOTISM. Henry Beebee Carrington, ed. (1894) 2-1
BLP *	BOOK OF LIVING POEMS, A. William R. Bowlin, ed. (1934) 5-4-3
BLPA	BEST LOVED POEMS OF THE AMERICAN PEOPLE, THE. Hazel Felleman, ed. (1936) 6-5-4-3
BLRP	BEST LOVED RELIGIOUS POEMS, THE. James Gilchrist Lawson, comp. (1933) 6-5-4-3
BLSH	BEST LOVED SONGS AND HYMNS. James Morehead & Albert Morehead, eds. (1965) E
BLSo	BEST LOVED SONGS OF THE AMERICAN PEOPLE. Denes Agay, ed. (1975) E
BluL	BLUES LINE, THE. Eric Sackheim, comp. (1969) E
BLV	BOOK OF LIGHT VERSE, A. Robert Maynard Leonard, ed. (1910) 2
BLV *	BOOK OF LIVING VERSE, THE. Louis Untermeyer, ed. (1932). For the revised editions of 1939 & 1945, see **BoLiVe** 5-4-3
BMC	BOOK OF MODERN CATHOLIC VERSE, THE. Theodore Maynard, comp. (1926) 4-3
BMEP	BOOK OF MODERN ENGLISH POETRY, THE. Edwin Markham, comp. (1934). See **PYM** 5-4-3
BMV	BOOK OF MOTHER VERSE, THE. Joseph Morris, pseud. [i.e., Joseph Morris Bachelor] & St. Clair Adams, comps. (1924) A
BNL	NEW LIBRARY OF POETRY AND SONG, A. William Cullen Bryant, ed. (Rev. & enl. ed., (1903). For the edition of 1925 under the title LIBRARY OF POETRY AND SONG, see **LPS 1-3** 2-1
BNP	See **BANP**
BoAN 1-2	BOOKS OF AMERICAN NEGRO SPIRITUALS,

THE; including THE BOOK OF AMERICAN NEGRO SPIRITUALS & THE SECOND BOOK OF NEGRO SPIRITUALS. James Weldon Johnson, ed. (1925; 2 vols. in 1, 1940)
6-5-4

BoAnP
BOOK OF ANIMAL POEMS, A. William Cole, ed. (1973)
E

BoAu
BOOK OF AUSTRALIAN AND NEW ZEALAND VERSE, A. Walter Murdoch, ed. (Rev. ed., 1945). Edition of 1918 had title THE OXFORD BOOK OF AUSTRALASIAN VERSE
6-5-4

BoAV
821.08
W93b
BOOK OF AUSTRALIAN VERSE, A. Judith Wright, ed. (1956)
6-5

BoB
BOOK OF BALLADS, THE. John R. Crossland, comp. (1940)
4

BOC
PN
6071
.C6 B6
BOOK OF CHRISTMAS, THE; with an introduction by Hamilton Wright Mabie, (1909)
2

BoC
BOOK OF COMFORT, A. Elizabeth Goudge, ed. (1964)
6-D

BoCaPo
BOOK OF CANADIAN POETRY, THE. A. J. M. Smith, ed. (1943; rev. ed., 1948)
5-4-B

BoChLi
BOOK OF CHILDREN'S LITERATURE, A. Lillian Hollowell, ed. (1939; 2d ed., 1950)
6-5-4-B

BoDaBa
839.81
O52
BOOK OF DANISH BALLADS, A. Axel Olrik, ed. (1939)
5-4-B

BoDS
BOOK OF DANISH VERSE, A SECOND. Charles Wharton Stork, tr. (1947)
5-4

BOF
BOOK OF FRIENDSHIP, THE; with an introduction by Samuel McChord Crothers. (1910)
2

BoFr
BOOK OF FRIENDSHIP, THE. Elizabeth Selden, comp. (1947)
5-4

BoHiPo	BOOK OF HISTORICAL POEMS, A. William R. Bowlin, comp. (1939) 5-4-B
BOHV	BOOK OF HUMOROUS VERSE, THE. Carolyn Wells, comp. (Rev. & enl. ed. 1934) 6-5-4-3
BOL	BOOK OF LOVE, THE. Jessie Reid, comp.; with an introduction by Madison Cawein. (1911) 2
BOL *	BOOK OF LULLABIES, A. Elva S. Smith, comp. (1925) 5-4-3-A
BoLiVe	BOOK OF LIVING VERSE, THE. Louis Untermeyer, ed. (Rev. ed., 1939; new [rev.] ed., 1945). For the edition of 1932, see **BLV** 6-5-4-B
BOLo	BLACK OUT LOUD. Arnold Adoff, ed. (1970) 6
BoLoP	BOOK OF LOVE POETRY, A. Jon Stallworthy, ed. (1974) E
BoLP	BOOK OF LOVE POEMS, A. William Cole, ed. (1965) 6-D
BoLV 1-3	BOOK OF LIVELY VERSE, A, Parts I-III. Alan Sauvain, comp. (1937) 4
BOM	YOUNG FOLKS' BOOK OF MIRTH, THE. Mary Roenah Thomas, comp. (1924) A
BoN	BOOK OF NONSENSE, THE. Roger Lancelyn Green, ed. (1956) 5
BoNaP	BOOK OF NATURE POEMS, A. William Cole, comp. (1969) 6
BoPe	BOOK OF PEACE, A. Elizabeth Goudge, ed. (1967) 6
BoPo	BOOK OF POEMS, A. Oliphant Gibbons, ed. (1938) 4-B

BoR *O*	BOOK OF RUSSIAN VERSE, A. Cecil Maurice Bowra, ed. (1943) 5-4
BoReV PR 1191 .633	BOOK OF RELIGIOUS VERSE, A. Helen Gardner, ed. (1972). Same as THE FABER BOOK OF RELIGIOUS VERSE E
BoRS *O*	BOOK OF RUSSIAN VERSE, A SECOND. Cecil Maurice Bowra, ed. (1948) 5-4
BoSA *O*	BOOK OF SOUTH AFRICAN VERSE, A. Guy Butler, comp. (1959) 6-5
BoTP *O*	BOOK OF A THOUSAND POEMS, THE. Jeannie Murray MacBain, ed. (1942) 6-5-4
BoW *O*	BOOK OF THE WINTER, THE. Edith Sitwell, comp. (1951) 6-5-C
BP *O*	BATTLE POEMS AND PATRIOTIC VERSES. George Goodchild, comp. (1915) 2
BP * PS 591 .N4B3	BLACK POETRY. Dudley Randall, ed. (1969) 6
BP-3 PR 1225 .B66	BEST POEMS OF 1923, THE. Leonard Alfred Strong, ed. (1924) A
BP-4 *same*	BEST POEMS OF 1924, THE. Leonard Alfred Strong, ed.(1925) A
BP-6 *same*	BEST POEMS OF 1926, THE. Leonard Alfred Strong, ed. (1927) A
BPB *O*	BLUE POETRY BOOK, THE. Andrew Lang. (1891) 3-2-1
BPM-30 *O*	BEST POEMS OF 1930, THE. Thomas Moult, ed. (1930). For earlier years see **MBP-22, 23, 24, 26.** 3
BPM-31 *O*	BEST POEMS OF 1931, THE. Thomas Moult, ed. (1931) 3

BPM-32 O	BEST POEMS OF 1932, THE. Thomas Moult, ed. (1932) 3
BPM-33 O	BEST POEMS OF 1933, THE. Thomas Moult, ed. (1933) 3
BPM-34 O	BEST POEMS OF 1934, THE. Thomas Moult, ed. (1934) 3
BPM-35 O	BEST POEMS OF 1935, THE. Thomas Moult, ed. (1935) 3
BPM-36 O	BEST POEMS OF 1936, THE. Thomas Moult, ed. (1936) 3
BPM-37 O	BEST POEMS OF 1937, THE. Thomas Moult, ed. (1937) 3
BPN O	BRITISH POETS OF THE NINETEENTH CENTURY. Curtis Hidden Page & Stith Thompson, eds. (New ed., 1929) 5-4-3
BPo PS 591 .N4 B5E	BLACK POETS, THE. Dudley Randall, ed. (1971)
BPP O	BOOK OF PERSONAL POEMS, A. William R. Bowlin, comp. (1936) 5-4-3
BR	ORIGINAL RECITATIONS WITH LESSON TALKS. Emma Dunning Banks. (1890; 2d ed., 1901; enl. ed., 1908) 2-1
BrAP O	BRIEF ANTHOLOGY OF POETRY, A. Stephen F. Fogle, ed. (1951) C
BrBE O	BROADWAY BOOK OF ENGLISH VERSE, THE. William Bowyer Honey, ed. (4th ed., 1946). Edition of 1939 had title THE SACRED FIRE 5-4
BrPB 6	BRITISH POPULAR BALLADS. John E. Housman, ed. (1952) C
BrPo O	BRITISH POETRY, 1880–1920. Paul L. Wiley &

	Harold Orel, eds. (1969) 6
BRR	BURBANK'S RECITATIONS AND READINGS. Alfred P. Burbank, ed. (18 - ?) 1
BrR	BRIDLED WITH RAINBOWS. Sara Brewton & John E. Brewton, eds. (1949) 6-5-4
BS	BRIGHT SIDE, THE. Charles R. Skinner, ed. (2d ed., 1909) 4-3
BS 1-27	SHOEMAKER'S BEST SELECTIONS, Vols. 1-27. Jacob W. Shoemaker & Rachel W. [Hinkle] Shoemaker, eds. (1887-1914). Same as BEST THINGS FROM BEST AUTHORS in 9 vols., see BTB 1-9 2-1
BSNS	BALLADS AND SEA SONGS FROM NOVA SCOTIA. W. Roy Mackenzie, comp. (1928) D
BSO	BALLADS AND SONGS FROM OHIO. Mary O. Eddy, comp. (1939) D
BSP	BEST SHORT POEMS OF THE NINETEENTH CENTURY. William Sinclair Lord, comp. (1899) 1
BSV	BOOK OF SCOTTISH VERSE, A. R. L. Mackie, ed. (1934) 5-4-3
BTB 1-9	BEST THINGS FROM BEST AUTHORS, Vols. 1-9. Jacob W. Shoemaker & Rachel W. [Hinkle] Shoemaker, eds. (1925). Same as SHOEMAKER'S BEST SELECTIONS in 27 vols., see BS 1-27 3
BTH [1]-2	FROM BEOWULF TO THOMAS HARDY, Vols. I-II. Robert Shafer, ed. (1924) A
BTP	BOOK OF TREASURED POEMS, A. William R. Bowlin, comp. (1928) 5-4-3

BTTM	BREATHES THERE THE MAN. Frank S. Meyer, ed. (1973)
0	E
BuBa	BUNDLE OF BALLADS, A. Ruth Manning-Saunders, comp. (1959)
0	6-D
BuTh	BURNING THORN, THE. Griselda Greaves, ed. (1971)
0	E
BVC	BOOK OF VERSES FOR CHILDREN, A. Edward Verrall Lucas, ed. (1897)
0	2-1
BWP	BEGINNING WITH POEMS. Reuben A. Brower, Anne D. Ferry, & David Kalstone, eds. (1966)
0	6
CaAE	CASSELL'S ANTHOLOGY OF ENGLISH POETRY. Margaret Flower & Desmond Flower, eds. (2d ed., 1946)
0	5-4
CAAP	CONTEMPORARY AMERICAN AND AUSTRALIAN POETRY. Thomas Shapcott, ed. (1976)
PS 615 .C65 1976	E
CABA	COLLEGE ANTHOLOGY OF BRITISH AND AMERICAN VERSE, THE. A. Kent Hieatt & William Park, eds. (1964)
0	6-D
CABL	COLLINS ALBATROSS BOOK OF LONGER POEMS. Edwin Morgan, ed. (1963)
6	6-D
CAD	CHRISTMAS. Alice Dalgliesh, comp. (1934)
0	3
CAD *	CITY IN ALL DIRECTIONS. Arnold Adoff, ed. (1969)
0	6
CaFP	CASE FOR POETRY, THE. Frederick L. Gwynn, Ralph W. Condee, & Arthur O. Lewis, Jr., eds. (1954; 2d ed., 1965)
0	6-D-C
CAG	CAP AND GOWN. 4th series. R. L. Paget, pseud. [i.e., Frederic Lawrence Knowles], comp. (1931). For earlier series, see **CG-1, CG-2, CG-3**
0	5-4-3
CAP	CHIEF AMERICAN POETS, THE. Curtis Hidden Page, ed. (1905)
0	3-2

CaP   CANADIAN POETRY IN ENGLISH. Bliss
          Carman, Lorne Pierce, & V. B. Rhodenizer, eds.
          (Rev. & enl. ed., 1954). Edition of 1935 had
          title OUR CANADIAN LITERATURE, see
          OCL.
          6-5-C
CAPP   CONTEMPORARY AMERICAN POETRY. A.
          Poulin, Jr., ed. (1971)
          E
CavP   CAVALIER POETS, THE. Robin Skelton, ed.
          (1970)
          6
CAW   CATHOLIC ANTHOLOGY, THE. Thomas Walsh,
          ed. (Rev. ed., 1932)
          6-5-4-3
CaYB   CATCH YOUR BREATH: A BOOK OF SHIVERY
          POEMS. Lilian Moore & Lawrence Webster,
          comps. (1973)
          E
CB   CHILDREN'S BOOK, THE. Frances (Hodgson)
          Burnett, ed. (1909)
          2
CBB   CHILDREN'S BOOK OF BALLADS. THE. Mary
          W. (Foote) Tileston, comp. (1883)
          2
CBE   CHISWELL BOOK OF ENGLISH POETRY, THE.
          Robert Bridges, comp. (1924)
          5-4-3-A [CEP in A]
CBEP   CASSELL BOOK OF ENGLISH POETRY, THE.
          James Reeves, ed. (1965)
          6-D
CBOP   CHILDREN'S BOOK OF POETRY. Henry Troth
          Coates, comp. (1879)
          2
CBOV   COLLEGE BOOK OF VERSE, THE, 1250-1925.
          Robert M. Gay, comp. (1927). Same as THE
          RIVERSIDE BOOK OF VERSE, see RBV
          5-4-3
CBP   CAMBRIDGE BOOK OF POETRY AND SONG,
          THE. Charlotte Fiske (Bates) Rogé [Charlotte
          Bates], comp. (1882)
          2
CBPC   CAMBRIDGE BOOK OF POETRY FOR CHIL-

CBV

DREN, THE. Kenneth Grahame, ed. (1933)
5-4-3-2

CBV   COLLEGE BOOK OF VERSE, A. C. F. Main, ed.
            (1970)
            6

CBV *   CRADLE BOOK OF VERSE, THE. Louise
            Hovde, comp. (1927)
            A

CCB   CAPE COD BALLADS. Joseph Crosby Lincoln.
            (1902)
            1

CCB *   CHILD'S CALENDAR BEAUTIFUL, THE.
            Rebecca Katherine Beeson, comp. (1906)
            2

CCP   CHIMNEY CORNER POEMS. Veronica S.
            Hutchinson, ed. (1929)
            3

CCR   CHOICE READINGS. Robert McLean Cumnock,
            ed. (1886; new ed., 1923)
            3-A-2-1 [CRC in A; CR in 2 & 1]

CCS   CORNHUSKERS, THE. Carl Sandburg. (1928)
            3

CD   CHOICE DIALECT AND OTHER CHARACTER-
            IZATIONS. Charles C. Shoemaker, comp.
            (1893)
            3-2-1

CDC   CAROLING DUSK. Countee Cullen, ed. (1927)
            6-5-4-3

CDD   CLASSIC DIALOGUES AND DRAMAS. Mrs. J.
            W. Shoemaker [Rachel W. (Hinkle) Shoemaker],
            comp. (1888)
            3-2-1

CDS   CHOICE DIALOGUES. Mrs. J. W. Shoemaker
            [Rachel W. (Hinkle) Shoemaker], ed. (1888)
            3-2-1 [CDs in 1]

CDs   See CDS

CDV   CHOICE DIALECT AND VAUDEVILLE STAGE
            JOKES. (1902) A. J. Drake & Co.
            1

CDW   CARRIERS OF THE DREAM WHEEL. Duane
            Niatum, ed. (1975)
            E

CE	CHRISTMAS ENTERTAINMENTS. Alice M. Kellogg, comp. (1918) 2
CEL	CHOICE ENGLISH LYRICS. James Baldwin, comp. (1894) 2-1
CenHV	CENTURY OF HUMOROUS VERSE, A, 1850-1950. Roger Lancelyn Green, ed. (1959) 6-5
CenL	CENTURY OF LYRICS, A. 1550-1650. D. C. Whimster, ed. (1938) 5-4
CEP	See CBE
CEP *	COLLECTION OF ENGLISH POEMS, A, 1660-1800. Ronald S. Crane, ed. (1932) 6-5-4-3
CFBP	CHILDREN'S FIRST BOOK OF POETRY, THE. Emilie Kip Baker, comp. (1915). For SECOND & THIRD books, see CSBP, CTBP 3-2
CG 821.08 P27c	CHILDREN'S GARLAND, THE. Coventry Patmore, comp. (1862) 5-4-3-2-1 [CGd in 2 & 1]
CG-1 811.084 H31	CAP AND GOWN. [1st series]. Joseph Le Roy Harrison, comp. (1897). For 4th series, see CAG 1
CG-2 811.4 K76c	CAP AND GOWN. 2d series. Frederic Lawrence Knowles, comp. (1897). For 4th series, see CAG 1
CG-3	CAP AND GOWN. 3d series. R. L. Paget, pseud. [i.e., Frederic Lawrence Knowles], comp. (1902). For 4th series, see CAG 1
CGd	See CG
CGOV	CHILDREN'S GARLAND OF VERSE, THE. Grace Rhys, comp. (1921) 3
CGP	CONTEMPORARY GERMAN POETRY. Babette Deutsch & Avrahm Yarmolinsky, eds. & trs. (1923) A
CGV 821.6 St4c	CHILD'S GARDEN OF VERSE. Robert Louis Stevenson. (1895) 1

CH   26

CH   COME HITHER. Walter De La Mare, comp. (Rev.
               ed., 1928; new ed., 1948; 3d ed., 1957)
               6-5-4-3-A [COH in A]
CH *   See CHS
ChAP   CHRISTMAS ANTHOLOGY OF POETRY AND
               PAINTING, A. Vivian Campbell, ed. (1947)
               4
CHB   CHRISTMAS HOLIDAY BOOK, A. Alice Dalgleish
               & Ernest Rhys, comps. (1934)
               4-3
ChBR   CHRISTMAS BELLS ARE RINGING. Sara
               Brewton & John E. Brewton, eds. (1951)
               6-5-C
ChER   CHOICE OF ENGLISH ROMANTIC POETRY, A.
               Stephen Spender, ed. (1947)
               6-5-4
ChIn   CHOICE INTERLUDES. Mildred Jones Keefe, ed.
               (1942)
               4-B
ChIP   CHRIST IN POETRY. Thomas Curtis Clark &
               Hazel Davis Clark, eds. (1952)
               6-5-C
ChLP   CHINESE LOVE POEMS. D. J. Klemer, ed. (1959)
               5
ChMo   CHIEF MODERN POETS OF ENGLAND AND
               AMERICA. Gerald DeWitt Sanders & John
               Herbert Nelson, eds. (3d ed., 1943). For edition
               of 1936, see CMP. For the edition of 1962, see
               CMoP.
               5-4-B
ChMP   CHATTO BOOK OF MODERN VERSE, THE,
               1915-1955. C. Day Lewis & John Lehmann,
               eds. (New ed., 1959)
               6-5
CHP   COMPLETE HOLIDAY PROGRAM FOR THE
               FIRST GRADE, A. Nancy May Burns & May
               Gertrude Nunney. (1911)
               2
ChPo   CHOICE POEMS FOR ELEMENTARY GRADES.
               Matilda Mahaffey Elsea, comp. (1943)
               4-B
ChrBoLe   CHRISTMAS BOOK OF LEGENDS AND

	STORIES, THE. Elva Sophronia Smith & Alice Isabel Hazeltine, eds. (1944). For edition of 1915, see **CLS** 6-5-4-B
CHS	CHOICE HUMOR FOR READING AND RECITATION. Charles C. Shoemaker, comp. (1886) 3-2-1 [CH in 2 & 1]
ChS	See **CS**
ChTr	CHERRY-TREE, THE. Geoffrey Grigson, comp. (1959) 6-5
CHV	CHILD'S HARVEST OF VERSE, THE. Mary W. (Foote) Tileston, comp. (1910) 2
CIV	See **AnIV**
CIV *	CAT IN VERSE, THE. Carolyn Wells & Louella D. Everett, comps. (1935) 6-5-4-3
CLS	CHRISTMAS IN LEGEND AND STORY. Elva Sophronia Smith & Alice Isabel Hazeltine, eds. (1915). For edition of 1944, see **ChrBoLe** 5-4-3-2
CLWM	COME LIVE WITH ME. Charles Norman, ed. (1966) 6
CMM	CONVERSATION AT MIDNIGHT. Edna St. Vincent Millay. (1937) 3
CMoP	CHIEF MODERN POETS OF ENGLAND AND AMERICA. Gerald D. Sanders, John H. Nelson, & M. L. Rosenthal, eds. (4th ed., 1962). For the edition of 1936, see **CMP**. For the edition of 1943, see **ChMo** 6
CMP	CHIEF MODERN POETS OF ENGLAND AND AMERICA. Gerald DeWitt Sanders & John Herbert Nelson, eds. (Rev. ed., 1936). For the edition of 1943, see **ChMo**. For the edition of 1962, see **CMoP** 5-4-3
COAH	CHRISTMAS (Our American Holidays Series). Robert Haven Schauffler, ed. (1907) 5-4-3-2 [OAC in 2]

CoAnAm   28

CoAnAm   COMPREHENSIVE ANTHOLOGY OF AMER-
              ICAN POETRY, A. Conrad Aiken, ed. (1944).
              Edition of 1929 had title AMERICAN POET-
              RY, 1671–1928, see **APA**
              6-5-4-B
CoAP   CONTEMPORARY AMERICAN POETS, THE.
              Mark Strand, ed. (1969)
              6
CoBA   COLLEGE BOOK OF AMERICAN LITERA-
              TURE, A. Milton Ellis & others, eds. (2d ed.,
              1949)
              6-5-4
CoBE   COLLEGE BOOK OF ENGLISH LITERATURE.
              James Edward Tobin & others, comps. (1949)
              6-5-4
CoBMV   COLLEGE BOOK OF MODERN VERSE, A.
              James K. Robinson & Walter B. Rideout, eds.
              (1958)
              6-5
CoDuFi   COAL DUST ON THE FIDDLE. George Korson,
              comp. (1943)
              B
CoEV   COLLECTED ENGLISH VERSE. Margaret Bot-
              trall & Ronald Bottrall, eds. (1946)
              5-4
CoFP   CONTEMPORARY FRENCH POETRY. Alexan-
              der Aspel & Donald Justice, eds. (1965)
              D
COH   See CH
CoIP   CONTEMPORARY ITALIAN POETRY. Carlo L.
              Golino, ed. (1962)
              D
CoMu   COMMON MUSE, THE. Vivian de Sola Pinto &
              Allan Edwin Rodway, eds. (1957)
              6-5
ConAP   CONTEMPORARY AMERICAN POETRY.
              Donald Hall, ed. (2d ed., 1972)
              E
CoPAm   CONTEMPORARY POETRY IN AMERICA.
              Miller Williams, ed. (1973)
              E
CoPo   CONTROVERSY OF POETS, A. Paris Leary &

	Robert Kelley, eds. (1965) 6-D
COS	CHILD'S OWN SPEAKER. Emma C. Rook & L. J. Rook [Elizabeth (Lizzie) J. Rook]. (1895). For composite edition, see **PPYP** 2-1
CoSo	COWBOY SONGS AND OTHER FRONTIER BALLADS. John A. Lomax & Alan Lomax, eds. (Rev. & enl. ed., 1938). For the edition of 1916, see **CSF** 6-5-4-B
CoSP	CONTEMPORARY SPANISH POETRY. Eleanor L. Turnbull, tr. (1945) 5-4
CoV	CONSCIOUS VOICE, THE. Albert D. Van Nostrand & Charles H. Watts, II, eds. (1959) 5
CP	CONTEMPORARY POETRY. Marguerite Wilkinson, ed. (1923) 5-4-3-A [CPW in A]
CP *	See **CPD**
CP-1	CHRISTMAS IN POETRY: CAROLS AND POEMS. 1st series. Carnegie Library School Association, comp. (1923) A
CP-2	CHRISTMAS IN POETRY. 2d series. Carnegie Library School Association, comp. (1923) A
CPAN 1-3	COLLECTED POEMS, Vols. I-III. Alfred Noyes. (1920) 3
CPB	COLLECTED POEMS. Rupert Brooke. (1915) 3
CPC	FIFTY CHRISTMAS POEMS FOR CHILDREN. Florence B. Hyett, ed. (1923) A
CPCS	CHICAGO POEMS. Carl Sandburg. (1916) 3
CPD	COMMENCEMENT PARTS. Harry Cassell Davis, comp. (1898, 1929) 3-2-1 [CP in 2 & 1]

CPG	CANADIAN POETS. John W. Garvin, ed. (Rev. ed., 1926) 5-4-3
CPL	CHOICE PIECES FOR LITTLE PEOPLE SUITABLE FOR SPEAKING AND READING IN SCHOOL, CHURCH & PARLOR ENTERTAINMENTS. (190-?) T. S. Denison & Co. 1
CPL *	COLLECTED POEMS. Vachel Lindsay. (1925) 3
CPN	CHILDREN'S POEMS THAT NEVER GROW OLD. Clement F. Benoit, comp. (1922) 4-3
CPOI	CERTAIN POEMS OF IMPORTANCE. Hattie Hecht Sloss, comp. (1929) 4-3
CPS	COMPLETE POEMS. Robert Service. (1921) 3
CPs	COLONIAL PLAYS FOR THE SCHOOL-ROOM. Blanche Shoemaker [Mrs. Blanche Shoemaker Wagstaff]. (1912) 2
CPW	See CP
CPWR	COMPLETE POETICAL WORKS OF JAMES WHITCOMB RILEY, THE. James Whitcomb Riley. (1937) 3
CR	See CCR
CR *	COPELAND READER, THE. Charles Townsend Copeland, ed. (1926) 3-A
CRAL	CENTURY READINGS FOR A COURSE IN AMERICAN LITERATURE. Fred Lewis Pattee, comp. (Rev. ed., 1926) 3
CRC	See CCR
CRE	CENTURY READINGS IN ENGLISH LITERATURE. John W. Cunliffe, J. F. A. Pyre & Karl Young, eds. (3d ed., 1929) 3
CrMA	CRITERION BOOK OF MODERN AMERICAN VERSE, THE. W. H. Auden, ed. (1956) 6-5

CRP	COLLEGE READINGS IN POETRY. Frances Kelley Del Plaine & Adah Georgina Grandy, eds. (1933) 4-3
CRR	COMIC READINGS AND RECITATIONS. Charles Walter Brown, comp. (1902) 1
CRYO	CHRISTMAS RECITATIONS FOR YOUNG AND OLD. Dorothy M. Shipman, ed. (1931) 4-3
CS	CHRISTMAS SELECTIONS FOR READING AND RECITATIONS. Rosamond Livingstone McNaught, ed. (1906) 4-3-2-[ChS in 2]
CS 1-40	See **OHCS 1-40**
CSBP	CHILDREN'S SECOND BOOK OF POETRY, THE. Emilie Kip Baker, ed. (1915). For FIRST & THIRD books, see **CFBP, CTBP** 3-2
CSF	COWBOYS SONGS AND OTHER FRONTIER BALLADS. John A. Lomax, comp. (New ed., 1916). For revised edition of 1944, see **CoSo** 5-4-3
CSL	CHORAL SPEAKING ARRANGEMENTS FOR THE LOWER GRADES. Louise Abney & Grace Rowe. (1937) 3
CSS	CUMNOCK'S SCHOOL SPEAKER. Robert M. Cumnock, comp. (1904) 2-1
CSU	CHORAL SPEAKING ARRANGEMENTS FOR THE UPPER GRADES. Louise Abney. (1937) 3
CTBA	CRAZY TO BE ALIVE IN SUCH A STRANGE WORLD. Nancy Larrick, comp. (1977) 3
CTBP	CHILDREN'S THIRD BOOK OF POETRY, THE. Emilie Kip Baker, ed. (1915). For FIRST & SECOND books, see **CFBP, CSBP** 3-2
CTC	CONFUCIUS TO CUMMINGS. Ezra Pound & Marcella Spann, eds. (1964) 6-D

CV	CONTEMPORARY VERSE, A. Marion Merrill & Grace E. W. Sprague, eds. (New ed., 1936) 5-4-3
CVG	COLLECTED VERSE. Edgar A. Guest. (1934) 3
CW	CHILD WORLD, A. James Whitcomb Riley. (1893) 1
CWAP	COMPLETE GEORGE WASHINGTON ANNIVERSARY PROGRAMS. Alma Laird, ed. (1931) 3
DaB	DAFFODIL POETRY BOOK, THE. Ethel L. Fowler, comp. (1920) 4
DaBS	DAFFODIL POETRY BOOK, THE SECOND. Ethel L. Fowler, comp. (1931) 4
DaDu	DAWN AND DUSK. Charles Causey, ed. (1963) D
DaM	DARK OF THE MOON. August Derleth, ed. (1947) 5-4
DB	DUBLIN BOOK OF IRISH VERSE, THE, 1728–1909. John Cooke, ed. (1909) 2
DCD	DICK'S COMIC DIALOGUES. William Brisbane Dick, ed. (1886) 1
DCP	DICK'S CHOICE PIECES FOR LITTLE CHILDREN. Harris B. Dick, comp. (1892) 1
DCR	DICK'S COMIC AND DIALECT RECITATIONS. William Brisbane Dick, ed. (1888) 1
DD	DAYS AND DEEDS. Burton Egbert Stevenson & Elizabeth Stevenson, comps. (1906; new & rev. ed., 1931) 6-5-4-3-2
DDA	DESK DRAWER ANTHOLOGY, THE. Alice Roosevelt Longworth & Theodore Roosevelt, comps. (1937) 5-4-3

DDD	DICK'S DIVERTING DIALOGUES. William Brisbane Dick, ed. (1888) 1
DDM	DICK'S DIALOGUES AND MONOLOGUES. William Brisbane Dick, ed, (1885) 1
DDR	DICK'S DRAMATIC RECITER. (1897) Dick & Fitzgerald Pub. Co. 1
DE	DICK'S ETHIOPIAN SCENES, VARIETY SKETCHES AND STUMP SPEECHES. William Brisbane Dick, ed. (1872) 1
DES	ELOCUTIONARY STUDIES. Anna T. (Randall) Diehl, comp. (1903) 1
DFR	DICK'S FESTIVAL RECITER. William Brisbane Dick, comp. (1892) 1
DFY	DICK'S DUTCH, FRENCH, AND YANKEE RECITATIONS. William Brisbane Dick, ed. (1879) 1
DI	DREAMS AND IMAGES. Joyce Kilmer, ed. (1917). For editions of 1926 & 1955 under the title JOYCE KILMER'S ANTHOLOGY OF CATHOLIC POETS, see JKCP A
DI*	DICK'S IRISH DIALECT AND RECITATIONS. William Brisbane Dick, ed. (1879) 1
DiM	DISTAFF, MUSE, THE. Clifford Bax & Meum Stewart, comps. (1949) 5-4
DiPo	DIMENSIONS OF POETRY, THE. James E. Miller, Jr., & Bernice Slote, eds. (1962) 6-D
DJS	DICK'S JUVENILE SPEAKER FOR BOYS AND GIRLS. William Brisbane Dick, comp. (1897) 1
DLD	DICK'S LITTLE DIALOGUES FOR LITTLE PEOPLE. Harris B. Dick, comp. (1890) 1
DLF	DICK'S LITTLE FOLKS' RECITER. William Bris-

DLS 34

bane Dick, comp. (1896)
1

DLS DICK'S LITTLE SPEECHES FOR LITTLE SPEAKERS. Harris B. Dick, comp. (1890)
1

DM DRILLS AND MARCHES. Emma Cecilia Rook & L. J. Rook [Elizabeth (Lizzie) J. Rook]. (1890)
2-1

DR See **DRB**

DRB DELSARTE RECITATION BOOK. Elsie M. Wilbor, comp. (4th ed. enl., 1905)
3-2-1 [DR in 2 & 1]

DRR DUTCH DIALECT; recitations, readings & jokes ... as related by our foremost Dutch comedians of to-day. (1902). A. J. Drake & Co.
1

DrRo DRINK FROM THE ROCK; selected poems from "Spirit" [1939-1944]. John Gilland Brunini, ed. (1944)
4-B

DS DELSARTE SPEAKER, THE. Henry Davenport Northrop, ed. (1895)
1

DSS DICK'S STUMP SPEECHES AND MINSTREL JOKES. William Brisbane Dick. (1889)
1

DST DICK'S SPEECHES FOR TINY TOTS. William Brisbane Dick, comp. (1895)
1

DT DRAWING ROOM THEATRICALS. Dick & Fitzgerald Pub. Co. (18-?)
1

DTC DYLAN THOMAS'S CHOICE; an anthology of verse spoken by Dylan Thomas. Ralph Maud & Aneirin Talfan Davies, eds. (1963)
6-D

DTo DARK TOWER, THE. Dairine Coffey, comp. (1967)
6

DTRN DICK TURPIN'S RIDE AND OTHER POEMS. Alfred Noyes. (1927)
3

DWC DAYS WE CELEBRATE, THE. Marie Irish.

	(1904)
	2
DWP	See WP
EA	ELOCUTION AND ACTION. Frank T. Southwick. (3d ed. rev. & enl., 1900)
	2-1
EA*	ENGLISH ANTHOLOGY OF PROSE AND POETRY, AN. Henry Newbolt, comp. (1921)
	3
EaAmPo	EARLY AMERICAN POETS. Louis Untermeyer, ed. (1952)
PS 586 .U62	C
EaLo	EARTH IS THE LORD'S, THE. Helen Plotz, comp. (1965)
	6-D
EAO	EARLY AMERICAN ORATIONS, 1760-1824. Louie Regina Heller, ed. (1902)
	2-1
EbR	EBONY RHYTHM. Beatrice M. Murphy, ed. (1948)
811.085 M95e	4
EBS	See EBSV
EBSV	EDINBURGH BOOK OF SCOTTISH VERSE, THE, 1300-1900. W. Macneile Dixon, ed. (1910)
821.08 D64	5-4-3-2 [EBS in 2]
ECBV	EVERY CHILD'S BOOK OF VERSE. Sarah Chokla Gross, comp. (1968)
	E
EcGr 1-3	ECHOING GREEN, THE, Books I-III. C. Day Lewis, ed. (1937-1943)
	4-B
ED	EXCELSIOR DIALOGUES. Phineas Garrett, ed. (1904)
	3-2-1
EDY	EVERY DAY IN THE YEAR. James Lauren Ford & Mary K. Ford, eds. (1902)
	2-1
EE	EASY ENTERTAINMENTS FOR YOUNG PEOPLE. (1892) Penn Pub. Co.
	2-1
EF	EUGENE FIELD BOOK, THE. Mary Elizabeth Burt & Mary B. Cable, eds. (1898)
	1

EFY	ENTERTAINMENTS FOR ALL THE YEAR. Clara J. [Fort] Denton. (1910) 2
EG	ENGLISH GALAXY OF SHORTER POEMS, THE. Gerald Bullett, ed. (1934) 6-5-4-3
EhP	ENGLISH POEMS. Edward Chauncey Baldwin & Harry G. Paul, eds. (1908) 2
EHT	ENGLISH HISTORY AS TOLD BY ENGLISH POETS. Katharine Lee Bates & Katharine Coman, comps. (1902) 2-1
EiCL	EIGHTEENTH CENTURY ENGLISH LITERATURE. Geoffrey Tillotson, Paul Fussell, Jr., & Marshall Waingrow, eds. (1969) 6
EiCP	EIGHTEENTH-CENTURY POETRY. Patricia Meyer Spacks, ed. (1964) 6-D
EiPP	EIGHTEENTH CENTURY POETRY AND PROSE. Louis J. Bredvold, Alan D. McKillop, & Lois Whitney, eds. (2d ed., 1956) 6-5
ElL	ELIZABETHAN LYRICS. Norman Ault, ed. (3d ed., 1949) 6-5-4
ElLy	ELIZABETHAN LYRICS; a critical anthology. Kenneth Muir, ed. (1953) C
ELP	ENGLISH LYRIC POEMS, 1500-1900. C. Day Lewis, ed. (1961) 6-D
ELP *	ENGLISH LYRIC POETRY, 1500-1700. Frederic Ives Carpenter, ed. (1897) 1
ElSeCe	ELIZABETHAN AND SEVENTEENTH-CENTURY LYRICS. Matthew W. Black, ed. (1938) 5-4-B
ELU	EIGHT LINES AND UNDER. William Cole, ed. (1967) 6

EM 1-2	ENGLISH MASTERPIECES, 700-1900, Vols. I-II. H. W. Herrington, ed. (Rev. ed., 1937) 5-4-3
EmBrPo	EMINENT BRITISH POETS OF THE NINETEENTH CENTURY. Paul Robert Lieder, ed. (2 vols. in 1, 1938) 5-4-B
EMS	EARLY MOON. Carl Sandburg. (1930) 3
EnH	ENGLISH HEART, THE. Clive Sansom, ed. (1946) 4
EnL	ENGLISH LITERATURE; a college anthology. Donald B. Clark, Leon T. Dickinson, Charles M. Hudson, & George B. Pace, eds. (1960) 6-5
EnLi 1-2	ENGLISH LITERATURE AND ITS BACKGROUNDS, Vols. I-II. Bernard D. N. Grebanier & Stith Thompson, eds. (1939). Bernard D. Grebanier, Samuel Middlebrook, Stith Thompson, & William Watt, eds. (Rev. ed., 1949) 6-5-4-B
EnLit	ENGLISH LITERATURE; a period anthology. Albert C. Baugh & George William McClelland, eds. (1954) 6-5
EnLoPo	ENGLISH LOVE POEMS. John Betjeman & Geoffrey Taylor, comps. (1957) 6-5
EnLP	ENGLISH LYRIC POETRY (Living Masterpieces of English Literature, Vol. III). Dorothy Bethurum & Randall Stewart, eds. (1954) 5-C
EnPE	ENGLISH POETRY OF THE MID AND LATE EIGHTEENTH CENTURY. Ricardo Quintana & Alvin Whitney, eds. (1963) 6-D
EnPo	ENGLISH POETRY 1400-1580. William Tydeman, ed. (1970) 6
EnPP	ENGLISH PASTORAL POETRY; from the beginnings to Marvell. Frank Kermode, ed. (1952) C

EnRePo	ENGLISH RENAISSANCE POETRY. John Williams, ed. (1963) 6-D
EnRP	ENGLISH ROMANTIC POETRY AND PROSE. Russell Noyes, ed. (1956) 6-5
EnSb	ENGLISH AND SCOTTISH BALLADS. Robert Graves, ed. (1957) 6-5
EnSW	ENGLISH, SCOTTISH, AND WELSH LANDSCAPE, 1700–c.1860. John Betjeman & Geoffrey Taylor, comps. (1944) 5-4
EOAH	EASTER (Our American Holidays Series). Susan Tracy Rice & Robert Haven Schauffler, eds. (1916) 5-4-3-2 [OAE in 2]
EP	EASTER IN POETRY. Carnegie Library School Association, comp. (1926) A
EP *	ENGLISH PASTORALS. Edmund Kerchever Chambers, comp. (1895) 1
EP **	ENGLISH POETRY 1550–1660. Fred Inglis, ed. (1965) 6
EP ***	ENGLISH POETRY, 1170–1892. John Matthews Manly, comp. (1907) 3-2 [EPY in 2]
EPC	ENGLISH POEMS FROM CHAUCER TO KIPLING. Thomas Marc Parrott & Augustus White Long, eds. (1902) 3-2
EPE	See EPEP
EPEP	ENGLISH POEMS, Vol. II. The Elizabethan age and the Puritan period. Walter C. Bronson, comp. (1909). For Vols. I, III, IV, see EPOM, EPRE, EPNC 3-2 [EPE in 2]
Epi	EPISODES IN FIVE POETIC TRADITIONS. R. G. Barnes, ed. (1972) E

EPN	ENGLISH POETRY OF THE NINETEENTH CENTURY. G. R. Elliott & Norman Foerster, eds. (1923) 6-5-4-3
EPN *	See **EPNC**
EPNC	ENGLISH POEMS, Vol. IV. The Nineteenth century. Walter C. Bronson, comp. (1907). For Vols. I, II, III, see **EPOM**, **EPEP**, **EPRE** 3-2 [EPN in 2]
EPO	See **EPOM**
EPOM	ENGLISH POEMS, Vol. I. Old English and middle English periods. Walter C. Bronson, comp. (1910). For Vols. II, III, IV, see **EPEP**, **EPRE**, **EPNC** 3-2 [EPO in 2]
EPP	ENGLISH PROSE AND POETRY. John Matthews Manly, comp. (1926) 5-4-3-A
EPR	See **EPRE**
EPRE	ENGLISH POEMS, Vol. III. The Restoration and the eighteenth century. Walter C. Bronson (1908). For Vols. I, II, IV, see **EPOM**, **EPEP**, **EPNC** 3-2 [EPR in 2]
EPS	ENGLISH POETRY OF THE SEVENTEENTH CENTURY. Roberta Florence Brinkley, ed. (1936; rev. ed., 1942) 5-4-3
EPs	PARNASSUS. Ralph Waldo Emerson, ed. (1874-) 2-1
EPW 1-5	ENGLISH POETS, THE, Vols. I-V. Thomas Humphrey Ward, ed. (1880-1918) 3-2 [WEP 1-4 in 2]
EPY	See **EP *****
ERoP 1-2	ENGLISH ROMANTIC POETRY, Vols. I-II. Harold Bloom, ed. (1963) 6
ERP	ENGLISH ROMANTIC POETS. James Stephens, Edwin L. Beck, & Royall H. Snow, eds. (1933) 5-4-3
ErPo	EROTIC POETRY. William Cole, ed. (1936) 6-D

ES 40

ES	ELIZABETHAN SONGS IN HONOUR OF LOVE AND BEAUTIE. Edmund Henry Garrett, comp., (1891)
	1
ES *	ENGLISH SONNETS. Arthur T. Quiller-Couch, ed. (1936)
	5-4-3
ESaP	ENGLISH SATIRIC POETRY: Dryden to Byron. James Kinsley & James T. Boulton, eds. (1966)
	E
ESB	See ESPB
ESCL	EVERY SOUL IS A CIRCUS. Vachel Lindsay. (1929)
	3
ESPB	ENGLISH AND SCOTTISH POPULAR BALLADS. Helen Child Sargent & George Lyman Kittredge, eds., from the collection of Francis James Child. (1904)
	6-5-4-3-2 [ESB in 2]
ESs	ENGLISH SATIRES. William Henry O. Smeaton, ed. (1899)
	1
EtPaEn	ETERNAL PASSION IN ENGLISH POETRY. Edith Wharton & Robert Norton, comps. (1939)
821.08 W55	5-4-B
EtS	ETERNAL SEA, THE. W. M. Williamson, ed. (1946)
	6-5-4
EuE	EUREKA ENTERTAINMENTS; containing a wide variety of new & novel entertainments. (1894) Penn Pub. Co.
	2-1
EV 1-5	ENGLISH VERSE, Vols. I-V. W. Peacock, ed. (1928-1931)
	5-4-3
EvOK	EVERYBODY OUGHT TO KNOW. Ogden Nash, ed. (1961)
	6-D
ExPo	EXPLORING POETRY. M. L. Rosenthal & A. J. M. Smith, eds. (1955)
	6-5-C

EY	ENCHANTED YEARS, THE. John Calvin Metcalf & James Southall Wilson, eds. (1921) A
FaBoBe	FAMILY BOOK OF BEST LOVED POEMS, THE. David L. George, ed. (1952) 6-5-C
FaBoCh	FABER BOOK OF CHILDREN'S VERSE, THE. Janet Adam Smith, comp. (1953). For the revised edition of 1959 under title THE LOOKING GLASS BOOK OF VERSE, see LoGBV 6-5-C
FaBoCo	FABER BOOK OF COMIC VERSE, THE. Michael Roberts & Janet Adam Smith, eds. (Rev. ed., 1974) E
FaBoEn	FABER BOOK OF ENGLISH VERSE, THE. John Hayward, ed. (1958) 6-5
FaBoMo	FABER BOOK OF MODERN VERSE, THE. Michael Roberts, ed. (2d ed., 1951, with a supplement of poems chosen by Anne Ridler) 6-5-C
FaBoTw	FABER BOOK OF TWENTIETH CENTURY VERSE, THE. John Heath-Stubbs & David Wright, eds. (1953) 6-5-C
FaBV	FAMILY BOOK OF VERSE, THE. Lewis Gannett, ed. (1961) 6-D
FaChP	FAVORITE CHRISTIAN POEMS. Donald T. Kauffman, ed. (1969) 6
FAD	FRIDAY AFTERNOON SERIES OF DIALOGUES. Thomas S. Denison, ed. (1907) 2-1
FAF	FLOWERING AFTER FROST. Michael McMahon, ed. (1975) E
FaFP	FAMILY ALBUM OF FAVORITE POEMS, THE. P. Edward Ernest, ed. (1959) 6-5

FAOV	FATHER. Margery Doud & Cleo M. Parsley, comps. (1931) 5-4-3
FaPL	FAMOUS POEMS AND THE LITTLE-KNOWN STORIES BEHIND THEM. Ralph L. Woods, ed. (1961) 6-D
FaPoFa	FAVORITE POEMS OF FAITH AND COMFORT. Barbara Moses Olds, ed. (1942) B
FaPON	FAVORITE POEMS OLD AND NEW. Helen Ferris, ed. (1957) 6-5
FAS	FRIDAY AFTERNOON SPEAKER, THE. Thomas S. Denison, ed. (1881) 2-1
FCP	FIVE COURTIER POETS OF THE ENGLISH RENAISSANCE. Robert M. Bender, ed. (1967) 6
FD 1-2	FIVE MINUTE DECLAMATIONS, Parts I-II. Walter K. Fobes, ed. (1885-1890) 2-1
FDY	DIALOGUES FOR YOUNG FOLKS. S. A. Frost [Sarah Annie (Frost) Shields]. (1867) 1
FEP	FIRESIDE ENCYCLOPEDIA OF POETRY. Henry Troth Coates, comp. & ed. (1901) 2-1
FF	FACING FORWARD. Joseph Morris, pseud. [i.e., Joseph Morris Bachelor] & St. Clair Adams, comps. (1925). For composite edition of 1928, see **POL** 3-A
FFTM	FEW FIGS FROM THISTLES, A. Edna St. Vincent Millay. (1922) 3
FHE	HUMOROUS AND EXHIBITION DIALOGUES. S. A. Frost [Sarah Annie (Frost) Shields]. (1870?) 1
FHS	FOR HIS SAKE. Anna E. Mack, ed. (1900) 2-1
FiBHP	FIRESIDE BOOK OF HUMOROUS POETRY,

	THE. William Cole, ed. (1959) 6-5
FiCP	FIFTY CONTEMPORARY POETS. Alberta Turner, ed. (1977) E
FIM	FATAL INTERVIEW. Edna St. Vincent Millay. (1931) 3
FiMAP	FIFTEEN MODERN AMERICAN POETS. George P. Elliott, ed. (1956) 6-5
FiP	FIFTEEN POETS; Chaucer to Arnold. (1941) Oxford Univ. Press 6-5-4
FiSC	FIRE AND SLEET AND CANDLELIGHT. August Derleth, ed. (1961) 6-D
FiYeLa	FIFTEEN YEARS FROM THE LANTERN. C. B. McAllister & Lefa Morse Eddy, eds. (1942) B
FlCo	FLYING COLOURS. Sir Charles G. D. Roberts, ed. (1942) 4-B
FLD	See FOAH
FLS	FOR LOVE'S SWEET SAKE. George Herbert Westley, ed. (1899) 2-1
FlW	FLOCK OF WORDS, A. David Mackay, ed. (1969) 6
FMR	FIVE MINUTE READINGS. Walter K. Fobes, ed. (1886) 2-1
FND	NEW BOOK OF DIALOGUES. S. A. Frost [Sarah Annie (Frost) Shields] (1872) 1
FOAH	FLAG DAY (Our American Holidays Series). Robert Haven Schauffler, ed. (1912) 5-4-3-2 [FLD & OAF in 2]
FoBA	FOURTEEN BRITISH AND AMERICAN POETS. Rowland L. Collins, ed. (1964) D

FOL	FROM OTHER LANDS. Al Hine, ed. (1969) 6
ForPo	FORM OF POETRY, THE. Thomas R. Arp, ed. (1966) 6
FoS	FORMAL SPRING. R. N. Currey, tr. (1950) 5
FosPo	FORMS OF POETRY. James L. Calderwood & Harold F. Tolliver, eds. (1968) 6
FoW 1-3	FOUR WINDS. Books I-III. Jean Edwards, comp. (1939) 4
FP	FAVORITE POEMS; selected from English & American authors. (Astor edition, 1883; compiled by Thomas Young Crowell, 1884) 2-1
FP *	FIFTY POETS. William Rose Benét, ed. (1933) 4-3
FPE	FAMOUS POEMS EXPLAINED. Waitman Barbe. (1909; rev. ed., 1930) 3-2
FPH	FIRESIDE POEMS. Veronica S. Hutchinson, ed. (1930) 3
FR	FIVE MINUTE DECLAMATIONS. Walter K. Fobes, ed. (1885) 2-1
FRC	FIRST READER OF CONTEMPORARY AMERICAN POETRY, A. Patrick Gleeson, ed. (1969) 6
FrOW	FROM ONE WORD; selected poems from "Spirit," 1944-1949. John Gilland Brunini, ed. (1950) 4
FS	FAVORITE SPEAKER, THE. T. G. La Moille & Eugene Parsons, comps. (1885) 2-1
FSFS	FOUR SEASONS FIVE SENSES. Elinor Parker, comp. (1974) E
FSN	FAVORITE SONGS OF THE NINETIES. Robert A. Fremont, ed. (1973) E

FT	FRIENDLY TOWN, THE. Edward V. Lucas, comp. (1905) 4-3-2
FTA	FOR THEE ALONE. Grace Hartshorne, comp. (1899) 2-1
FTB	FOUR AND TWENTY BLACKBIRDS. Helen Dean Fish, ed. (1937) 6-5-4-3
FTR	CHOICE READINGS FROM STANDARD AND POPULAR AUTHORS. Robert Irwin Fulton & Thomas Clarkson Trueblood, comps. (1887) 2-1
FTT	FROM TOTS TO TEENS. Clara J. [Fort] Denton. (1897) 2-1
FuAF	FUN IN AMERICAN FOLK RHYMES. Ray Wood, ed. (1952) C
GA	GREAT AMERICANS, AS SEEN BY THE POETS. Burton Egbert Stevenson, ed. (1933) 5-4-3
GaP	GAILY WE PARADE. John E. Brewton, comp. (1940) 6-5-4
GatP	GATEWAY TO POETRY. Elizabeth Sturch, comp. (1946) 4
GBL	GAMBIT BOOK OF LOVE POEMS, THE. Geoffrey Grigson, ed. (1975). Same as THE FABER BOOK OF LOVE POEMS E
GBOV	GARDEN BOOK OF VERSE, THE. William Griffith & Mrs. John Walton Paris, eds. (1932) 4-3
GBP	GAMBIT BOOK OF POPULAR VERSE, THE. Geoffrey Grigson, ed. (1971). Same as THE FABER BOOK OF POPULAR VERSE E
GBV	GIRL'S BOOK OF VERSE, THE. Mary Gould Davis, comp., (1922; rev. ed., 1952) 6-5-C-4-3-A
GC	GARLAND OF CHILHOOD, THE. Percy Withers,

	comp. (1910) 2
GDAH	GRADUATION DAY (Our American Heritage Series). A. P. Sanford & Robert Haven Schauffler, eds. (1930) 5-4-3
GEP	See GEPM
GEPC	GREAT ENGLISH POETS; Oscar James Campbell & J. F. A. Pyre, comps. (1928) 5-4-3
GEPM	GREAT ENGLISH POETS, A SELECTION FROM THE. Sherwin Cody, ed. (1905) 3-2 [GEP in 2]
GFA	GOLDEN FLUTE, THE. Alice Hubbard & Adeline Babbitt, comps. (1932) 6-5-4-3
GG	GOLDEN GLEAMS OF THOUGHT. S. Pollock Linn, comp. (1882) 2-1
GH	GOOD HUMOR FOR READING AND RECITATION. Henry Firth Wood, comp. (1893) 3-2-1
GMAS	GOOD MORNING, AMERICA. Carl Sandburg. (1927) 3
GMs	GRADED MEMORY SELECTIONS. S. D. Waterman, J. W. McClymonds, & C. C. Hughes, comps. (1903) 1
GN	GOLDEN NUMBERS. Kate Douglas Wiggin & Nora Archibald Smith, eds. (1902) 6-5-4-3-2-1
GnP-1	GEORGIAN POETRY, 1911-1912. Prefactory note by E. H. Marsh ("E. H.") (1914) 2
GnP-2	GEORGIAN POETRY, 1913-1915. Prefactory note by E. H. Marsh ("E. H.") (1916) 2
GoBC	GOLDEN BOOK OF CATHOLIC POETRY, THE. Alfred Noyes, ed. (1946) 6-5-4
GoBP	GOLDEN BOOK OF POETRY, THE. Jane Werner, ed. (1949) 5-4

GoJo	GOLDEN JOURNEY, THE. Louise Bogan & William Jay Smith, comps. (1965) 6-D
GoSl	GOLDEN SLIPPERS. Arna Bontemps, comp. (4th ed., 1941) 6-5-4-B
GoTL	GOLDEN TREASURY OF LONGER POEMS, THE. Ernest Rhys, ed. (1939; rev. ed., 1949) 6-5-4
GoTP	GOLDEN TREASURY OF POETRY, THE. Louis Untermeyer, ed. (1959) 6-5
GoTS	GOLDEN TREASURY OF SCOTTISH POETRY, THE. Hugh MacDiarmid, pseud.[(i.e., Christopher Murray Grieve], ed. (1941) 6-5-4
GoYe	GOLDEN YEAR, THE. Melville Cane, John Farrar, & Louise Townsend Nicholl, eds. (1960) 6-5
GP	GOLDEN POEMS BY BRITISH AND AMERICAN AUTHORS. Francis F. Browne, ed. (1882; new ed., 1906) 2-1
GPE	GREAT POEMS OF THE ENGLISH LANGUAGE. Wallace Alvin Briggs, comp. (1927; new ed., 1936; enl. ed. with a supplement of recent poetry by William Rose Benét, 1941) 3-A
GPWW	GREAT POEMS OF THE WORLD WAR. William Dunseath Eaton, ed. (1922). Published in 1918 under the title THE WAR IN VERSE & PROSE 3
GR 1-2	GOOD READINGS FOR HIGH SCHOOLS, Vol. 1. Adventure & Vol. 2. Achievement. Tom Peete Cross, Reed Smith, & Elmer Stauffer, eds. (1931) 3
GR-a	GOOD READINGS FOR HIGH SCHOOLS, Vol. 3. American writers. Tom Peete Cross, Reed Smith, & Elmer Stauffer eds. (1931) 3
GR-e	GOOD READINGS FOR HIGH SCHOOLS, Vol. 4.

	English writers. Tom Peete Cross, Reed Smith, & Elmer Stauffer, eds. (1931) 3
GrCo 1-2	GREAT COMPANIONS, Vols. I-II. Robert French Leavens & Mary Agnes Leavens, comps., (1927- 1941 5-4-B
GrL	GREEK LITERATURE IN TRANSLATION. Whitney Jennings Oates & Charles Theophilus Murphy, eds. (1944) 5-4
GrPE	GREEK POETRY FOR EVERYMAN. F. L. Lucas, ed. & tr. (1951) 5-C
GrPo	GREEK POETS, THE. Moses Hadas, ed. (1953) 5-C
GrR	GREEK READER, THE. A. L. Whall, ed. (1943) 5-4
GrRo	GRANDFATHER ROCK. David Morse, ed. (1972) E
GS	GOLDEN SONGS OF THE GOLDEN STATE. Marguerite Wilkinson, comp. (1917) 2
GS *	GOLDEN STAIRCASE, THE. Louey Chisholm, comp. (1906) 3-2 [GSP in 2]
GS **	GRAHAM'S SCHOOL DIALOGUES FOR YOUNG PEOPLE. George C. Graham. (1878) 1
GSP	GREAT STORY-POEMS. Theodoric Jones, comp. (1966) 6
GSP *	See GS *
GSRC	GRACE MARIE STANISTREET'S RECITATIONS FOR CHILDREN. Grace Marie Stanistreet, comp. (1930) 3
GT	GYPSY TRAIL, THE. [Vol. I]. Pauline Goldmark & Mary Hopkins, comps. (1914) 2
GT-2	GYPSY TRAIL, THE. Vol. II. Pauline Goldmark & Mary Hopkins, comps. (1930) 4-3

GTBS	GOLDEN TREASURY OF THE BEST SONGS AND LYRICAL POEMS IN THE ENGLISH LANGUAGE, THE. Francis Palgrave, comp. (1929) Oxford Univ. Press 6-5-4-3
GTBS-D	GOLDEN TREASURY OF THE BEST SONGS AND LYRICAL POEMS IN THE ENGLISH LANGUAGE, THE. Francis Turner Palgrave, comp. With additional poems selected by C. Day Lewis. (1954) 6-5-C
GTBS-P	GOLDEN TREASURY OF THE BEST SONGS AND LYRICAL POEMS IN THE ENGLISH LANGUAGE, THE. Francis Turner Palgrave, comp. With a fifth book selected by John Press. (1964) 6-D
GTBS-W	F. T. PALGRAVE'S THE GOLDEN TREASURY OF THE BEST SONGS AND LYRICAL POEMS. Revised and enlarged by Oscar Williams. (1953) 6-5-C
GTIV	GOLDEN TREASURY OF IRISH VERSE, A. Lennox Robinson, ed. (1925) 5-4-3-A [TIV in A]
GTML	GOLDEN TREASURY OF MODERN LYRICS, A. Laurence Binyon, comp. (New ed., 1924) 5-4-3-A
GTSE	GOLDEN TREASURY (Everyman's Library). Francis T. Palgrave, comp. (1934) 6-5-4-3
GTSL	GOLDEN TREASURY OF SONGS AND LYRICS, THE. Francis T. Palgrave, comp. (Rev. & enl. ed., 2 vols. in 1928) 6-5-4-3-2 [PGT 1-2 in 2]
GTWL	GOOD THINGS FOR WASHINGTON AND LINCOLN BIRTHDAYS. Marie Irish. (1907) 2
HaMV	HARRAP BOOK OF MODERN VERSE, THE. Maurice Wollman & Kathleen B. Parker, comps. (1959) 6-5
HAP	HARPER'S ANTHOLOGY FOR COLLEGE

	COURSES IN COMPOSITION AND LITERATURE, Vol. 2. Poetry. Frederick A. Manchester & William F. Giese, eds. (1926) A
HaSV	HARRAP BOOK OF SEA VERSE, THE. Ronald Hope, ed. (1960) D
HB	HEROIC BALLADS. David Henry Montgomery, ed. (1890) 2-1
HB *	HOMESPUN. Anite Brown, comp. (1936) 3
HBMV	HOME BOOK OF MODERN VERSE, THE. Burton Egbert Stevenson, ed. (1925; 2d ed., 1953) 6-5-4-3-A [HMV in A]
HBP	HOUSEHOLD BOOK OF POETRY, THE. Charles A. Dana, comp. (1858) 2-1
HBR	HANDBOOK OF BEST READINGS. Solomon Henry Clark, ed. (1902) 3-2-1
HBV	HOME BOOK OF VERSE, THE. Burton Egbert Stevenson, ed. (3d ed., 1918; 5th ed., 1922; 6th ed., 1926; 8th ed. 1949, 2 vols.) 6-5-4-3-A-2
HBVY	HOME BOOK OF VERSE FOR YOUNG FOLKS, THE. Burton Egbert Stevenson, ed. (1915; rev. & enl. ed., 1929) 6-5-4-3-2 [HBVy in 2]
HBVy	See HBVY
HCTC	HOW TO CELEBRATE THANKSGIVING AND CHRISTMAS. Alice M. Kellogg, ed. (1894) 3-2
HD	HUMOROUS DIALOGUES AND DRAMAS. Charles C. Shoemaker, comp. (1888) 2-1
HDL	HEAVEN'S DISTANT LAMPS. Anna E. Mack, comp. (1900) 2-1
HE	HOLIDAY ENTERTAINMENTS. Charles C. Shoemaker, ed. (1888) 3-2-1
HeIP	HEATH INTRODUCTION TO POETRY, THE.

	Joseph de Roche, ed. (1975) E
HeS	HEARTLAND II: poets of the midwest. Lucien Stryk, ed. (1975) E
HeT	HEROIC TALES IN VERSE. E. J. Pratt, ed. (1941) 5-4
HGP	HUNDRED GREAT POEMS, A. Richard James Cross, comp. (1907) 2
HGV	HARVEST OF GERMAN VERSE, A. Margarete Munsterberg, ed. & tr. (1916) 2
HH	HIGHWAYS AND HOLIDAYS. Florence Adams & Elizabeth McCarrick, comps. (1927) 6-5-4-3-A
HH *	See HHHA
HHHA	HUMOROUS HITS AND HOW TO HOLD AN AUDIENCE. Grenville Kleiser. (1908) 3-2 [HH in 2]
HiLiAm	HIGHLIGHTS IN AMERICAN LITERATURE. Ola Pauline Srygley & others, eds. (1940) 5-4-B
HiLiEn	HIGHLIGHTS IN ENGLISH LITERATURE. Ola Pauline Srygley & Otsie Verona Betts, eds. (1940) 5-4-B
HMSP	HOLYROOD; a garland of modern Scots poetry. W. H. Hamilton, ed. (1929) 4-3
HMV	See HBMV
HNS	NEW SCIENCE OF ELOCUTION, THE. S. S. Hamill. (1886; rev. ed., 1914) 2-1
HOAH	HALLOWE'EN (Our American Holidays Series). Robert Haven Schauffler, ed. (1933) 5-4-3
HoPM	HOW DOES A POEM MEAN? John Ciardi, ed. (1959) 6-5
HP-1	HUMBLER POETS, THE, 1870-1885. Slason Thompson, comp. (1885) 2-1

HP-2	HUMBLER POETS, THE, 1885-1910 [2d series]. Wallace Rice & Frances Rice, comps. (1911) 2
HPB	HISTORIC POEMS AND BALLADS. Rupert Sargent Holland, ed. (1912) 2
HPE	HUMOROUS POETRY OF THE ENGLISH LANGUAGE, THE, FROM CHAUCER TO SAXE. James Parton, ed. (13th ed., 1884) 2-1
HR	HOWARD'S RECITATIONS. Clarence J. Howard, ed. (1872) 1
HS	HOLIDAY SELECTIONS FOR READING AND RECITATION. Sara Sigourney Rice, ed. (1892) 4-3-2-1
HSP	HUMOROUS SPEAKER, THE. Paul M. Pearson, comp. (1909) 3-A-2 [HSp in 2]
HSp	See HSP
HSPS	HIGH SCHOOL PRIZE SKEAKER, THE. William Leonard Snow, ed. (1916) 3-2
HSS 1-3	HARPER'S SCHOOL SPEAKER, Vols. I-III. James Baldwin comp. (1890-1891) 1
HT	HEART THROBS IN PROSE AND VERSE. Joseph Mitchell Chapple, comp. (1905). Published also with MORE HEART THROBS in a 1 vol. edition, TREASURE CHEST OF MEMORIES, see MHT 3-2 [HTb-1 in 2]
HT *	HERE AND THERE. Elinor Parker, ed (1967) 6
HT **	See HTR
Htb-1	See HT
HTP	See TPH
HTR	HIGH TIDE. Mrs. Waldo Richards [Gertrude Moore Richards], comp. (1916) 3-2 [HT in 2]
HW	HIGH WEDLOCK THEN BE HONOURED. Virginia Tufte, ed. (1970) 6

HWC	HERE WE COME A' PIPING. Rose Fyleman, ed. (1937) 3
HWM	HARP-WEAVER, THE. Edna St. Vincent Millay. (1923) 3
HYD	HOLMES'S VERY LITTLE DIALOGUES FOR VERY LITTLE FOLKS. Alice Holmes. (1875) 1
HYE	HOLDING YOUR EIGHT HANDS. Edward Lucie-Smith, ed. (1969) 6
IAP	INTRODUCTION TO AMERICAN POETRY, AN. Frederick C. Prescott & Gerald DeWitt Sanders, eds. (1932) 5-4-3
ICBD	IT CAN BE DONE. Joseph Morris, pseud. [i.e., Joseph Morris Bachelor] & St. Clair Adams, comps. (1921) 3-A [ICD in A]
ICD	See ICBD
IcP	ICELANDIC POEMS AND STORIES. Richard Beck, ed. (1943) 5-4
ID	IDEAL DRILLS. Marguerite W. Morton, comp. (1900) 2-1
IDAH	INDEPENDENCE DAY (Our American Holidays Series). Robert Haven Schauffler, ed. (1912) 5-4-3-2 [OAI in 2]
IDB	I AM THE DARKER BROTHER. Arnold Adoff, ed. (1968) 6
IHA	I HEAR AMERICA SINGING. Ruth Barnes, comp. (1937) 6-5-4-3
IHMS	I HEAR MY SISTERS SAYING: poems by 20th century women. Carol Knoek & Dorothy Walters, eds. (1976) E
ILP	INTRODUCTION TO LITERATURE: POEMS. Lynn Altenbernd & Leslie L. Lewis, eds. (1963) 6-D
ImOP	IMAGINATION'S OTHER PLACE. Helen Plotz,

	comp. (1955) 6-5-C
InME	INNOCENT MERRIMENT. Franklin P. Adams, comp. (1942) 6-5-4-B
InP	INTRODUCTION TO POETRY, AN. Jay B. Hubbell & John O. Beaty, eds. (Rev. ed. 1936) 6-5-4
InPK	INTRODUCTION TO POETRY, AN. X. J. Kennedy, ed. (3d ed., 1974) E
InPo	INTRODUCTION TO POETRY. Mark Van Doren, ed. (1951) 6-5-C
InPS	INTRODUCTION TO POETRY, AN. Louis Simpson, ed. (2d ed., 1972) E
IPWM	INTRODUCING POETRY. Linda W. Wagner & C. David Mead, eds. (1976) E
InV	INVITATION TO VERSE, A. E. M. Bayliss, ed. (1944) 4
InvP	INVITATION TO POETRY. Lloyd Frankenberg, ed. (1956) 6-5
IR	INTERPRETIVE READING. Cora Marsland. (1902) 2-1
IrP	IRISH POEMS OF TODAY. Geoffrey Taylor, ed. (1944) 4
IrPN	IRISH POETS OF THE NINETEENTH CENTURY. Geoffrey Taylor, ed. (1951) 6-5-C
ISi	I SING OF A MAIDEN. Sister M. Therese, ed. (1947) 6-5-4
ISP	INTRODUCTION TO THE STUDY OF POETRY, AN. Richard Ray Kirk & Roger Philip McCutcheon, eds. (1934) 4-3
JAWP	JUNIOR ANTHOLOGY OF WORLD POETRY, A. Mark Van Doren & Garibaldi M. Lapolia, eds. (1929). Same as **WBP** 6-5-4-3
JB	JUMP BAD. Gwendolyn Brooks, ed. (1971) E

JHP	JUNIOR HIGH SCHOOL POETRY. John A. O'Keefe & Frederick A. Guindon, comps. (1927) 3-A [JHSP in A]
JHSP	See JHP
JK 1-2	JOYCE KILMER, Vols. I-II. Robert Cortes Holliday, ed. (1918) 3
JKCP	JOYCE KILMER'S ANTHOLOGY OF CATHOLIC POETS. Joyce Kilmer, ed. (New ed., 1926; with a new supplement by James Edward Tobin, 1955). Edition of 1917 had title DREAMS AND IMAGES, see DI 6-5-C-4-3
JPC	JUNIOR POETRY CURE, THE. Robert Haven Schauffler, comp. (1931) 3
Kal	KALEIDOSCOPE. Robert Hayden, ed. (1967) 6
KC	KAVANAUGH'S COMIC DIALOGUES & PIECES FOR LITTLE CHILDREN. Mrs. Russell Kavanaugh. (1887) 1
KER	KAVANAUGH'S EXHIBITION RECITER FOR VERY LITTLE CHILDREN. Mrs. Russell Kavanaugh. (1881) 1
KH	KAVANAUGH'S HUMOROUS DRAMAS. Mrs. Russell Kavanaugh. (1878) 1
KiLC	KINGS, LORDS, & COMMONS. Frank O'Connor, pseud. [i.e., Michael O'Donovan], ed. & tr. (1959) 6-5
KJ	KAVANAUGH'S JUVENILE SPEAKER. Mrs. Russell Kavanaugh. (1877) 1
KN	KNAPSACK, THE. Herbert Read, ed. (1939; 7th ed., 1947) 5-4
KNE	KIDD'S NEW ELOCUTION AND VOCAL CULTURE. Robert Kidd. (1883) 1
KNS	KAVANAUGH'S NEW SPEECHES AND DIALOGUES. Mrs. Russell Kavanaugh. (1884) 1

LA	LYRIC AMERICA, 1630-1930. Alfred Kreymborg, ed. (1930). Revised editions of 1935 and 1941 have title AN ANTHOLOGY OF AMERICAN POETRY, see **AnAmPo**
LaA	LATE AUGUSTANS, THE. Donald Davie, ed. (1958) 6-5
LaNeLa	LAYS OF THE NEW LAND. Charlie May Simon, ed. (1943) 6-5-4-B
LaP	LATIN POETRY IN VERSE TRANSLATION. L. R. Lind, ed. (1957) 5
LAuP	LATE AUGUSTAN POETRY. Patricia Meyer Spacks, ed. (1973) E
LauV	LAUGHING VERSE. Fairfax Douwney, comp. (1946) 5-4
LAV	See **LEAP**
LBA	See **LBAP**
LBAH	LINCOLN'S BIRTHDAY (Our American Holidays Series). Robert Haven Schauffler, ed. (1909) 5-4-3-2- [OAL in 2]
LBAP	LITTLE BOOK OF AMERICAN POETS, THE, 1787-1900. Jessie B. Rittenhouse, ed. (1915) 5-4-3-2 [LBA in 2]
LBB	BALLADS OF BOOKS. Andrew Lang, ed. (1888) 1
LBBV	LITTLE BOOK OF MODERN BRITISH VERSE, THE. Jessie B. Rittenhouse, comp. (1924) 5-4-3-A
LBMV	LITTLE BOOK OF MODERN VERSE, THE. Jessie B. Rittenhouse, ed. (1913). See also **SBMV, TBM** 5-4-3-2
LBN	LITTLE BOOK OF NECESSARY NONSENSE, A. Burges Johnson, comp. (1929) 6-5-4-3
LC	LISTENING CHILD, THE. Lucy W. Thacher, comp. (1899) 3-A-2-1
LCL	LISTEN, CHILDREN, LISTEN. Lyra Cohn Livingstone, ed. (1972) E

LCS	CHILDHOOD SONGS. Lucy Larcom. (1874) 1
LEAP	LE GALLIENNE BOOK OF ENGLISH AND AMERICAN POETRY, THE. Richard Le Gallienne, ed. (2 vols. in 1, 1935). First published as THE LE GALLIENNE BOOK OF ENGLISH VERSE (1922) & THE LE GALLIENNE BOOK OF AMERICAN VERSE (1925) 5-4-3-A [BEV & LAV in A]
LFL	LITTLE-FOLK LYRICS. Frank Dempster Sherman. (1897) 2-1
LFS	LITTLE FOLKS SPEAKER. Charles W. Brown, comp. (1903) 2
LH	LYRA HEROICA. William Ernest Henley, ed. (1891) 5-4-3-2-1
LHT	LYRA HISTORICA. M. E. Windsor & J. Turral, eds. (1911) 2
LHV	LITTLE BOOK OF AMERICAN HUMOROUS VERSE, A. T. A. Daly, comp. (1926) 6-5-4-3-A
LHW	LOVE'S HIGH WAY. Mrs. Waldo Richards [Gertrude Moore Richards], comp. (1927) 3-A
LiA	LIMITS OF ART, THE. Huntington Cairns, ed. (1948) 5-4
LiAnCa	LITTLE ANTHOLOGY OF CANADIAN POETS, A. Ralph Gustafson, ed. (1943) B
LiBL	LITTLE BOOK OF LIMERICKS, THE. H. I. Brock, comp. (1947) 6-5-4
LiL	LITTLE LAUGHTER, A. Katherine Love, comp. (1957) 5
LiPo	LINCOLN AND THE POETS. William W. Betts, Jr., ed. (1965) 6-D
LiTA	LITTLE TREASURY OF AMERICAN POETRY,

	A. Oscar Williams, ed. (1948) 6-5-4
LiTB	LITTLE TREASURY OF BRITISH POETRY, A. Oscar Williams, ed. (1951) 6-5-C
LiTG	LITTLE TREASURY OF GREAT POETRY, A. Oscar Williams, ed. (1947) 6-5-4
LiTL	LITTLE TREASURY OF LOVE POEMS, A. John Holmes, ed. (1950) 6-5-4
LiTM	LITTLE TREASURY OF MODERN POETRY, A, ENGLISH AND AMERICAN. Oscar Williams, ed. (1946; rev. ed., 1950. 3d ed., 1970) 6-5-C-4
LiTW	LITTLE TREASURY OF WORLD POETRY, A. Hubert Creekmore, ed. (1952) 6-5-C
LL	LITTLE LINES FOR LITTLE SPEAKERS. Clara J. [Fort] Denton. (1891) 1
LL 1-4	LITERATURE AND LIFE, Vols. I-IV. Edwin A. Greenlaw, William H. Elson, Christine M. Keck, Dudley Miles, Clarence Stratton, & Robert C. Pooley, eds. (Rev. ed., 1933-1936) 3
LLC	LINCOLN LITERARY COLLECTION. John Piersol McCaskey, ed. (1897) 3-2-1
LO	LOVE. Walter de la Mare, ed. (1946) 6-5-4
LoAs	LOVE'S ASPECTS. Jean Garrigue, comp. (1975) E
LoBV	LONDON BOOK OF ENGLISH VERSE, THE. Herbert Read & Bonamy Dobrée, comps. (1949; 2d rev. ed., 1952) 6-5-4
LoDa	LOOK TO THIS DAY. The Poetry Society of Southern California. (1944) B
LoEn	LOVE'S ENCHANTMENT. Helen Ferris, comp. (1944) 6-5-4-B
LoGBV	LOOKING GLASS BOOK OF VERSE, THE. Janet

	Adam Smith, comp. (1959). Revised edition of **FaBoCh** 6-5
LoP	LOVE POEMS. [Elizabeth Riley, comp.] (1945) 4
LoPo	LOVE POEMS, OLD AND NEW. Catharine Connell, comp. (1943) 5-4-B
LoPS	LOVE POEMS OF SIX CENTURIES. Helen Husted, ed. (1950) 5-4
LOS 1-3	LAND OF SONG, THE, Books I-III. Katharine Henry Shute, comp. Larkin Dunton, ed. (1898-1899) 2
LOW	LEAN OUT OF THE WINDOW. Sara Hannum & Gwendolyn E. Reed, comps. (1965) 6-D
LOW *	LIGHT OF THE WORLD. Joseph Morris, pseud. [i.e., Joseph Morris Bachelor] & St. Clair Adams, comps. (1928). For composite edition of 1928, see **POL** 3
LP	LIVING POETS. Michael Morpurgo & Clifford Simmons, comps. (1974) E
LPC	LAMB'S POETRY FOR CHILDREN. Charles Lamb & Mary Lamb. William MacDonald, ed. (1903) 1
LPD	LITTLE PEOPLE'S DIALOGUES. Clara J. [Fort] Denton. (1888) 2-1
LPP	LITTLE PRIMARY PIECES FOR WEE FOLKS TO SPEAK. Caroline Stearns Griffin, comp. (1904) 3-2
LPS	LITTLE PEOPLE'S SPEAKER. Mrs. J. W. Shoemaker [Rachel W. (Hinkle) Shoemaker]. (1886). For composite edition, see **PPYP** 2-1
LPS 1-3	LIBRARY OF POETRY AND SONG, Vols. I-III. William Cullen Bryant, ed. (Rev. & enl. ed., 1925). For edition of 1903 under title A NEW

	LIBRARY OF POETRY AND SONG, see BNL 5-4-3
LS	LOVE SONGS OF CHILDHOOD. Eugene Field. (1894) 1
LS *	LYRIC SOUTH, THE. Addison Hibbard, ed. (1928) 5-4-3
LTV	LOVER'S TREASURY OF VERSE. John White Chadwick & Annie Hathaway Chadwick, comps. (1891) 2
LV	LYRIC VERSE. Edwin Rakow, ed. (1962) D
LVN	LAST VOYAGE, THE (Book III of THE TORCH BEARERS). Alfred Noyes. (1930) 3
LY	LYRIC YEAR. Ferdinand Earle, ed. (1912) 2
LyMA	LYRICS OF THE MIDDLE AGES. Hubert Creekmore, ed. (1959) 5
LyMo	LYRIC MODERNS. Tom Boggs, ed. (1940) 4-B
LyPI	LYRIC POETRY OF THE ITALIAN RENAIS- SANCE. L. R. Lind, ed. (1954) 5-C
MaAnDe	MAN ANSWERS DEATH. Corliss Lamont, ed. (2d & enl. ed., 1952) C
MaC	MAGIC CIRCLE, THE. Louis Untermeyer, ed. (1952) 6-5-C
MAD	ALL KINDS OF DIALOGUES. H. Elliott McBride. (1874) 1
MAL	MASTERPIECES OF AMERICAN LITERATURE. Horace E. Scudder, ed. (1891) 3-2-1
MAL *	MODERN AMERICAN LYRICS. Stanton A. Coblentz, comp. (1924) A
MaMe	MAJOR METAPHYSICAL POETS OF THE SEVENTEENTH CENTURY, THE. Edwin

	Honig & Oscar Williams, eds. (1968) 6
MAmP	MAJOR AMERICAN POETS TO 1914. Francis Murphy, ed. (1967) 6
MAP	MODERN AMERICAN POETRY. Louis Untermeyer, ed. (5th rev. ed., 1936). For the 6th & 7th revised editions, see **MoAmPo**. For the 3d revised edition, see **UAP** 6-5-4-3
MAP *	See **MAPA**
MAPA	MODERN AMERICAN POETS. Conrad Aiken, ed. (1927). Enlarged edition of 1963 has title TWENTIETH-CENTURY AMERICAN POETRY, see **TwAmPo** 6-5-4-3-A [MAP in A]
MaPo	MAJOR POETS, THE. Charles M. Coffin & Gerrit Hubbard Roelofs, eds. (1954, 2d ed., 1969) 6-5-C
MaRV	MASTERPIECES OF RELIGIOUS VERSE. James Dalton Morrison, ed. (1948) 6-5-4
MasP	MASTER POEMS OF THE ENGLISH LANGUAGE. Oscar Williams, ed. (1966) 6
MAT	MESSAGES: a thematic anthology of poetry. X. J. Kennedy, ed. (1973) E
MAuV	MAP OF AUSTRALIAN VERSE, A. James McAuley, ed. (1975) E
MaVP	MAJOR VICTORIAN POETS, THE. William H. Marshall, ed. (1966) 6
MBB	BALLADS OF BOOKS. Brander Matthews, ed. (1886) 1
MBD	LATEST DIALOGUES. H. Elliott McBride. (1889) 2
MBL	MASTERPIECES OF BRITISH LITERATURE. Horace E. Scudder, ed. (1895) 3-2-1

MBL *

MBL *	MODERN BRITISH LYRICS. Stanton A. Coblentz, comp. (1925) A
MBOP 1-2	BOOK OF POETRY, THE. Vols. I-II. Edwin Markham, comp. (1926-1927) A
MBP	MODERN BRITISH POETRY. Louis Untermeyer, ed. (4th rev. ed., 1936). For the 5th, 6th & 7th revised editions, see **MoBrPo**. For the revised edition of 1925, see **UBP** 5-4-3
MBP-22	BEST POEMS OF 1922, THE. Thomas Moult, ed. (1923) A
MBP-23	BEST POEMS OF 1923, THE. Thomas Moult, ed. (1924) A
MBP-24	BEST POEMS OF 1924, THE. Thomas Moult, ed. (1925) A
MBP-26	BEST POEMS OF 1926, THE. Thomas Moult, ed. (1926). For later years, see **BPM 30-37** A
MBPR	MAJOR BRITISH POETS OF THE ROMANTIC PERIOD. William Heath, ed. (1973) E
MBW 1-2	MAJOR BRITISH WRITERS, Vols. I-II. G. B. Harrison, ed. (1959) 6
MC	McBRIDE'S CHOICE DIALECTS. H. Elliott McBride. (1893) 1
MC *	MY COUNTRY. Burton Egbert Stevenson, ed. (1932) 6-5-4-3
MC **	See MCT
MCCG	MAGIC CASEMENTS. George S. Carhart & Paul A. McGhee, comps. (1926). Same as THROUGH MAGIC CASEMENTS, see **TMC** 6-5-4-3
MCD	McBRIDE'S COMIC DIALOGUES FOR SCHOOL EXHIBITIONS AND LITERARY ENTERTAIN-

	MENTS. H. Elliott McBride. (1873) 1
MCG	MY CARAVAN. Eulalie Osgood Grover, ed. (1931) 3
MCS	COMIC SPEECHES AND RECITATIONS. H. Elliott McBride. (1878) 1
MCT	MAGIC CARPET, THE. Mrs. Waldo Richards [Gertrude Moore Richards], comp. (1924) 3-A [MC in A]
MD	MODEL DIALOGUES. William M. Clark, comp. (1897) 3-2-1
MDAH	MEMORIAL DAY (Our American Holidays Series). Robert Haven Schauffler, ed. (1911) 5-4-3-2 [OAM in 2]
MDD	MARTINE'S DROLL DIALOGUES AND LAUGHABLE RECITATIONS. Arthur Martine. (1870) 1
MDIP	MEMORIAL DAY IN POETRY. Carnegie Library School Association, comp. (1924) A
MDP	MOTHER'S DAY IN POETRY. Carnegie Library School Association, comp. (1926) A
ME	MELODY OF EARTH, THE. Mrs. Waldo Richards [Gertrude Moore Richards], comp. (1918) 3-A
MeEL	MEDIEVAL ENGLISH LYRICS. R. T. Davies, ed. (1964) 6-D
MeEV	MEDIEVAL ENGLISH VERSE AND PROSE, IN MODERNIZED VERSIONS. Roger Sherman Loomis & Rudolph Willard, eds. (1948) 6-5-4
MeLP	METAPHYSICAL LYRICS AND POEMS OF THE SEVENTEENTH CENTURY. Herbert J. C. Grierson, ed. (1921) 6-5-4
MeMeAg	MERRY MEET AGAIN. Elizabeth Hough Sechrist, ed. (1941) 5-4-B

MemP	MEMORABLE POETRY. Sir Francis Meynell, ed. (1965) 6
MeP	MEDITATIVE POEM, THE. Louis L. Martz, ed. (1963) D
MePo	METAPHYSICAL POETS, THE. Helen Gardner, ed. (1957) 6-5
MERP	MAJOR ENGLISH ROMANTIC POETS, THE. William H. Marshall, ed. (1966) 6
MeRV	MENTOR BOOK OF RELIGIOUS VERSE, THE. Horace Gregory & Marya Zaturenska, eds. (1956) 5
MetP	METAPHYSICAL POETS, THE. Margaret Willy, ed. (1971) E
MeWo	MEN AND WOMEN. Louis Untermeyer, ed. (1970) 6
MFD	McBRIDE'S FUNNY DIALOGUES. H. Elliott McBride. (1899) 1
MFP	MODERN FRENCH POETRY. Joseph T. Shipley, comp. (1926) A
MG	MOTHER GOOSE NURSERY RHYMES. Arthur Rackham, ed. & illus. (1913, 1975) E
MGP	MODERN GERMAN POETRY, 1910-1960. Michael Hamburger & Christopher Middleton, eds. (1962) D
MHD	HUMOROUS DIALOGUES. H. Elliott McBride. (1879) 1
MHR	HUMOROUS READINGS. Lewis B. Monroe, ed. (1871) 2-1
MHT	MORE HEART THROBS. Joseph Mitchell

	Chapple, comp. (1911). Published also with HEART THROBS in a 1 vol. edition, TREASURE CHEST OF MEMORIES, see HT 3-2 [MTb 2 in 2]
MiAP	MID-CENTURY AMERICAN POETS. John Ciardi, ed. (1950) 6-5-4
MiCF	MID-CENTURY FRENCH POETS. Wallace Fowlie, ed. & tr. (1955) 5-C
MiFP	MIRROR FOR FRENCH POETRY, A, 1840-1940. Cecily Mackworth, pseud., ed. [i.e., Cecily De Chabannes La Palice] (1947) 5-4
MiMiPa	MINSTRELS OF THE MINE PATCH. George Korson, comp. (1938) B
MiP	MINDSCAPES: POEMS FOR THE REAL WORLD. Richard Peck, ed. (1971) E
MIS	MADE IN SCOTLAND. Robert Harioch, ed. (1974) E
MiSk	MINNESOTA SKYLINE. Carmen Nelson Richards, ed. (1944) B
MIT	MARK IN TIME: PORTRAITS AND POETRY/ SAN FRANCISCO. Nick Harvey, ed. (1971) E
ML	MARVELOUS LIGHT, THE. Helen Plotz, ed. (1970) 6
MLP	MODERN LYRIC POETRY. Herbert Bates, ed. (1929) 4-3
MM	MODERN MUSE, THE. Published for the English Association. (1934) 5-4-3
MMA	MEN WHO MARCHED AWAY. I. M. Parsons, ed. (1965) 6-D

MMD	MOUNTAIN MOVING DAY: POEMS BY WOMEN. Elaine Gill, ed. (1973) E
MMR	MISCELLANEOUS READINGS. Lewis B. Monroe, ed. (1872) 2-1
MMV	MASTERPIECES OF MODERN VERSE. Edwin Du Bois Shurter & Dwight Everett Watkins, comps. (1926) 4-3-A
MN	MONOLOGUES AND NOVELITIES. B. L. C. Griffith (et al), eds. (1896) 2-1
MND	McBRIDE'S NEW DIALOGUES. H. Elliott McBride. (1883) 1
MoAB	MODERN AMERICAN AND MODERN BRITISH POETRY. Louis Untermeyer, ed., in consultation with Karl Shapiro & Richard Wilbur. (Rev. shorter ed., 1955). For 4th edition, see **NeMa** 6-5-C
MOAH	MOTHER'S DAY (Our American Holidays Series). Susan Tracy Rice, comp., Robert Haven Schauffler, ed. (1915) 5-4-3-2 [OAMs in 2]
MoAmPo	MODERN AMERICAN POETRY. Louis Untermeyer, ed. (6th rev. ed., 1942; mid-century ed. [7th rev. ed.], 1950; 8th rev. ed., 1962). For the 5th revised edition, see **MAP**. For the 3d rev. ed., see **UAP**. See also **MoAB** 6-5-4-B
MOAP	MASTERPIECES OF AMERICAN POETS. Mark Van Doren, ed. (1936). Editions of 1932 & 1940 have title AMERICAN POETS, 1630-1930 5-4-3
MoAuPo	MODERN AUSTRALIAN POETRY. H. M. Green, comp. (2d ed., rev., 1952) 6-5-C
MOB	MAGIC OF BOOKS, THE (Our American Holidays Series). A. P. Sanford & Robert Haven Schauffler, eds. (1929) 5-4-3

MoBrPo	MODERN BRITISH POETRY. Louis Untermeyer, ed. (5th rev. ed., 1942; mid-century ed. [6th rev. ed.], 1950; 7th rev. ed., 1962). For the 4th revised edition, see **MBP**. For the revised edition of 1925, see **UBP**. See also **MoAB** 6-5-4-B
MoBS	MODERN BALLADS AND STORY POEMS. Charles Causley, ed. (1965). English edition has title RISING EARLY (1964) 6-D
MoCV	MODERN CANADIAN VERSE. Arthur James Marshall Smith, ed. (1967) 6
MoGo	MOTHER GOOSE. William Rose Benét, comp. (1943) B
MoGoRh	MOTHER GOOSE RHYMES. Margot Austin, illus. (1939) B
MoGoRi	MOTHER GOOSE ON THE RIO GRANDE. Frances Alexander (et al), comps. & trs. (1944) B
MoGP	MODERN GREEK POETRY. Rae Dalven, tr. & ed. (1949) 5-4
MoLP	MODERN LOVE POEMS. D. J. Klemer, ed. (1961) 6-D
MOM	MASTER OF MEN, THE. Thomas Curtis Clark, comp. (1930) 3
Moon	MOONSTRUCK: AN ANTHOLOGY OF LUNAR POETRY. Robert Phillips, ed. (1974) E
MooP	MOORISH POETRY; a translation of The Pennants, an anthology compiled in 1243 by the Andalusian Ibn Sa'id. A. J. Arberry, ed. & tr. (1953) 5-C
MoP	MODERN POET, THE. Gwendolyn Murphy, ed. (1938) 5-4

MoPo	MODERN POETRY. Kimon Friar & John Malcolm Brinnin, eds. (1951) 6-5-C
MoPW	MODERN POETS' WORLD, THE. James Reeves, ed. (1957) 6-5
MoRP	MODERN RELIGIOUS POEMS. Jacob Trapp, ed. (1964) 6-D
MoShBr	MOON IS SHINING BRIGHT AS DAY, THE. Ogden Nash, ed. (1953) 6-5-C
MoSiPe	MORE SILVER PENNIES. Blanche Jennings Thompson, comp. (1938) 6-5-4-B
MotAn	MOTHERS' ANTHOLOGY, THE. William Lyon Phelps, comp. (1941) 5-4-B
MoVE	MODERN VERSE IN ENGLISH, 1900–1950. David Cecil & Allen Tate, eds. (1958) 6-5
MoWP	MODERN WELSH POETRY. Keidrych Rhys, ed. (1954) 5
MP	MODERN POETS, THE. John Malcom Brinnin & Bill Read, eds. (1963). Revised edition of 1970 has title TWENTIETH CENTURY POETRY (1900–1970), see **TwCP** 6-D
MPB	MY POETRY BOOK. Grace Thompson Huffard, Laura Mae Carlisle, & Hellen Ferris, comps. (1934; rev. ed., 1956) 6-5-4-3
MPC 1-14	MODERN POETRY FOR CHILDREN, Vols. 1-14. James J. Reynolds, ed. (1928) 3
MPD	DIALOGUES AND DRAMAS. Lewis B. Monroe, ed. (1873) 2-1
MPo	MODERN POETRY. John Rowe Townsend, comp. (1974) E

MR	MY RECITATIONS. Cora Urquhart Potter. (1886) 3-2-1
MRS	MODERN READER AND SPEAKER, A. George Riddle, ed. (1900) 2-1
MRV	MODERN RELIGIOUS VERSE AND PROSE. Fred Merrifield, ed. (1925) 3-A
MTb	See MHT
MTD	TEMPERANCE DIALOGUES. H. Elliott McBride. (1877) 1
MuM	MUSIC MAKERS, THE. Stanton A. Coblentz, (1945) 5-4
MuP	MUSIC OF POETRY, THE. Alfred H. Body, comp. (1940) 5-4
MuSP	MUSIC AND SWEET POETRY. John Bishop, comp. (1968) 6
MV 1-2	MANY VOICES, Books I-II. Mona Swann, ed. (1934) 4-3
MW	MAGIC WORLD, A. Margery Gordon & Marie B. King, eds. (1930) 5-4-3
MWA 1-2	MAJOR WRITERS OF AMERICA, Vols. I-II. Perry Miller & others, eds. (1962) 6
MYF	YOUNG FOLKS' READINGS. Lewis B. Monroe, ed. (1877) 2-1
MyFE	MY FAVOURITE ENGLISH POEMS. John Masefield, ed. (1950) 6-5-4
NA	NONSENSE ANTHOLOGY, A. Carolyn Wells, ed. (1902) 6-5-4-3-2-1
NAE	NEW ARBOR DAY EXERCISES. Alice Maude Kellogg. [No. 2 in Arbor Day Programs] (1901). For Arbor Day Program, No. 1, see **ADP** * 2

NAL	NARRATIVE AND LYRIC POETRY. James W. Tupper, ed. (1927) 3
NAMP	NEW ANTHOLOGY OF MODERN POETRY, A. Selden Rodman, ed. (1938) 6-5-4-3
NaP	NAKED POETRY. Stephen Berg & Robert Mezey, eds. (1969) 6
NBE	NEW BOOK OF ENGLISH VERSE, THE. Charles Williams (et al), eds. (1936) 5-4-3
NBM	19th CENTURY MINOR BRITISH POETS. W. H. Auden, ed. (1966) 6
NBP	NEW BLACK POETRY, THE. Clarence Major, ed. (1970) 6
NC	NEW CENTURY SPEAKER, THE. Henry A. Frink. (1898) 2-1
NCEP	NEW CANON OF ENGLISH POETRY, A. James Reeves & Martin Seymour-Smith, eds. (1967) 6
NCSH	NEW COASTS AND STRANGE HARBORS. Helen Hill & Agnes Perkins, comps. (1974) E
NDP	NEW DIALOGUES AND PLAYS. Binney Gunnison. (1905) 3-A-2-1
NE	NATIONAL EPICS. Kate Milner Rabb. (1896) 2-1
NeAC	NEW AMERICAN AND CANADIAN POETRY. John Gill, ed. (1971) E
NeAP	NEW AMERICAN POETRY, THE, 1945-1960. Donald M. Allen, ed. (1960) 6-5
NeBP	NEW BRITISH POETS, THE. Kenneth Rexroth, ed. (1949) 6-5-4

NeCa	NEGRO CARAVAN, THE. Sterling A. Brown (et al), eds. (1941) 4-B
NeHB	NEW HOME BOOK OF BEST LOVED POEMS, THE. Richard Charlton MacKenzie, ed. (1946) 6-5-4
NeIP	NEW IRISH POETS. Devin A. Garrity, ed. (1948) 6-5-4
NeLNL	NEW LAND, NEW LANGUAGE. Judith Wright, comp. (1957) 6-5
NeMA	NEW MODERN AMERICAN & BRITISH POETRY, THE. Louis Untermeyer, ed. (Mid-century ed. [4th ed.], 1950). For edition of 1955, see MoAB 6-5-4
NeMiVe	NEW MICHIGAN VERSE. Carl Edwin Burkland, ed. (1940) 4-B
NePA	NEW POCKET ANTHOLOGY OF AMERICAN VERSE FROM COLONIAL DAYS TO THE PRESENT, THE. Oscar Williams, ed. (1955) 6-5-C
NePo	NEW POEMS, 1942. Oscar Williams, ed. (1942) B
NePoAm	NEW POEMS BY AMERICAN POETS. Rolfe Humphries, ed. (1953) 6-5-C
NePoAm-2	NEW POEMS BY AMERICAN POETS #2. Rolfe Humphries, ed. (1957) 6-5
NePoEA	NEW POETS OF ENGLAND AND AMERICA. Donald Hall, Robert Pack, & Louis Simpson, eds. (1957) 6-5
NePoEA-2	NEW POETS OF ENGLAND AND AMERICA, Second Selection. Donald Hall & Robert Pack, eds. (1962) 6-D
NeTW	NEW TREASURY OF WAR POETRY, THE; poems of the Second World War. George Herbert Clarke, ed. (1943) 5-4

NLK	NATURE LOVER'S KNAPSACK, THE. Edwin Osgood Grover, ed. (1927; enl. ed., 1947) 5-4-3
NM	NEGRO MINSTRELS, A COMPLETE GUIDE TO NEGRO MINSTRELSY. Jack Haverly. (1902) 2
NMM	NO MORE MASKS! AN ANTHOLOGY OF POEMS BY WOMEN. Florence Howe & Ellen Bass, eds. (1973) E
NMP	NEW MODERN POETRY, THE. M. L. Rosenthal, ed. (1967) 6
NNP	NEW NEGRO POETS: U. S. A. Langston Hughes, ed. (1964) 6-D
NoAM	NORTON ANTHOLOGY OF MODERN POETRY, THE. Richard Ellmann & Robert O'Clair, eds. (1973) E
NOBA	NEW OXFORD BOOK OF AMERICAN VERSE, THE. Richard Ellmann, ed. (1976). For the edition of 1927 edited by Bliss Carman, see OBAV; for the edition of 1950 edited by F. O. Matthiessen, see OxBA E
NOBE	NEW OXFORD BOOK OF ENGLISH VERSE, THE, 1250–1950. Helen Gardner, ed. (1972). For the editions of 1900 & 1939 edited by Arthur Quiller-Couch, see OBEV E
NoCaPo	See PoNC
NoP	NORTON ANTHOLOGY OF POETRY, THE. Arthur M. Eastman (et al), eds. (1970) 6
NowV	NOW VOICES, THE. Angelo Carli & Theodore Kilman, eds. (1971) E
NP	See NPSC; see NPTP
NP *	NEW POETRY, THE. Harriet Monroe & Alice Corbin Henderson, eds. (1917; new ed., rev. & enl., 1932) 6-5-4-3-A-2 [NPA in A & 2]

NPA	See NP *
NPC	NEW PLAYS FOR CHRISTMAS. Anne Putnam Sanford, comp. (1935) 3
NPH	NARRATIVE POEMS. Max J. Herzberg, ed. (1930) 4-3
NPS	NEW POPULAR SPEAKER. Henry Davenport Northrup, comp. (1900) 1
NPSC	NEW POEMS THAT WILL TAKE PRIZES IN SPEAKING CONTESTS. Edwin DuBois Shurter & Dwight Everett Watkins, eds. (1926) 3-A [NP in A]
NPTP	NEW PIECES THAT WILL TAKE PRIZES IN SPEAKING CONTESTS. Harriet Blackstone, comp. (1901) 3-2-1 [NP in 2 & 1]
NPW	NEW POEMS: WOMEN. Terry Wetherby, ed. (1976) E
NT	NEW GOLDEN TREASURY OF SONGS AND LYRICS, THE. Ernest Rhys, ed. (1914) 2
NV	NATURE IN VERSE. Mary I. Lovejoy, comp. (1895) 2-1
NV *	NEW VOICES. Marguerite Wilkinson, ed. (New ed., rev. & enl., 1928) 5-4-3-A [NVW in A]
NVAP	NEW VOICES IN AMERICAN POETRY. David Allen Evans, ed. (1973) E
NVW	See NV *
NYBP	NEW YORKER BOOK OF POEMS, THE. (1969) 6
NYBV	NEW YORKER BOOK OF VERSE, THE. (1935) 4-3
NYM	NEW YEAR AND MIDWINTER EXERCISES. Alice M. Kellogg, ed. (1907) 2
NYTB	NEW YORK TIMES BOOK OF VERSE, THE. Thomas Lask, ed. (1970) 6

OA	OKLAHOMA ANTHOLOGY FOR 1929, THE. Joseph Francis Paxton, ed. (1929) 3
OA *	OUT OF THE ARK. Gwendolyn Reed, comp. (1970) 6
OAA	See ADAH
OAE	See EOAH
OAEP	OXFORD ANTHOLOGY OF ENGLISH POETRY, AN. Howard Foster Lowry & Willard Thorp, eds. (1935); 2d ed., 1956) 6-5-4-3
OAF	See FOAH
OAI	See IDAH
OAL	See LBAH
OAM	See MDAH
OAMs	See MOAH
OAT	See TOAH
OAW	See WOAH
OB	See OBEV
OBAV	OXFORD BOOK OF AMERICAN VERSE, THE. Bliss Carman, ed. (1927). For the edition of 1950 edited by F. O. Matthiessen, see OxBA; for the edition of 1976 edited by Richard Ellmann, see NOBA 5-4-3-A
OBB	OXFORD BOOK OF BALLADS, THE. Arthur Quiller-Couch, ed. (1910). For the edition of 1969 edited by James Kinsley, see OxBB 6-5-4-3-2
OBCV	OXFORD BOOK OF CANADIAN VERSE IN ENGLISH AND FRENCH, THE. A. J. M. Smith, ed. (1960). For the edition of 1914 edited by William Wilfred Campbell, see OCV 6-D
OBEC	OXFORD BOOK OF EIGHTEENTH CENTURY VERSE, THE. David Nichol Smith, ed. (1926) 6-5-4-3-A [OBV in A]
OBEV	OXFORD BOOK OF ENGLISH VERSE, THE. Arthur Quiller-Couch, ed. (1900; new ed., rev. & enl., 1939). For the edition of 1972 edited by Helen Gardner, see NOBE 6-5-4-3-2-1 [OB in 2 & 1]

OBMV	OXFORD BOOK OF MODERN VERSE, THE. 1892–1935. William Butler Yeats, ed. (1936) 6-5-4-3
OBNC	OXFORD BOOK OF NINETEENTH-CENTURY ENGLISH VERSE, THE. John Hayward, ed. (1964) 6-D
OBP	ONE HUNDRED BRITISH POETS. Selden Rodman, ed. (1974) E
OBRV	OXFORD BOOK OF REGENCY VERSE, THE, 1798–1837. H. S. Milford, ed. (1928). Edition of 1935 has title OXFORD BOOK OF ENGLISH VERSE OF THE ROMANTIC PERIOD, 1798–1837 6-5-4-3
OBS	OXFORD BOOK OF SEVENTEENTH CENTURY VERSE, THE. H. J. C. Grierson & G. Bullough, eds. (1934) 6-5-4-3
OBSC	OXFORD BOOK OF SIXTEENTH CENTURY VERSE, THE. E. K. Chambers, comp. (1932) 6-5-4-3
OBV	See **OBEC**
OBVV	OXFORD BOOK OF VICTORIAN VERSE, THE. Sir Arthur Quiller-Couch, comp. (1912) 6-5-4-3-2 [OVV in 2]
OCL	OUR CANADIAN LITERATURE. Bliss Carman & Lorne Pierce, eds. (Rev. ed., 1935). Revised edition of 1954 has title CANADIAN POETRY IN ENGLISH, see **CaP** 5-4-3
OCP	OUR COUNTRY IN POEM AND PROSE. Eleanor Alice Persons. (1899) 2
OCS	ON CITY STREETS. Nancy Larrick, comp. (1968) 6
OCV	OXFORD BOOK OF CANADIAN VERSE, THE. William Wilfred Campbell, comp. (1914). For the edition of 1960 edited by A. J. M. Smith, see **OBCV** 2

ODP	OPEN DOOR TO POETRY, THE. Mrs. Anne [Knott] Stokes. (1931) 3
OEB	OLD ENGLISH BALLADS. Introduction by Hamilton Wright Mabie. (1896) 2-1
OEL	OLD ENGLISH LOVE SONGS. Introduction by Hamilton Wright Mabie. (1897) 2-1
OES	OLD ENGLISH SONGS. Austin Dobson, ed. (1894) 1
OFD	O FRABJOUS DAY!: poetry for holidays & special occasions. Myra Cohn Livingston, ed. (1977) E
OFG 1-4	OFF THE GROUND, Book I-IV. William Kerr & Alexander Haddow, comps. (1945) 4
OFPE	OVER ONE HUNDRED FAMOUS POEMS AND THE ENTERTAINMENT SPEAKER. William Montgomery Major, ed. Sometimes listed as THE ENTERTAINMENT SPEAKER (1927) 3
OG	OPEN GATES. Susan Thompson Spaulding & Francis Trow Spaulding, comps. (1924) 3
OH	OUT OF THE HEART. John White Chadwick & Annie Hathaway Chadwick, eds. (1891) 1
OHCS 1-40	ONE HUNDRED CHOICE SELECTIONS IN POETRY AND PROSE, Vols. 1-40. Phineas Garrett, ed. (1866-1914). Same as THE SPEAKER'S GARLAND, Vols. 1-10 (1910-1926) 3-2-1 [CS 1-40 in 2 & 1]
OHFP	ONE HUNDRED AND ONE FAMOUS POEMS. Roy J. Cook, comp. (1929; rev. ed., 1958) 6-5-4-3-A
OHIP	OUR HOLIDAYS IN POETRY. Mildred P. Harrington & Josephine Thomas, comps. (1929) 6-5-4-3
OHNP	ONE HUNDRED NARRATIVE POEMS. George E. Teter, ed. (1918) 4-3

OHPI	ONE HUNDRED POEMS OF IMMORTALITY. Thomas Curtis Clark & Winfred Ernest Garrison, comps. (1935) 4-3
OHPP	ONE HUNDRED POEMS OF PEACE. Thomas Curtis Clark & Winfred Ernest Garrison, comps. (1934) 4-3
OlF	OLD FAVORITE SONGS AND HYMNS. Richard Charlton MacKenzie, ed. (1946) 5-4
OlPN	OLD POEMS AND NEW VERSE. E. F. Kingston, ed. (1954) C
OLR	ONE LITTLE ROOM, AN EVERYWHERE. Myra Cohn Livingston, ed. (1975) E
OM	ORATOR'S MANUAL, THE. George L. Raymond. (1879; rev. ed., 1910) 2-1
OnAP	100 AMERICAN POEMS. Selden Rodman, ed. (1948) 5-4
OnCuPl	ONIONS AND CUCUMBERS AND PLUMS. Sarah Zweig Betsky, ed. (1958) 5
OnGR	100 GREAT RELIGIOUS POEMS. Randolph Ray, ed. (1951) C
OnHM	100 MODERN POEMS. Selden Rodman, comp. (1949) 6-5-4
OnHT	ONE HUNDRED AND TEN FAVORITE CHILDREN'S POEMS. H. G. Platt, ed. (1943) 5-4
OnMSP	100 MORE STORY POEMS. Elinor Parker, comp. (1960) 6-D
OnP	100 POEMS. A. J. M. Smith, ed. (1965) D
OnPC	ONE HUNDRED POEMS FROM THE CHINESE. Kenneth Rexroth, tr. (1956) 5

OnPJ	ONE HUNDRED POEMS FROM THE JAPANESE. Kenneth Rexroth, tr. (1955) 5-C
OnPM	ONE THOUSAND AND ONE POEMS OF MANKIND. Henry W. Wells, comp. (1953) 6-5-C
OnPP	100 POEMS ABOUT PEOPLE. Elinor Parker, comp. (1955) 6-5-C
OnSP	100 STORY POEMS. Elinor Parker, comp. (1951) 6-5-C
OnYI	1000 YEARS OF IRISH POETRY. Kathleen Hoagland, ed. (1947) 6-5-4
OPoP	100 POSTWAR POEMS. M. L. Rosenthal, ed. (1968) 6
OPP	OF POETRY AND POWER. Erwin A. Glikes & Paul Schwaber, eds. (1964) D
OQP	1000 QUOTABLE POEMS. Thomas Curtis Clark, ed. (1937). Includes **QP-1**, **QP-2** 6-5-4-3
OR	OPEN ROAD, THE. Edward V. Lucas, comp. (1905) 2
OrM	OUR MOTHERS. Mary Allette Ayer, comp. (1916) 2
OS 1-3	OPEN SESAME, Parts I-III. Blanche W. Bellamy & Maude W. Goodwin, eds. (1889-1890) 2-1
OTA	OFF TO ARCADY. Max J. Herzberg, ed. (1933) 4-3
OTD	ON THIS DAY. Phyllis Detz & Kermit M. Stover, eds. (1970) 6
OtMeF	OTHER MEN'S FLOWERS. A. P. Wavell, Earl Wavell, comp. (1944) 6-5-4-B
OTPC	ONE THOUSAND POEMS FOR CHILDREN.

	Roger Ingpen, ed. (1903; rev. & enl. ed., 1923) Elizabeth Hough Sechrist, ed. (1946) 6-5-4-3-2
OuHeWo	OUR HERITAGE OF WORLD LITERATURE. Stith Thompson & John Gassner, eds. (Rev. ed., 1942, 2 books in 1). Also published separately 6-5-4-B
OuSiCo	OUR SINGING COUNTRY. John A. Lomax & Alan Lomax, comps. (1941) 6-5-4-B
OVV	See OBVV
OxBA	OXFORD BOOK OF AMERICAN VERSE, THE. F. O. Matthiessen, ed. (1950). For the edition of 1927 edited by Bliss Carman, see **OBAV**; for the edition of 1976 edited by Richard Ellmann, see **NOBA** 6-5-4
OxBB	OXFORD BOOK OF BALLADS, THE. James Kinsley, ed. (1969). For the edition of 1910 edited by Arthur Quiller-Couch, see **OBB** 6
OxBChV	OXFORD BOOK OF CHILDREN'S VERSE, THE. Iona Opie & Peter Opie, eds. (1973) E
OxBG	OXFORD BOOK OF GREEK VERSE IN TRANSLATION, THE. T. F. Higham & C. M. Bowra, eds. (1938) 5-4
OxBI	OXFORD BOOK OF IRISH VERSE, THE; XVIIth-XXth Century. Donagh MacDonagh & Lennox Robinson, comps. (1958) 6-5
OxBM	OXFORD BOOK OF MEDIEVAL ENGLISH VERSE, THE. Celia Sisam & Kenneth Sisam, eds. (1970) E
OxBoCh	OXFORD BOOK OF CHRISTIAN VERSE, THE. Lord David Cecil, ed. (1940) 6-5-4-B
OxBoLi	OXFORD BOOK OF LIGHT VERSE, THE. W. H. Auden, ed. (1938; repr. with corr., 1939) 6-5-4-B
OxBS	OXFORD BOOK OF SCOTTISH VERSE, THE.

	John MacQueen & Tom Scott, comps. (1966) 6
OxBTC	OXFORD BOOK OF TWENTIETH-CENTURY ENGLISH VERSE, THE. Philip Larkin, ed. (1973) E
OxNR	OXFORD NURSERY RHYME BOOK, THE. Iona Opie & Peter Opie, comps. (1955) 6-5-C
PA	PARODY ANTHOLOGY, A. Carolyn Wells, comp. (1904) 5-4-3-2
PaA	PATRIOTIC ANTHOLOGY, THE. Introduced by Carl Van Doren. (1941) 6-5-4
PaAn	PATRIOTIC ANTHOLOGY, A. (1940). The Peter Pauper Press B
PAH	POEMS OF AMERICAN HISTORY. Burton Egbert Stevenson, ed. (1908; rev. ed., 1922) 6-5-4-3-2
PAIC	POETRY AND ITS CONVENTIONS. John T. Shawcross & Frederick R. Lapides, eds. (1972) E
PAL	PATRIOTIC POEMS AMERICA LOVES. Jean Anne Vincent, comp. (1968) 6
PAn	POETRY ANTHOLOGY, A. Marlies K. Danziger & Wendell Stacy Johnson, eds. (1968) 6
PaOS	PAGEANT OF OLD SCANDINAVIA, A. Henry Goodard Leach, ed. (1946) 5-4
PAP	POEMS OF AMERICAN PATRIOTISM. Brander Matthews, ed. (1882; rev. & enl. ed., 1922) 6-5-4-3-2-1
PAPm	POEMS OF AMERICAN PATRIOTISM, 1776-1898. R. L. Paget, pseud. [i.e., Frederic Lawrence Knowles], ed. (1898) 4-3-2-1
PaPo	PARLOUR POETRY. Michael R. Turner, ed. (1969) 6

Par	PARODIES. Dwight Macdonald, ed. (1960) 6-D
PASC	POETRY ARRANGED FOR THE SPEAKING CHOIR. Marion Parsons Robinson & Rozetta Lura Thurston. (1936) 3
PB 1-9	POETRY BOOK, THE, Vols. 1-9. Miriam Blanton Huber, Herbert B. Bruner, & Charles Madison Curry, eds. (1926) 3
PBA	POEMS FROM BLACK AFRICA. Langston Hughes, ed. (1963) 6
PBGG	POEMS BY GRADES, Vol. 2. For grades 5, 6, 7, 8 (Grammar). Ada Van Stone Harris & Charles B. Gilbert, comps. (1907) 3-2 [PGGR in 2]
PBGP	POEMS BY GRADES, Vol. 1. For grades 1, 2, 3, 4 (Primary). Ada Van Stone Harris & Charles B. Gilbert, comps. (1907) 3-2 [PGpr in 2]
PBMP	PREMIER BOOK OF MAJOR POETS, THE. Anita Dore, ed. (1970) E
PBV	PINK BOOK OF VERSE FOR VERY LITTLE CHILDREN, THE. Augusta Monteith, comp. (1934) 3
PC	POETRY FOR CHILDREN. Samuel Eliot, ed. (1879) 2-1
PC *	POETRY CURE, THE. Robert Haven Schauffler, comp. (1925) 5-4-3-A [SPC in A]
PCat	POETRY OF CATS, THE. Samuel Carr, ed. (1974) E
PCD	POET'S CRAFT, THE. Helen Fern Daringer & Anne Thaxter Eaton, comps. (1935) 6-5-4-3
PCH	POEMS FOR THE CHILDREN'S HOUR. Josephine Bouton, comp. (1927) 6-5-4
PCK	See **PECK**

PCL	POEMS CHILDREN LOVE. Penrhyn W. Coussens, comp. (1908) 2
PCN	POEMS, CHIEFLY NARRATIVE. W. L. Macdonald & F. C. Walker, eds. (New rev. ed., 1938). Edition of 1925 had title NARRATIVE ENGLISH POEMS 5-4
PCW	POEMS BY CONTEMPORARY WOMEN. Theodora Roscoe & Mary Winter Were, comps. (1944) 4
PD	POPULAR DIALOGUES. Phineas Garrett, comp. (1898) 3-2-1
PDK	PRACTICAL DIALOGUES. Amos M. Kellogg, comp. (1908) 3
PDN	POEMS FOR DAILY NEEDS. Thomas Curtis Clark, ed. (1936) 4-3
PDV	PIPING DOWN THE VALLEYS WILD. Nancy Larrick, ed. (1968) 6
PE	PRACTICAL ELOCUTION. Jacob W. Shoemaker. (1880; enl. ed., 1893) 3-2-1 [SPE in 2 & 1]
PEB 1-4	POPULAR ENGLISH BALLADS, Vols. 1-4. R. Brimley Johnson, ed. (1894) 1
PeBB	PENGUIN BOOK OF BALLADS, THE. Geoffrey Grigson, ed. (1975) E
PeBoSo	PENGUIN BOOK OF SONNETS, THE. Carl Withers, ed. (1943) 5-4-B
PECK	POEMS EVERY CHILD SHOULD KNOW. Mary E. Burt, ed. (1904) 5-4-3-2 [PCK in 2]
PeCV	PENGUIN BOOK OF CANADIAN VERSE, THE. Ralph Gustafson, ed. (1958; rev. ed., 1967) 6-5

PEDC	PIECES FOR EVERY DAY THE SCHOOLS CELEBRATE. Norman H. Deming & Katharine I. Bemis, comps. (Rev. ed., 1924; enl. ed., 1931; rev. & enl. ed., 1949) 6-5-4-3-A
PeER	PENGUIN BOOK OF ENGLISH ROMANTIC VERSE, THE. David Wright, ed. (1968) 6
PEF	POEMS OF EUGENE FIELD, THE. [Complete edition.] (1906) 3
PEM	PIECES FOR EVERY MONTH OF THE YEAR. Mary I. Lovejoy & Elizabeth Adams, comps. (1921) 3
PEO	See PEOR
PEOR	PIECES FOR EVERY OCCASION. Caroline Bigelow LeRow, comp. (1901; rev. & enl. ed., 1927) 5-4-3-A-2-1 [PEO in A-2-1]
PEP	See PPSC
PeP	PERSIAN POEMS. A. J. Arberry, ed. (1954) 5-C
PER	PARNASSUS EN ROUTE. Mrs. Kenneth Horan, comp. (1929) 4-3
PeRV	PENGUIN BOOK OF RESTORATION VERSE, THE. Harold Love, ed. (1968) 6
PeSA	PENGUIN BOOK OF SOUTH AFRICAN VERSE, THE. Jack Cope & Uys Krige, eds. (1968) 6
PeVV	PENGUIN BOOK OF VICTORIAN VERSE, THE. George MacBeth, ed. (1969) 6
PF	POETICAL FAVORITES—YOURS AND MINE. Warren Snyder, comp. (1910) 2
PFD	POEMS OF FAITH AND DOUBT. R. L. Brett, ed. (1965) E

PFE	POEMS FOR ENJOYMENT. Elias Lieberman, ed. (1931) 5-4-3
PFIr	POEMS FROM IRELAND. William Cole, comp. (1972) E
PFY	POEMS FOR YOUTH. William Rose Benét, comp. (1925) 6-5-4-3
PG	POET'S GOLD. David Ross, ed. (1933; rev. & enl. ed., 1945; 2d rev. ed., 1956) 6-5-4-3
PGD	POEMS FOR THE GREAT DAYS. Thomas Curtis Clark & Robert Earle Clark, comps. (1948) 6-5-4
PGGR	See PBGG
PGpr	See PBGP
PGT 1-2	See GTSL
PGW	POEMS OF THE GREAT WAR. John W. Cunliffe, ed. (1916) A
PHS	POETRY FOR HOME AND SCHOOL. Anna C. Brackett & Ida M. Eliot, comps. (1876) 2-1
PIA	POETRY. Hazard Adams, ed. (1968) 6
PIAE	POETRY: ITS APPRECIATION AND ENJOYMENT. Louis Untermeyer & Carter Davidson, eds. (1934) 5-4-3
PiAm	POET IN AMERICA, THE. Albert Gelpi, ed. (1973) E
PiDr	PIPE AND DRUM. Rose Fyleman, ed. (1940) 4-B
PIR	POEMS I REMEMBER. John Kieran, comp. (1942) 5-4
PJH 1-2	POETRY FOR JUNIOR HIGH SCHOOLS, Vols. I-II. Elias Leberman, ed. (1926) 3-A

PLD	POINT LACE AND DIAMONDS. George A. Baker, Jr. (1875) 1
PM	POEMS [Complete edition]. John Masefield. (1935) 3
PNW	POETIC NEW-WORLD, THE. Lucy H. Humphrey, comp. (1910) 2
Po	POEM, THE. Josephine Miles, ed. (1959) 6-5
PoA	POEMS OF ACTION. Vere Henry Collins, comp. (1913) 2
PoAn	POEM, THE. Stanley B. Greenfield & A. Kingsley Weatherhead, eds. (1968) 6
PoAu 1-2	POETRY IN AUSTRALIA, Vols. I-II. Vol. I. From the ballads to Brennan. T. Inglis Moore, comp. Vol. II. Modern Australian verse. Douglas Stewart, comp. (1965) 6-D
PoBA	POETRY OF BLACK AMERICA, THE. Arnold Adoff, ed. (1973) E
PoBoAm	POCKET BOOK OF AMERICA, THE. Philip Van Doren Stern, ed. (1942) B
PoBoVe	POCKET BOOK OF VERSE, THE. M. E. Speare, ed. (1940) B
PoC	POET'S CAT, THE. Mona Gooden, comp. (1946) 5-4
PoCH	POET'S CHOICE. Paul Engle & Joseph Langland, eds. (1962) 6-D
PoCo	POCKET COMPANION, THE. Philip Van Doren Stern, ed. (1942) B
PoD	POEMS OF DEATH. Phoebe Pool, comp. (1945) 5-4

PoDB	POEMS OF DOUBT AND BELIEF. Tom F. Driver & Robert Pack, eds. (1964) 6-D
PoE	POEMS IN ENGLISH, 1530-1940. David Daiches & William Charvat, eds. (1950) 6-5-4
PoEL 1-5	POETS OF THE ENGLISH LANGUAGE, Vols. I-V. W. H. Auden & Norman Holmes Pearson, eds. (1950) 6-5-4
PoeLi	POETRY AND LIFE. Clyde S. Kilby, ed. (1953) C
PoeMoYo	POEMS FOR MODERN YOUTH. Adolph Gillis & William Rose Benét, eds. (1938) 5-4-B
PoeP	POETS & POEMS. Herbert Goldstone & Irving Cummings, eds. (1967) 6
PoeT	POEMS OF TO-DAY. Published for the English Association. (1915) 5-4
PoEx	POETRY AS EXPERIENCE. Norman C. Stageberg & Wallace L. Anderson, eds. (1952) C
PoF	POETRY OF FLIGHT, THE. Selden Rodman, ed. (1941) 5-4-B
PoFr	POETRY OF FREEDOM, THE. William Rose Benét & Norman Cousins, eds. (1945) 6-5-4
PoFS	POEMS FOR STUDY. Leonard Unger & William Van O'Connor, eds. (1953) 6-5-C
PoG	POET'S GARDEN, THE. Stevie Smith, ed. (1970) 6
PoHN	POEMS OF THE HUNDRED NAMES. Henry H. Hart, ed. (3d ed., 1954). Originally published in 1933 as THE HUNDRED NAMES 5-C
POI	POEMS OF INSPIRATION. Joseph Morris, pseud. [i.e., Joseph Morris Bachelor] & St. Clair Adams, comps. (1928). Includes FACING FOR-

	WARD, SILVER LININGS, & LIGHT OF THE WORLD, see FF, SL, LOW * (1928)
PoIE	POETRY IN ENGLISH. Warren Taylor & Donald Hall, eds. (1963; 2d ed., 1970) 6-D
POL	POEMS ONE LINE AND LONGER. William Cole, ed. (1973) E
POL *	PRAISE OF LINCOLN, THE. A. Dallas Williams, ed. (1911) 2
PoLa	POETS LAUREATE, THE. Kenneth Hopkins. (1954) C
PoLF	POEMS THAT LIVE FOREVER. Hazel Felleman, ed. (1965) 6-D
PoLFOT	POETRY FROM LITERATURE FOR OUR TIME, THIRD EDITION. Harlow O. Waite & Benjamin P. Atkinson, eds. (1958) 5
PoLi	POETRY AND LIFE. F. J. Sheen, comp. (1942) 6-5-4
PoLJ	POETRY OF LIVING JAPAN, THE. Takamichi Ninomiya & D. J. Enright, eds. (1958) 5
PoMa	POEMS FOR A MACHINE AGE. Horace J. McNeil, ed. (1941). Edition of 1949 has title LIVING POETRY 6-5-4-B
PoMeSp	POETRY FOR MEN TO SPEAK CHORALLY. Marion Parsons Robinson & Rozetta Lura Thurston, eds. (1939) 4-B
PoMS	POEMS OF MAGIC AND SPELLS. William Cole, ed. (1960) 6-5
PoMyRe	POCKET MYSTERY READER, THE. Lee Wright, ed. (1942) B

PON	POETRY OF THE NINETIES. C. E. Andrews & M. O. Percival, eds. (1926) A
PoN	POETRY NOW. G. S. Fraser, ed. (1956) 5
PoNC	POETS OF NORTH CAROLINA. Richard Gaither Walser, ed. (1963). Edition of 1941 & revised edition of 1951 had title NORTH CAROLINA POETRY D-5-C-4-B [NoCaPo in 5-C-4-B]
PoNe	POETRY OF THE NEGRO, THE, 1746–1970. Langston Hughes & Arna Bontemps, eds. (1949; rev. ed., 1970) 6-5-4
PoNiLa	POEMS–1940 FROM THE "LANTERN." C. B. McAllister, ed. (1940) B
POOI	PRINCIPLES OF ORAL INTERPRETATION, THE. Dana Thurlow Burns. (1936) 3
POOT	POETRY OF OUR TIMES. Sharon Brown, ed. (1928) 4-3
PoOW	POEMS OF THE OLD WEST. Levette J. Davidson, ed. (1951) 6-5-C
PoP	POET PHYSICIANS. Mary Lou McDonough, comp. (1945) 5-4
PoPl	POETRY FOR PLEASURE; the Hallmark book of poetry. (1960) 6-D
PoPo	POEMS AND POETS. David Aloian, ed. (1965) 6-D
POR	See PRWS
PoRA	POEMS TO READ ALOUD. Edward Hodnett, ed. (1957, rev. ed., 1967) 6-5
PoRe	POCKET READER, THE. Philip Van Doren Stern, ed. (1941) B
PoRh	POCKETFUL OF RHYMES, A. Katherine Love, ed. (1946) 6-5-4

PoRL	POEMS FOR RED LETTER DAYS. Elizabeth Hough Sechrist, comp. (1951) 6-5-C
PoRo	POP/ROCK SONGS OF THE EARTH. Jerry L. Walker, ed. (1972) E
POS	POETRY OF THE SEASONS. Mary I. Lovejoy, comp. (1898) 2-1
PoSa	POETRY SAMPLER, A. Donald Hall, ed. (1962) 6-D
PoSC	POEMS FOR SEASONS AND CELEBRATIONS. William Cole, ed. (1961) 6-D
PoSp	POETS SPEAK, THE, 1943. Introduced by May Sarton. (1943) B
PoSS	POETRY FOR SENIOR STUDENTS; an anthology of shorter poems. J. L. Gill & L. H. Newell, eds. (1953) C
POT	POEMS OF TODAY. Alice Cecilia Cooper, ed. (1924). For new enlarged edition of 1939, see **PoTo** 5-4-3-A
PoTa	POET'S TALES, THE. William Cole, ed. (1971) E
POTE	POEMS OF OUR TIME, 1900-1942. Richard Church & M. M. Bozman, eds. (1945) POEMS OF OUR TIME, 1900-1960. Richard Church, Mildred Bozman, & Edith Sitwell, eds. (1959) 6-5-4
POTi	POETS OF OUR TIME. F. E. S. Finn, comp. (1965) 6
PoTo	POEMS OF TODAY. Alice Cecilia Cooper, ed. (New enl. ed., 1939). For the edition of 1924, see **POT** 5-4-B
PoToHe	POEMS THAT TOUCH THE HEART. A. L. Alex-

	ander, comp. (1941; new enl. ed., 1956) 6-5-4-B
PoTR	POEMS TO REMEMBER. E. F. Kingston, ed. (1951) C
POTT	POETRY OF THE TRANSITION, 1850-1914. Thomas Marc Parrott & Willard Thorp, eds. (1932) 5-4-3
PoVP	POETRY OF THE VICTORIAN PERIOD. George Benjamin Woods & Jerome Hamilton Buckley, eds. (Rev. ed., 1955) 6-5
POW	POETIC OLD-WORLD, THE. Lucy H. Humphrey, comp. (1908) 2
PoWorKn	POEMS WORTH KNOWING. Claude E. Lewis, comp. (1941) 4-B
PoWoSp	POETRY FOR WOMEN TO SPEAK CHORALLY. Marion Parsons Robinson & Rozetta Lura Thurston, eds. (1940) 4-B
POY	POEMS OF YOUTH. Alice Cecilia Cooper, ed. (1928) 3
PP	POEMS ON POETRY. Robert Wallace & James G. Taafe, eds. (1965) 6-D
PP *	PRIZE POEMS, 1913-1929. Charles A. Wagner, ed. (1930) 3
PPA	POETRY'S PLEA FOR ANIMALS. Frances E. Clarke, ed. (1927) 3-A
PPD 1-2	PROSE, POETRY, AND DRAMA FOR ORAL INTERPRETATION, Vols. I-II. William J. Farma, ed. (1930-1936) 4-3
PPGW	PATRIOTIC PIECES OF THE GREAT WAR. Edna D. Jones, comp. (1918) 3

PPh	PIPE AND POUCH. Joseph Knight, comp. (1894) 1
PPL	PINAFORE PALACE. Kate Douglas Wiggin & Nora Archibald Smith, eds. (1907) 6-5-4-3-2 [PPl in 2]
PPl	See **PPL**
PPoD	POETRY: POINTS OF DEPARTURE. Henry Taylor, ed. (1974) E
PPoe	PLEASURE OF POETRY, THE. Donald Hall, ed. (1971) E
PPON	POEMS OF PROTEST OLD AND NEW. Arnold Kenseth, ed. (1968) 6
PPP	POETRY: PAST AND PRESENT. Frank Brady & Martin Price, eds. (1974) E
PPP *	POPULAR PLATFORM POEMS. Ellis Clipson, comp. (1928) 3
PPS	PRACTICAL PUBLIC SPEAKING. Solomon H. Clark & Frederic M. Blanchard. (1899) 3-2-1
PPSC	PIECES FOR PRIZE SPEAKING. Asa H. Craig & Binney Gunnison, comps. & eds. (1931). Edition of 1899 had title PIECES FOR PRIZE SPEAKING CONTESTS 3-2-1 [PEP in 2 & 1]
PPSr	PRIZE POETICAL SPEAKER, THE. (1901) H. A. Dickerman & Son (Pub.) 1
PPV	PRO PATRIA, A BOOK OF PATRIOTIC VERSE. Wilfrid Joseph Halliday, comp. (1915) 2
PPYP	PROSE AND POETRY FOR YOUNG PEOPLE; comprising CHILD'S OWN SPEAKER, LITTLE PEOPLE'S SPEAKER, YOUNG PEOPLE'S SPEAKER, YOUNG FOLK'S RECITATIONS [4 parts] (1892). See **COS, LPS, YPS, YFR** 3-2-1
PR	PEERLESS RECITER. Henry Davenport Northrup, ed. (1894) 1

PR *	PATRICIAN PHYMES. Clinton Scollard & Jessie B. Rittenhouse, eds. (1932) 5-4-3
PraNu	PRAISE OF NUNS, IN. James M. Hayes, ed. (1942) 5-4-B
PraP	PRAYER POEMS. O. V. Armstrong & Helen Armstrong, comp. (1942) 5-4
PreP	PREFACE TO POETRY. Charles W. Cooper, in consultation with John Holmes. (1946) 5-4
Prf	PREFERENCES. Richard Howard, ed. (1974) E
PriVe	PRINCETON VERSE BETWEEN THE WARS. Allen Tate, ed. (1942) B
PRK	PRACTICAL RECITATIONS. Amos M. Kellogg, comp. (1903) 3-2 [PRs in 2]
PrPoCR	PROSE AND POETRY OF THE CONTINENTAL RENAISSANCE IN TRANSLATION. Harold Hooper Blanchard, ed. (2d ed., 1955) 5-C
PrPoTo	PROSE AND POETRY OF TODAY; regional America. Harriet Marcelia Lucas, ed. (1941) 4-B
PRR	PATRIOTIC READINGS AND RECITATIONS. Josephine Stafford, ed. (1902) 2-1
PrRL	PRE-RAPHAELITES IN LITERATURE AND ART, THE. D. S. R. Welland, ed. (1953) C
PrWP	PRESENTING WELSH POETRY. Gwyn Williams, ed. (1959) 6-5
PRWS	POSY RING, THE. Kate Douglas Wiggin & Nora Archibald Smith, eds. (1903) 6-5-4-3-2-1 [PoR in 2 & 1]
PS	PROGRESSIVE SPEAKER, THE. (1897). National Pub. Co. Also published under titles CHAUTAUQUA INSTRUCTOR OF ELOCUTION & DRAMATIC ART (1897) and ENTERTAIN-

	MENTS & AMUSEMENTS (1897) 1
PSA	POETRY SOCIETY OF AMERICA ANTHOLOGY, THE. Amy Bonner (et al), eds. (1946) 4
PSh	POETS OF THE SOUTH. Franklin V. N. Painter. (1903) 2
PSN	POEMS SINCE 1900. Colin Falck & Ian Hamilton, ed. (1975) E
PSO	POEMS FOR SPECIAL DAYS AND OCCASIONS. Thomas Curtis Clark, comp. (1930) 5-4-3
PSoN	POPULAR SONGS OF NINETEENTH-CENTURY AMERICA. Richard Jackson, ed. (1976) E
PSR	POETRY FOR SCHOOL READINGS. Marcus White, ed. (1889) 1
Psy	PSYCHE: THE FEMININE POETIC CONSCIOUSNESS. Barbara Segnitz & Carol Rainey, eds. (1973) E
PT	POETRY OF TO-DAY. Rosa M. R. Mikels & Grace Shoup, eds. (1927) 4-3-A
PTA 1-2	POEMS TEACHERS ASK FOR, Vols. I-II. (1925?) F. A. Owens Pub. Co. 5-4-3
PTER	POEMS OF THE ENGLISH RACE. Raymond MacDonald Alden, ed. (1921) 4-3
PTK	POETRY TO KNOW. Editors of the Book of Knowledge. (1966) 6
PtOT	POETS OF OUR TIME. Eric Gillett, comp. (1932) 5-4
PtP	POET TO POET. Houston Peterson & William S. Lynch, eds. (1945) 5-4
PtPa	POETS OF THE PACIFIC: 2d Series. Yvor Winters, ed. (1949) 5-4

PTS	PIECES TO SPEAK. Harlan H. Ballard. (1897) 1
PtTo	POETS OF TODAY. Walter Lowenfels, ed. (1964) D
PTWP	PIECES THAT HAVE WON PRIZES. Frank McHale, comp. (Enl. ed., 1930) 3-A [PWP in A]
PuPrPo	PULITZER PRIZE POEMS. Marjorie Barrows, comp. (1941) 4-B
PV	PITH AND VINEGAR. William Cole, ed. (1969) 6
PVD	POEMS OF HENRY VAN DYKE. (1920) 3
PVS	PROSE AND VERSE FOR SPEAKING AND READING. William Palmer Smith, ed. (1930) 4-3
PWB	POETICAL WORKS OF ROBERT BRIDGES. (2d ed. in 1 vol., 1936) 3
PWP	See PTWP
PYM	POETRY OF YOUTH. Edwin Markham, comp. (1935). Included in ANTHOLOGY OF THE WORLD'S BEST POEMS. Edwin Markham, comp. Memorial ed., 6 vols., 1948 5-4-3
PYO	POEMS YOU OUGHT TO KNOW. Elia W. Peattie, comp. (1902) 2-1
PyR	PRIMARY RECITATIONS. Amos M. Kellogg, comp. (1897) 2
PYS	PEOPLE, YES, THE. Carl Sandburg. (1936) 3
PyS	PRIMARY SPEAKER. Amos S. Kellogg, comp. (1903) 2
QAH	QUICKLY AGING HERE. Geof Hewitt, ed. (1969) 6
QFR	QUEST FOR REALITY. Yvor Winters & Kenneth Fields, eds. (1969) 6

QH	QUIET HOUR, THE. FitzRoy Carrington, ed. (1915) 2
QKB	QUIZ KIDS' BOOK, THE. (1947) The Viking Press 4
QP 1-2	QUOTABLE POEMS, Vols. I-II. Thomas Curtis Clark & Esther A. Gillespie, comps. (1928-1931). For one-volume edition, see **OQP** 5-4-3
QS	QUESTING SPIRIT, THE. Halford E. Luccock & Frances Breantano, eds. (1947) 5-4
RAC	RECITATIONS FOR ASSEMBLY AND CLASSROOM. Anna Theodore Lee O'Neill, comp. (1909) 2
RAE	ROUND ABOUT EIGHT. Geoffrey Palmer & Noel Lloyd, eds. (1972) E
RAR	RING-A-ROUND. Mildred P. Harrington, comp. (1930) 5-4-3
RBL	RENAISSANCE AND BAROQUE LYRICS. Harold Martin Priest, ed. (1962) D
RBV	RIVERSIDE BOOK OF VERSE, THE. Robert M. Gay, comp. (1927). Same as THE COLLEGE BOOK OF VERSE, 1250-1925, see **CBOV** A
RCR	RILEY CHILD RHYMES. James Whitcomb Riley. (1898) 1
RDAH	ROOSEVELT DAY (Our American Heritage Series). Hilah Paulmier & Robert Haven Schauffler, comps. & eds. (1932) 3
RDB	RICHARD DYER-BENNET FOLK SONG BOOK, THE. Richard Dyer-Bennet, ed. (1971) E
REAL	READINGS IN ENGLISH AND AMERICAN LITERATURE. Gerald E. Seboyar, comp. (2d ed., 1945) 5-4

ReaPo	READING POEMS. Wright Thomas & Stuart Gerry Brown, eds. (1941) 5-4-B
ReC	RESTORATION CARNIVAL. Vivian de Sola Pinto, ed. (1954) C
ReEn	RENAISSANCE ENGLAND. Roy Lamson & Hallett Smith, ed. (1956). Edition of 1942 had title THE GOLDEN HIND 6-5
ReIE	RENAISSANCE ENGLAND, THE. Hyder E. Rollins & Herschel Baker, comps. (1954) 6-5
REL	READINGS IN EUROPEAN LITERATURE. Gerald E. Seboyar & Rudolph F. Brosius, eds. (2d ed., 1946) 4
ReMoGo	REAL MOTHER GOOSE, THE. Blanche Fisher Wright, illus. (1916) Rand McNally & Co. B
ReMP	READING MODERN POETRY. Paul Engle & Warren Carrier, eds. (1955) 6-5-C
RePo	READING OF POETRY, THE. William D. Sheldon, Nellie Lyons, & Polly Roualt, eds. (1963) 6-D
ReTS	RECITER'S TREASURY OF SCENES AND POEMS, THE. Ernest Guy Pertwee, ed. (1934) 5-4
RFM	ROOM FOR ME AND A MOUNTAIN LION. Nancy Larrick, comp. (1974) E
RG	RAINBOW GOLD. Sara Teasdale, comp. (1922) 6-5-4-3-A
RH	RED HARVEST, THE. Vincent Godfrey Burns, ed. (1930) 4-3
RiBV	RINEHART BOOK OF VERSE, THE. Alan Swallow, ed. (1952) 5-C
RIS	RAINBOW IN THE SKY. Louis Untermeyer, ed. (1935) 6-5-4-3

RiTi	RISING TIDES. Laura Chester & Sharon Barba, eds. (1973) E
RKV	RUDYARD KIPLING'S VERSE, 1885-1932. (1934) 3
RLP	RED LETTER POEMS, by English men and women. Thomas Young Crowell, comp. (1884) 2
RM	READINGS AND MONOLOGUES OF DISTINCTION. Frances Leedom Hess, comp. (1925) A
RM *	RENASCENCE AND OTHER POEMS. Edna St. Vincent Millay. (1917) 3
RNP	READINGS FROM THE NEW POETS. William Webster Ellsworth, ed. (1928) 3
RO	ROMANTICS, THE. Geoffrey Grigson, ed. (1942) 5-4
RoGo	ROOFS OF GOLD. Padraic Colum, ed. (1964) 6-D
RoL	ROMAN LITERATURE IN TRANSLATION. George Howe & Gustave Adolphus Harrer, eds.; revised by Albert Suskin. (Rev. ed., 1959) 5
RON	RECITATIONS, OLD AND NEW, FOR BOYS AND GIRLS. Grace Gaige, comp. (1924) 3-A
RoTe	ROAD TO TEXAS, THE. Whitney Montgomery, ed. (1940) B
RRA	ROSES RACE AROUND HER NAME, THE. Jonathan Cott, ed. (1974) E
RT	RADIANT TREE, THE. Marguerite Wilkinson, ed. (1927) 4-3-A
RTI	RECITER'S TREASURY OF IRISH VERSE AND PROSE, THE. Albert Perceval Graves & Ernest Guy Pertwee, comps. (1915) 2

RTV	RECITER'S TREASURY OF VERSE, SERIOUS AND HUMOROUS, THE. Ernest Pertwee, comp. (1904) 2
RuPo	RUSSIAN POETRY, 1917-1955. Jack Lindsay, ed. & tr. (1957) 5
RYC	RECITATIONS FOR YOUNGER CHILDREN. Grace Gaige, comp. & ed. (1927) 3-A
S	SUNFLOWERS. Willard Wattles, comp. (1916) 2
SA	SCIENCE AND ART OF ELOCUTION. Frank H. Fenno. (1878) 2-1
SA *	SETTLING AMERICA, David Kherdian, ed. (1974) E
SAE	See AE
SaFP	SAINT FRANCIS AND THE POET. Elizabeth B. Patterson, ed. (1956) 5
SaL	SALAMANDER. Keith Bullen & John Cromer, eds. (1947) 4
SAM	SECOND APRIL. Edna St. Vincent Millay. (1921) 3
SAP	STORIES AND POEMS FOR CHILDREN. Celia Thaxter. (1883) 1
SAS	SUGAR AND SPICE. Mary Wilder Tileston, comp. (1928) 6-5-4-3
SaSa	SAUCY SAILOR AND OTHER DRAMATIZED BALLADS, THE. Alice M. G. White & Janet E. Tobitt, comps. (1940) 6-5-4-B
SASS	SMOKE AND STEEL AND SLABS OF THE SUN-BURNT WEST. Carl Sandburg. (1922) 3
SAy	SATIRE ANTHOLOGY, A. Carolyn Wells, ed. (1905) 2

SBA	STANDARD BOOK OF BRITISH AND AMERICAN VERSE, THE. Nella Braddy, comp. (1932) 4-3
SBG	SALT AND BITTER AND GOOD. Cora Kaplan, ed. (1975) E
SBMV	SECOND BOOK OF MODERN VERSE, THE. Jessie B. Rittenhouse, ed. (1919). See also **LBMV**, **TBM** 5-4-3-A
SBOS	SONGS AND BALLADS FROM OVER THE SEA. E. A. Helps, comp. (1912) 2
SC	SCHOOL AND COLLEGE SPEAKER. Wilmot Brookings Mitchell, ed. (1901) 2-1
SC *	SPEECH CHOIR, THE. Marjorie Gullan, comp. (1937) 3
SCAP	SEVENTEENTH-CENTURY AMERICAN POETRY. Harrison T. Meserole, ed. (1968) 6
SCC	SONGS OF THE CATTLE TRAIL AND COW CAMP. John A. Lomax, comp. (1919; new ed., 1950) 6-5-4-3
SCEP 1-2	17th CENTURY ENGLISH POETRY, Vols. I-II. Miriam K. Sparkman, ed. (1967) 6
SCP 1-2	SIGNET CLASSIC POETS OF THE 17th CENTURY, Vols. I-II. John Broadbent, ed. (1974) E
SCS	SPENCER'S COMIC SPEECHES. Dick & Fitzgerald. 1
SD	SPRINTS AND DISTANCES. Lillian Morrison, comp. (1965) 6-D
SD *	STANDARD DIALOGUES. Alexander Clark, comp. (1898) 3-2-1

SDC	STERLING DIALOGUES. William M. Clark, comp. (1898; 1929) 3-2-1 [StD in 2 & 1]
SDD	SCHOOLDAY DIALOGUES. Alexander Clark, comp. (1897) 3-2-1
SDE	˙SPECIAL DAY EXERCISES. Amos M. Kellogg, comp. (1903-1908) 3-2 [SpDE in 2]
SDH	STARDUST AND HOLLY. Dorothy Middleton Shipman, comp. (1932) 5-4-3
SDR	DIALECT READINGS. Henry M. Soper, ed. (19-?) 2-1
SE	SCHOOL ELOCUTION. John Swett. (1884) 1
SeCePo	SEVEN CENTURIES OF POETRY. A. N. Jeffares, ed. (1955) 6-5
SeCeV	SEVEN CENTURIES OF VERSE, ENGLISH AND AMERICAN. A. J. M. Smith, ed. (2d ed., rev. & enl., 1957; rev. & enl. ed., 1967) 6-5
SeCL	SEVENTEENTH CENTURY LYRICS. Norman Ault, ed. (2d ed., 1950) 6-5-4
SeCP	SEVENTEENTH CENTURY POETRY. Hugh Kenner, ed. (1964) 6-D
SeCSL	SEVENTEENTH CENTURY SONGS AND LYRICS. John P. Cutts, ed. (1959) 6-5
SeCV 1-2	SEVENTEENTH-CENTURY VERSE AND PROSE, Vols. I-II. Helen C. White, Ruth C. Wallerstein, & Ricardo Quintana, eds. (1951, 1952) 6-5-C
SED	STEELE'S EXHIBITION DIALOGUES. Silax Sexton Steele. (1882) 1
SeEP	SEVENTEENTH-CENTURY ENGLISH POETRY. R. C. Bald, ed. (1959) 6-5

SEP	STANDARD ENGLISH POEMS; Spenser to Tennyson. Henry S. Pancoast, ed. (1899) 4-3-2
SePoSe	SEVEN POETS IN SEARCH OF AN ANSWER. Thomas Yoseloff, ed. (1944) 4-B
SeUD	SEALED UNTO THIS DAY. John Gilland Brunini, ed. (1955) C
SFC	SELECTIONS FOR CHORAL SPEAKING. Agnes Curren Hamm, comp. (1935) 3
SFF	SINCE FEELING IS FIRST. James Mecklenburger & Gary Simmons, eds. (1971) E
SFM	SELECTIONS FOR MEMORIZING. Avery Warner Skinner, comp. (1906) 2
SG	SAILOR'S GARLAND, A. John Masefield, ed. (New ed., 1924) 5-4-3
SGB	SONGS AND BALLADS OF GREATER BRITAIN. E. A. Helps, comp. (1913) 2
SGR	SONGS OF THE GOLD RUSH, THE. Richard A. Dwyer & Richard E. Lingenfelter, eds. (1964) 6-D
ShBV 1-4	SHELDON BOOK OF VERSE, THE. Books I-IV. P. G. Smith & J. F. Wilkins, comps. (1959) 6-5
ShGoBo	SHORTER GOLDEN BOOK OF NARRATIVE VERSE, THE. Frank Jones, ed. (1943) 5-4-B
ShM	SHRIEKS AT MIDNIGHT. Sara Brewton & John E. Brewton, eds. (1969) 6
ShS	SHANTYMEN AND SHANTYBOYS. William Main Doerflinger, comp. (1951) 6-5-C
SiB	SILVER BRANCH, THE. Sean O'Faolain, comp. (1938) 5-4

SiCE	SIXTEENTH-CENTURY POETRY. Norman E. McClure, ed. (1954) 6-5-C
SiGo	SINGING AND THE GOLD, THE. Elinor Parker, comp. (1962) D
SiMeYo	SING ME YOUR SONG, O! Janet E. Tobitt, comp. (1941) B
SiPS	SILVER POETS OF THE SIXTEENTH CENTURY. Gerald Bullett, ed. (1947) 6-5-4
SiSoSe	SING A SONG OF SEASONS. Sara Brewton & John E. Brewton, eds. (1955) 6-5
SiSw	SILVER SWAN, THE. Horace Gregory & Marya Zaturenska, eds. (1968) 6
SiTL	SILVER TREASURY OF LIGHT VERSE, THE. Oscar Williams, ed. (1957) 6-5
SIV	STORIES IN VERSE. Max T. Hohn, ed. (1961) D
SiWo	SINGING WORDS. Alice G. Thorn, comp. (1941) B
SL	SILVER LININGS. Joseph Morris, pseud. [i.e., Joseph Morris Bachelor] & St. Clair Adams, comps. (1927). For composite edition, see POL 3-A [SLHC in A]
SL *	SMILES. Alice Lewis Richards. (1899) 1
SLHC	See SL
SLP	SCOTTISH LOVE POEMS. Antonia Fraser, ed. (1975) E
SM	SELECTIONS FOR MEMORIZING. Luther Clark Foster & Sherman Williams, comps. (1892) 1
SMG	SELECTED MEMORY GEMS. William Andrew Wilson, comp. (1911) 2

SMP	SHORTER MODERN POEMS, 1900–1931. David Morton, comp. (1932) 4-3
SN	SONGS OF NATURE. John Burroughs, comp. (1901). Edition of 1938 has title BOOK OF SONGS OF NATURE 5-4-3-2
SO	STEPS TO ORATORY. F. Townsend Southwick, ed. (1900) 1
SoAF	SONGS OF AMERICAN FOLKS. Satis N. Coleman & Adolph Bregman, eds. (1942) 5-4
SoAmSa	SONGS OF AMERICAN SAILORMEN. Joanna C. Colcord, ed. (Enl. & rev. ed., 1938). Edition of 1924 had title ROLL AND GO, SONGS OF AMERICAN SAILORMEN 6-5-4-B
SOC	SONGS OF CHILDHOOD. Walter Ramal, pseud. [i.e., Walter De La Mare]. (1902) 1
SoLD	SONGS FROM THE LAND OF DAWN. Lois J. Erickson, tr. (1949) 5-4
Sonn	SONNET, THE. Robert M. Bender & Charles L. Squier, eds. (1965) 6
SoP	SOURCEBOOK OF POETRY. Al Bryant, comp. (1968) 6
SoPo	SOUND OF POETRY, THE. Mary C. Austin & Queenie B. Mills, eds. (1963) 6-D
SoSe	SOUND AND SENSE. Laurence Perrine, ed. (4th ed., 1973) E
SoV	SOLDIERS' VERSE. Patric Dickinson, comp. (1945) 5-4
SP	SILVER PENNIES. Blanche Jennings Thompson, comp. (1925) 6-5-4-3-A

SP 1-8	See SPE 1-8
SPC	See PC *
SPC *	SCHOOL AND PARLOR COMEDIES. Benjamin L. C. Griffith. (1894) 2-1
SpDE	See SDE
SPE	See PE
SPE 1-8	SPEAKER, THE. Vols. 1-8. Paul M. Pearson, ed. (1925) 3-2 [SP 1-8 in 2]
SPo	SPORTS POEMS. R. R. Knudson & P. K. Ebert, eds. (1971) E
SPP	SOUTHERN POETS. Edd Winfield Parks, ed. (1936) 5-4-3
SpRo	SPEAK ROUGHLY TO YOUR LITTLE BOY. Myra Cohn Livingston, ed. (1971) E
SPS	SELECTIONS FOR PUBLIC SPEAKING. Leslie C. Proctor & Gladys Trueblood Stroop, comps. (1930) 3
SPT	STAR-POINTS. Mrs. Waldo Richards [Gertrude Moore Richards], comp. (1921) 3-A [STP in A]
SR	SELECTED READINGS. Anna Morgan, comp. (1909) 3-2
SR 1-15	SCRAP-BOOK RECITATIONS, Numbers I-XV. Henry M. Soper & others, comps. (1879-1919) 2-1
SS	SOUNDS AND SILENCES. Robert W. Boynton & Maynard Mack, eds. (1975) E
SS *	STANDARD SPEAKER, THE. Epes Sargent, comp. (1852) 2-1
SS **	See SSS
SSD	SELECT SPEECHES FOR DECLAMATION. John B. Bechtel, comp. (1898) 2-1

SSE	SUNDAY SCHOOL ENTERTAINMENTS, together with 99 other choice readings & recitations. (1901). Henneberry Co. 2-1
SSR	SCHOOL SPEAKER AND READER, THE. William DeWitt Hyde, ed. (1900) 2
SSS	SARA SHRINER'S SELECTIONS. Sara Venore Shriner, comp. (1924) 3-A [SS in A]
SSS *	SUNDAY SCHOOL SELECTIONS. John H. Bechtel, ed. (1892) 2-1
SSSC	SONGS OF THE SEA AND SAILORS' CHANTEYS. Robert Frothingham, comp. (1924) A
SSSC *	SPRING AND SUMMER SCHOOL CELEBRATIONS. Alice M. Kellogg, ed. (1895) 3-2
ST	SILVER TREASURY, THE. Jane Manner, ed. (1934) 4-3
StaSt	STARS TO STEER BY. Louis Untermeyer, ed. (1941) 6-5-4-B
STB	STORY-TELLING BALLADS. Frances Jenkins Olcott, comp. (1920) 3
STC	SONGS OF THREE CENTURIES. John Greenleaf Whittier, ed. (1875) 2
StD	See SDC
StDa	STEAMBOATIN' DAYS. Mary Wheeler, comp. (1944) 5-4-B
STF	SPEAKER'S TREASURY OF 400 QUOTABLE POEMS, THE. Croft M. Pentz, comp. (1963) 6-D
StJW	STORY OF JESUS IN THE WORLD'S LITERATURE, THE. Edward Wagenknecht, ed. (1946) 6-5-4
STP	See SPT
STP *	STORY-TELLING POEMS. Frances Jenkins Ol-

	cott, comp. (1913) 3-2
StP	STUDYING POETRY. Karl Kroeber & John O. Lyons, eds. (1965) 6-D
StPo	STORY POEMS, NEW AND OLD. William Cole, ed. (1957) 6-5
StS	STANDARD SELECTIONS. Robert I. Fulton & Thomas C. Trueblood, comps. (1907) 2
StVeCh	STORY AND VERSE FOR CHILDREN. Miriam Blanton Huber, ed. (1940; rev. ed. 1955) 6-5-4-B
SuAmHu	SUBTREASURY OF AMERICAN HUMOR, A. E. B. White & Katharine S. White, eds. (1941) 4-B
SUS	SUNG UNDER THE SILVER UMBRELLA. Association for Childhood Education. (1935) 6-5-4-3
SWC	See TSWC
SyP	SYMBOLIST POEM, THE. Edward Engelburg, ed. (1967) 6
SYS	SMILES YOKED WITH SIGHS. Robert Jones Burdette. (1900) 1
TaBoMg	TALL BOOK OF MOTHER GOOSE, THE. Feodor Rojankovsky, illus. (1942) B
TAS	TREASURY OF AMERICAN SACRED SONG. W. Garrett Horder, ed. (1896) 1
TAV	See AV
TAV *	TREASURY OF AMERICAN VERSE, A. Walter Learned, ed. (1897) 1
TB	TRIAL BALANCES. Ann Winslow, ed. (1935) 4-3
TBM	THIRD BOOK OF MODERN VERSE, THE. Jessie B. Rittenhouse, ed. (1927). See also LBMV & SBMV 5-4-3

TBV	TRAVELER'S BOOK OF VERSE, THE. Frederick E. Emmons & T. W. Huntington, eds. (1928) 4-3
TCEP	TWELVE CENTURIES OF ENGLISH POETRY AND PROSE. Aphonso Gerald Newcomer, Alice E. Andrews, & Howard Judson Hall, comps. (Rev. ed., 1928) 5-4-3
TCAP	THREE CENTURIES OF AMERICAN POETRY AND PROSE. Alphonso Gerald Newcomer, Alice E. Andrews, & Howard Judson Hall, eds. (Rev. ed., 1929) 5-4-3
TCP	TABLEAUX, CHARADES AND PANTOMIMES. Emma C. Rook, comp. (1889) 2-1
TCP *	TWENTIETH CENTURY POETRY. Carol Marshall, ed. (1971) E
TCPD	TWENTIETH-CENTURY POETRY. John Drinkwater, Henry Seidel Canby, & William Rose Benét, eds. (1929) 5-4-3
TCV	TREASURY OF CANADIAN VERSE, A. Theodore H. Rand, comp. (1900) 2-1
TDP	THREE DIMENSIONS OF POETRY. Vincent Stewart, ed. (1969) 6
TDT	BOOK OF TABLEAUX. Tony Dernier. (1868) 1
TeCS	TEN CENTURIES OF SPANISH POETRY. Eleanor L. Turnbull, ed. (1955) 5-C
TFS	TOMMY'S FIRST SPEAKER. Thomas W. Handford, ed. (1885) 2-1
TFY	THIS IS FOR YOU. William Sinclair Lord, comp. (1902) 2-1
TH	TAKE HOLD! Lee Bennett Hopkins, comp. (1974) E

ThDr	THUDDING DRUMS. G. M. Miller, comp. (1942) 4-B
ThGo	THREAD OF GOLD, A. Eleanor Graham, comp. (1964) 6-D
ThHaHo	THIS HAPPY HOME. C. S. Goodsman, comp. (1944) B
ThLM	THIS LAND IS MINE. Al Hine, ed. (1965) 6-D
ThO	31 NEW AMERICAN POETS. Ron Schreiber, ed. (1969) 6
THP	TREASURY OF HUMOROUS POETRY, A. Frederic Lawrence Knowles, ed. (1902) 4-3-2-1
ThRuPo	THREE RUSSIAN POETS. Vladimir Nabokov, tr. (1944) B
THV	TREASURY OF HELPFUL VERSE, A. John White Chadwick & Annie H. Chadwick, eds. (1896) 2
ThWaDe	THIS WAY, DELIGHT. Herbert Read, ed. (1956) 6-5
TIHL	THESE I HAVE LOVED. Gilbert Hay, comp. (1969) 6
TIP	TREASURY OF IRISH POETRY, A. Stopford Brooke & T. W. Rolleston, eds. (1900; rev. & enl. ed., 1932) 5-4-3-2-1
TiPo	TIME FOR POETRY. May Hill Arbuthnot, comp. (General ed., 1952; rev. ed., 1959) 6-5-C
TIWP	THROUGH ITALY WITH THE POETS. Robert Haven Schauffler, comp. (1908) 2
TK	TALKS. George Thatcher. (1890) 1
TL	TAKEN FROM LIFE. (1897) Doubleday, Page & Co. 1

TL *	TODAY'S LITERATURE. Dudley Chadwick Gordon, Vernon Rupert King, & William Whittingham Lyman, eds. (1935) 4-3
TM	TO MOTHER. Elizabeth McCracken, ed. (1917) 2
TMC	THROUGH MAGIC CASEMENTS. George S. Carhart & Paul A. McGhee, comps. (1926). Same as MAGIC CASEMENTS, see MCCG A
TMD	THREE MINUTE DECLAMATIONS FOR COLLEGE MEN. Harry Cassell Davis & John C. Bridgeman, eds. (1890) 2-1
TMEV	TREASURY OF MIDDLE ENGLISH VERSE. Margot Robert Adamson, comp. (1930) 5-4-3
TMR	THREE MINUTE READINGS FOR COLLEGE GIRLS. Harry Cassell Davis, ed. (1897) 2-1
TNP	NEW PATRIOTISM, THE. Thomas Curtis Clark & Esther A. Gillespie, comps. (1927) A
TNV	TODAY'S NEGRO VOICES. Beatrice M. Murphy, ed. (1970) 6
TOAH	THANKSGIVING (Our American Holidays Series). Robert Haven Schauffler, ed. (1907) 5-4-3-2 [OAT in 2]
TOP	TYPES OF POETRY. Jacob Zeitlin & Clarissa Rinaker, comps. (1926) 6-5-4-3-A
ToPo	TODAY'S POETS. Chad Walsh, ed. (1964) 6-D
TOV	See TVSH
TP	THANKSGIVING IN POETRY. Carnegie Library School Association, comp. (1925) A
TPH	TYPES OF POETRY. Howard Judson Hall, ed. (1927) 4-3-A [HTP in A]

TPM	TO PLAY MAN NUMBER ONE. Sara Hannum & John Terry Chase, comps. (1969) 6
TrAB	TREASURY OF AMERICAN BALLADS, A. Charles O'Brien Kennedy, ed. (1954) C
TrAS	TREASURY OF AMERICAN SONG, A. Olin Downes & Elie Siegmeister, comps. (2d ed., rev. & enl., 1943) 6-5-4
TrBrHu	TREASURY OF BRITISH HUMOR, A. Morris Bishop, ed. (1942) 4-B
TrCh	TRANSLATIONS FROM THE CHINESE. Arthur Waley, tr. (1941) 5
TreF	TREASURY OF THE FAMILIAR, A. Ralph L. Woods, ed. (1942) 6-5-4
TreFS	TREASURY OF THE FAMILIAR, A SECOND. Ralph L. Woods, ed. (1950) 6-5-4
TreFT	TREASURY OF THE FAMILIAR, A THIRD. Ralph L. Woods, ed. (1970) 6
TrEV	TREASURY OF ENGLISH VERSE, NEW AND OLD. A. S. Collins, ed. (1931) 4
TrFP	TREASURY OF FRENCH POETRY, A. Alan Conder, ed. & tr. (1951) 5-C
TrGrPo	TREASURY OF GREAT POEMS, ENGLISH AND AMERICAN, A. Louis Untermeyer, ed. (1942; rev. & enl. ed., 1955) 6-5-C-4-B
TriL	TRIUMPH OF LIFE, THE. Horace Gregory, ed. (1943) 5-4
TrJP	TREASURY OF JEWISH POETRY, A. Nathan Ausubel & Maryann Ausubel, eds. (1957) 6-5

TrNE	TREASURY OF NEW ENGLAND FOLKLORE, A. B. A. Botkin, ed. (1947) 4
TrPWD	TREASURY OF POEMS FOR WORSHIP AND DEVOTION, A. Charles L. Wallis, ed. (1959) 6-5
TrRuLi	TREASURY OF RUSSIAN LITERATURE, A. Bernard Guilbert Guerney, ed. (1943) 4-B
TrRV	TREASURY OF RUSSIAN VERSE, A. Avraham Yarmolinsky, ed. (1949) 5-4
TrS	TREASURY OF SATIRE, A. Edgar Johnson, ed. (1945) 4
TRV	TREASURY OF RELIGIOUS VERSE, THE. Donald T. Kauffman, comp. (1962) 6-D
TS	TEMPERANCE SELECTIONS. John B. Bechtel, ed. (1893) 3-2-1
TSS	TOMMY'S SECOND SPEAKER. Thomas W. Handford, comp. (190-?) 2
TSW	THIS SINGING WORLD. Louis Untermeyer, ed. (1923) 6-5-4-3-A
TSWA	TO SEE THE WORLD AFRESH. Lilian Moore & Judith Thurman, comps. (1974) E
TSWC	THIS SINGING WORLD FOR YOUNGER CHILDREN. Louis Untermeyer, ed. (1926) 5-4-3-A [SWC in A]
TT	TINY TOTS SPEAKER. Elizabeth (Lizzie) J. Rook & E. J. H. Goodfellow. (1895) 2-1
TTY	3000 YEARS OF BLACK POETRY. Alan Lomax & Raoul Abdul, eds. (1970) 6
TuPP	TUDOR POETRY AND PROSE. J. William Hebel, Hoyt H. Hudson, Francis R. Johnson, A. Wigfall Green, & Robert Hoopes, eds. (1953). Edition

	of 1929 had title POETRY OF THE ENGLISH RENAISSANCE. 6-5-C
TVC	TREASURY OF VERSE FOR LITTLE CHILDREN, A. M. G. Edgar, ed. (Rev. & enl. ed., 1927; new ed., 1946) 6-5-4-3-A
TVS	TUDOR VERSE SATIRE. K. W. Gransden, ed. (1970) E
TVSH	TREASURY OF VERSE FOR SCHOOL AND HOME, A. M. G. Edgar & Eric Chilman, comps. (1926, 1936) 5-4-3-A [TOV in A]
TwAmPo	TWENTIETH-CENTURY AMERICAN POETRY. Conrad Aiken, ed. (rev. ed., 1963). Edition of 1927 had title MODERN AMERICAN POETS, see MAPA 6-5-4-B
TwCaPo	TWENTIETH CENTURY CANADIAN POETRY. Earle Birney, ed. (1953) 6-5-C
TwCP	TWENTIETH CENTURY POETRY (1900–1970). John Malcolm Brinnin & Bill Read, eds. (rev. ed., 1970). Edition of 1963 had title THE MODERN POETS, see MP 6
TwCrTr	TWO CREATIVE TRADITIONS IN ENGLISH POETRY. Seymour M. Pitcher, & others, eds. (1939) 5-4-B
TwCV	TWENTIETH CENTURY VERSE. Ira Dilworth, ed. (1945) 5-4
TwGP	TWENTY GERMAN POETS. Walter Kaufmann, ed. (1962) D
TwGV	TWENTIETH-CENTURY GERMAN VERSE. Herman Salinger, ed. & tr. (1952) 5-C
TwHP	TWO HUNDRED POEMS. Ricardo Quintana, ed. (1947) 5-4

TwMBP	TWENTY-THREE MODERN BRITISH POETS. John Matthias, ed. (1971) E
TwP	12 POETS. Glenn Leggett, ed. (1958) 5
TWP-1	TREASURY OF WAR POETRY, A. 1st series. George Herbert Clarke, ed. (1917) A
TWP-2	TREASURY OF WAR POETRY, A. 2d series. George Herbert Clarke, ed. (1919) A
TwSpPo	12 SPANISH AMERICAN POETS. H. R. Hays, ed. & tr. (1943) 5-4-B
TyEnPo	TYPES OF ENGLISH POETRY. Rudolf Kirk & Clara Marburg Kirk, eds. (1940) 5-4-B
TYP	THREE YEARS WITH THE POETS. Bertha Hazard, comp. (1904) 4-3-2
UAP	MODERN AMERICAN POETRY. Louis Untermeyer, ed. (3d rev. ed., 1921). For later editions, see **MoAmPo** A
UBP	MODERN BRITISH POETRY. Louis Untermeyer, ed. (rev. ed., 1925). For later editions, see **MoBrPo** A
UFE	UP FROM THE EARTH. Sylvia Spencer, comp. (1935) 4-3
UnPo	UNDERSTANDING POETRY. Cleanth Brooks & Robert Penn Warren, eds. (1938; 3d ed., 1960) 6-5-4-B
UnS	UNTUNE THE SKY. Helen Plotz, comp. (1957) 6-5
UnTE	UNINHIBITED TREASURY OF EROTIC POETRY, AN. Louis Untermeyer, ed. (1963) 6-D
UnW	UNSEEN WINGS. Stanton A. Coblentz, comp. (1949) 5-4
UTS	UNDER THE TENT OF THE SKY. John E.

	Brewton, comp. (1937) 6-5-4-3
VA	VICTORIAN ANTHOLOGY, A, 1837–1895. Edmund Clarence Stedman, ed. (1895) 6-5-4-3-2-1
VaPo	VARIETY OF POETRY, THE. Edward A. Bloom, Charles H. Philbrick, & Elmer M. Blistein, eds. (1964) 6-D
VE	VISTA OF ENGLISH VERSE. Henry S. Pancoast, comp. (1911) 2
VeChBo	VERMONT CHAP BOOK. Helen Hartness Flanders, comp. (1941) B
VeV	VERSE OF VALOUR. John L. Hardie, ed. (1943) 4
VF	VOICES FROM THE FIELDS. Russell Lord, ed. (1937) 4-3
VGW	VOICE THAT IS GREAT WITHIN US, THE. Hayden Carruth, ed. (1970) E
ViBoFo	VIKING BOOK OF FOLK BALLADS OF THE ENGLISH-SPEAKING WORLD, THE. Albert B. Friedman, ed. (1956) 6-5
ViBoPo	VIKING BOOK OF POETRY OF THE ENGLISH-SPEAKING WORLD, THE. Richard Aldington, ed. (1941; rev. mid-century ed., 1959, in 2 vols.) 6-5-4-B
ViL	VERSES I LIKE. Major Edward Bowes, comp. (1937) 4-3
ViP	VICTORIAN POETRY. Arthur J. Carr, ed. (1959) 5
ViPo	VICTORIAN POETRY. E. K. Brown & J. O. Bailey, eds. (1942; 2d ed., 1962) 6-5-4-B
ViPP	VICTORIAN POETRY AND POETICS. Walter E. Houghton & G. Robert Stange, eds. (1959) 6-5
ViV	VINTAGE VERSE. Clifford Bax, comp. (1945) 4

VLEP	VICTORIAN AND LATER ENGLISH POETS. James Stephens, Edwin L. Beck, & Royall H. Snow, eds. (1934) 5-4-3
VM	VALIANT MUSE, THE. Frederick W. Ziv, ed. (1936) 4-3
VOD	VERSE OF OUR DAY. Margery Gordon & Marie B. King, eds. (Rev. ed., 1913; 2d rev. ed., 1935) 5-4-3
VoFP	VOICES FROM THE PAST. James Maclean Todd & Janet Maclean Todd, eds. (1955) C
VoPo	VOICES OF POETRY. Allen Kirschner, ed. (1970) E
VP	VERSE FOR PATRIOTS. Jean Broadhurst & Clara Lawton Rhodes, comp. (1919) A
VP *	VICTORIAN POETRY. Robert Bernard Martin, ed. (1964) 6-D
VPC	VICTORIAN POETRY: "THE CITY OF DREADFUL NIGHT" AND OTHER POEMS. N. P. Messenger & J. R. Watson, eds. (1974) E
VS	VICTORIAN SONGS. Edmund H. Garrett, comp. (1895) 1
VSA	VERS DE SOCIETE ANTHOLOGY, A. Carolyn Wells, ed. (1907) 2
VSG	VOICE, SPEECH, AND GESTURE. Hugh Campbell, Robert F. Brewer, & Henry G. Neville (1895) 1
VW	VOICES FROM WAH'KON-TAH. Robert K. Dodge & Joseph B. McCullough, eds. (2d ed., 1976) E

WA	WHIMSEY ANTHOLOGY, A. Carolyn Wells, comp. (1906) 2
WaaP	WAR AND THE POET . . . FROM ANCIENT TIMES TO THE PRESENT. Richard Eberhart & Selden Rodman, eds. (1945) 6-5-4
WaKn	WAY OF KNOWING, A. Gerald D. McDonald, comp. (1959) 6-5
WaL	WAGGON OF LIFE, THE, AND OTHER LYRICS BY RUSSIAN POETS OF THE NINETEENTH CENTURY. Sir Cecil Kisch, tr. (1947) 5-4
WaP	WAR POETS, THE. Oscar Williams, ed. (1945) 6-5-4
WaPE	WAYSIDE POEMS OF THE EARLY EIGHTEENTH CENTURY. Edmund Blunden & Bernard Mellor, eds. (1964) 6-D
WBLP	WORLD'S BEST-LOVED POEMS, THE. James Gilchrist Lawson, comp. (1927) 6-5-4-3
WBN	WE BECOME NEW. Lucille Iverson & Kathryn Ruby, eds. (1975) E
WBP	WORLD'S BEST POEMS, THE. Mark Van Doren & Garibaldi M. Lapolla, eds. (1929, 1946) Same as **JAWP** 6-5-4-3
WCL	CHILD LIFE. John Greenleaf Whittier, ed. (1871) 2-1
WCLG 1-2	WILLIAMS'S CHOICE LITERATURE . . . FOR GRAMMAR GRADES, Vols. I-II. Sherman Williams, comp. (1898) 1
WCLI 1-2	WILLIAMS'S CHOICE LITERATURE . . . FOR INTERMEDIATE GRADES, Vols. I-II. Sherman Williams, comp. (1898) 1
WCS	WREATH OF CANADIAN SONGS, A. Mrs. C. M. Whyte-Edgar, ed. (1910) 2

WDM	WILSON'S DRILLS AND MARCHES. Bertha M. Wilson. (1895) 1
WeCh	WELCOME CHRISTMAS! Anne Thaxter Eaton, comp. (1955) C
WEP 1-4	See **EPW 1-5**
WePo	WEALTH OF POETRY, A. Winifred Hindley, ed., with the assistance of John Betjeman. (1963) 6-D
WFG	WINE FROM THESE GRAPES. Edna St. Vincent Millay. (1934) 3
WGRP	WORLD'S GREAT RELIGIOUS POETRY, THE. Caroline Miles Hill, ed. (1923) 6-5-4-3-A [WRP in A]
WGS	WORLD'S GREATEST SHORT STORIES, THE. Sherwin Cody, ed. (1902) 1
WHA	WINGED HORSE ANTHOLOGY, THE. Joseph Auslander & Frank Ernest Hill, eds. (1929) 6-5-4-3
WhBS	WHERE BIRDS SING. Ada L. F. Snell, comp. (1959) 5
WhC	WHAT CHEER. David McCord, ed. (1945) 6-5-4
WHL	WITH HARP AND LUTE. Blanche Jennings Thompson, comp. (1935) 6-5-4-3
WHO	WHITE HOUSE HANDBOOK OF ORATORY. Charles Chadman, comp. (1899) 2
WhP	WHITE PONY, THE. Robert Payne, ed. (1947) 5-4
WHW	WIND HAS WINGS, THE. Mary Alice Downie & Barbara Robertson, eds. (1968) 6
WIF	WORDS IN FLIGHT. Richard Abcarian, ed. (1972) E
WiR	WIND AND THE RAIN, THE. John Hollander & Harold Bloom, eds. (1961) 6-D

WIRo	WIND IS ROUND, THE. Sara Hannum & John Terry Chase, comps. (1970) 6
WLIP	WHAT I LIKE IN POETRY. William Lyon Phelps, comp. (1934) 4-3
WLO	WHEN THE LESSONS ARE OVER. Clara J. Denton. (1891) 2-1
WN	WINKS. Alice Lewis Richards. (1900) 1
WOAH	WASHINGTON'S BIRTHDAY. (Our American Holidays Series). Robert Haven Schauffler, ed. (1910) 5-4-3-2 [OAW in 2]
WoL	WORLD LITERATURE. Arthur R. Christy & Henry W. Wells, eds. (1947) 6-5-4
WoMu	WORLDLY MUSE, THE. A. J. M. Smith, ed. (1951) C
WOW	WRITING ON THE WALL, THE. Walter Lowenfels, ed. (1969) 6
WP	WAY OF POETRY. John Drinkwater, comp. (1922) 5-4-3-A [DWP in A]
WPB	WELSH POEMS AND BALLADS. George Henry Borrow, tr. (1915) 2
WPE	WOMEN POETS IN ENGLISH, THE. Ann Stanford, ed. (1972) E
WR	See WRR 1-58
WrChPo	WREATH OF CHRISTMAS POEMS, A. Albert M. Hayes & James Laughlin, eds. (1942) 4-B
WRD	WILSON'S RECITATIONS AND DIALOGUES. Floyd Baker Wilson, comp. (188-?) 1
WRP	See WGRP
WRR 1-58	WERNER'S READINGS AND RECITATIONS, Nos. 1-58. (1910) 4-3-2 [WR in 2]

WSL	WE SPEAK AS LIBERATORS. Orde Coombs, ed. (1970) 6
WSN	WATCHERS OF THE SKY (Book I of THE TORCH-BEARERS). Alfred Noyes. (1922) 3
WTD	WITH TRUMPET AND DRUM. Eugene Field. (1892) 1
WTP 1-10	WORLD'S BEST POEMS, THE, Vols. 1-10. Berton Braley, ed. (1929) 3
YA	YOUNG AMERICAN SPEAKER. Henry Davenport Northrup, comp. & ed. (1895) 1
YaCaBo	YALE CAROL BOOK, THE. H. Frank Bozyan & Sidney Lovett, eds. (1944) 6-5-4-B
YaD	YANKEE DOODLES. Ted Malone, pseud. [i.e., F. A. Russell], ed. (1943). Edition of 1948 has title THE ALL-AMERICAN BOOK OF VERSE 6-5-4
YAP	YOUNG AMERICAN POETS, THE. Paul Carroll, ed. (1968) 6
YAT	YOUNG AMERICAN'S TREASURY OF ENGLISH POETRY, A. Shirley E. Marshall, ed. (1967) 6
YBF	YEAR BOOK OF FAMOUS LYRICS. Frederic Lawrence Knowles, comp. (1901) 1
YBT	YEAR OF BEAUTIFUL THOUGHTS FOR BOYS AND GIRLS. Jeanie A. B. Greenough, comp. (1902) 1
YBV	YALE BOOK OF AMERICAN VERSE. Thomas R. Lounsbury, ed. (1912) 2
YC	YULE TIDE CHEER. Edward A. Bryant, comp. (1912) 2 [Also listed as **YTC**]

YeAr	YEAR AROUND, THE. Alice I. Hazeltine & Elva S. Smith, comps. (1956) 6-5
YF	YULE FIRE. Marguerite Wilkinson, comp. (1925) 4-3-A
YFD	YOUNG FOLKS' DIALOGUES. Charles C. Shoemaker, ed. (1885) 3-2-1
YFE	YOUNG FOLKS' ENTERTAINMENTS. Emma C. Rook & Elizabeth (Lizzie) J. Rook. (1886) 2-1
YFR	YOUNG FOLKS' RECITATIONS. Mrs. J. W. Shoemaker [Rachel W. (Hinkle) Shoemaker], comp. (1888). For composite edition, see **PPYP** 3-2-1
YP	YOUNG PEOPLE'S SPEAKER. Henry Davenport Northrup, comp. & ed. (1895) 1
YPS	YOUNG PEOPLE'S SPEAKER. Emma C. Rook & Elizabeth (Lizzie) J. Rook, comps. (1892). For composite edition, see **PPYP** 3-2-1
YT	YESTERDAY AND TODAY. Louis Untermeyer, ed. (1926) 6-5-4-3-A
YTC	See **YC**
YTE	YULETIDE ENTERTAINMENTS. Ellen M. Willard. (1910) 2

TITLE LIST

Directions for Use: Each work is listed alphabetically by its title as used in *Granger's* as well as by any other titles under which it may have been published. Wrong or erroneous titles given in *Granger's* (an occasional occurence in the earlier editions) have been corrected.

The title entry gives only the Granger Symbol for the work. Reference to the principal list is necessary to ascertain full details of the work, including author and variant titles (if any).

Articles at the beginning of titles are not retained but appear at the end of the title and are disregarded in the alphabeting.

ADAM AMONG THE TELEVISION TREES. AATT
ADVANCED ELOCUTION. AE
ALL DAY LONG. AlDL
ALL IN A LIFETIME. ALG
ALL KINDS OF DIALOGUES. MAD
ALL KINDS OF EVERYTHING. AKE
ALL SORTS OF DIALOGUES. ASD
ALL THE BEST DOG POEMS. AlBD
ALL-AMERICAN BOOK OF VERSE, THE. YaD
AMERICA FOREVER NEW. AmFN
AMERICA IS NOT ALL TRAFFIC LIGHTS. ANTL
AMERICAN ANTHOLOGY, AN, 1787-1900. AA
AMERICAN BALLADS AND FOLK SONGS. ABF
AMERICAN BALLADS AND SONGS. ABS
AMERICAN DECADE. AmD
AMERICAN FAMILIAR VERSE, A VERS DE SOCIETE. AFV
AMERICAN FOLK POETRY. AmFP
AMERICAN HISTORY BY AMERICAN POETS. AH 1-2
AMERICAN IDEA, THE. AI
AMERICAN LYRIC POEMS. AmLP
AMERICAN LYRICS. AL
AMERICAN MYSTICAL VERSE. AMMV
AMERICAN NEGRO POETRY. AmNP
AMERICAN PATRIOTIC PROSE AND VERSE. APPV

AMERICAN POEMS (1625-1892). AP
AMERICAN POEMS (1776-1922). APL
AMERICAN POEMS. AP *
AMERICAN POEMS; a contemporary collection. AmPC
AMERICAN POETRY, 1671-1928. APA
AMERICAN POETRY. G.W. Allen (et al). AP **
AMERICAN POETRY. P. Boynton. APB
AMERICAN POETRY. A. B. DeMille. APD
AMERICAN POETRY. K. Shapiro. AmP
AMERICAN POETRY. R. Stewart & D. Bethurum. AmPo
AMERICAN POETRY, 1922; a miscellany. AP-2
AMERICAN POETRY, 1925; a miscellany. AP-4
AMERICAN POETRY, 1927; a miscellany. AMA
AMERICAN POETRY AND PROSE. AmPP
AMERICAN POETRY ANTHOLOGY, THE. AmPA
AMERICAN POETRY FROM THE BEGINNING TO WHITMAN. APW
AMERICAN POETS, THE, 1800-1900. AmePo
AMERICAN PROSE. APr
AMERICAN SEA SONGS AND CHANTEYS. AmSS
AMERICAN SONGBAG, THE. AS
AMERICAN STAR SPEAKER, THE. AmSS *
AMERICAN VERSE OF THE NINETEENTH CENTURY. AmVN
AMERICAN VOICE. AmVo
AMERICAN WAR BALLADS AND LYRICS. AWB
AMERICAN WRITING, 1943. AmWr
ANALYTICAL ELOCUTION. AE *
ANCHOR ANTHOLOGY OF SEVENTEENTH CENTURY VERSE, THE. AnAnS 1-2
ANCHOR ANTHOLOGY OF SIXTEENTH-CENTURY VERSE, THE. AAS
ANCIENT ENGLISH CHRISTMAS CAROLS, MCCCC to MDCC. AnEC
ANCIENTS AND MODERNS. AnMo
ANOTHER BOOK OF VERSES FOR CHILDREN. ABVC
ANSWERING VOICE, THE. AV
ANTHOLOGY FOR THE ENJOYMENT OF POETRY. AnEnPo
ANTHOLOGY OF AMERICAN NEGRO LITERATURE. ANL
ANTHOLOGY OF AMERICAN POETRY,THE. AnAmPo
ANTHOLOGY OF CANADIAN POETRY. AnCaPo
ANTHOLOGY OF CATHOLIC POETS, AN. ACP
ANTHOLOGY OF COMMONWEALTH VERSE, AN. ACV
ANTHOLOGY OF CONTEMPORARY LATIN-AMERICAN

POETRY. AnCL
ANTHOLOGY OF CONTEMPORARY VERSE, AN. AnCV
ANTHOLOGY OF ENGLISH POETRY, AN: DRYDEN TO BLAKE. AEP-D
ANTHOLOGY OF ENGLISH POETRY: WYATT TO DRYDEN. AEP-W
ANTHOLOGY OF ENGLISH VERSE, AN. AEV
ANTHOLOGY OF FAMOUS ENGLISH AND AMERICAN POETRY, AN. AnFE
ANTHOLOGY OF FRENCH POETRY. AFP
ANTHOLOGY OF FRENCH POETRY FROM NERVAL TO VALERY IN ENGLISH TRANSLATION, AN. AnFP
ANTHOLOGY OF GERMAN POETRY FROM HOLDERLIN TO RILKE IN ENGLISH TRANSLATION, AN. AnGP
ANTHOLOGY OF GERMAN POETRY THROUGH THE 19th CENTURY. AGP
ANTHOLOGY OF IRISH LITERATURE, AN. AnIL
ANTHOLOGY OF IRISH VERSE, AN. AnIV
ANTHOLOGY OF ITALIAN AND ITALO-AMERICAN POETRY. AnIA
ANTHOLOGY OF LIGHT VERSE, AN. ALV
ANTHOLOGY OF MAGAZINE VERSE FOR 1913, 1914, 1915 & 1916. AMV 1-4
ANTHOLOGY OF MAGAZINE VERSE FOR 1924, 1925 & 1926. AMV 24-26
ANTHOLOGY OF MAGAZINE VERSE FOR 1935, 1936 & 1937. AMV 35-37
ANTHOLOGY OF MAGAZINE VERSE FOR 1938-1942. AnMaVe
ANTHOLOGY OF MEDIEVAL LYRICS, AN. AnML
ANTHOLOGY OF MEXICAN POETRY. AnMP
ANTHOLOGY OF MODERN POETRY. AnMoPo
ANTHOLOGY OF THE NEW ENGLAND POETS, AN. AnNE
ANTHOLOGY OF NEW YORK POETS, AN. ANYP
ANTHOLOGY OF NEW ZEALAND VERSE, AN. AnNZ
ANTHOLOGY OF NORWEGIAN LYRICS. AnNoLy
ANTHOLOGY OF OLD ENGLISH POETRY, AN. AnOE
ANTHOLOGY OF RECENT POETRY, AN. AnRP
ANTHOLOGY OF SPANISH POETRY FROM GARCILASO TO GARCIA LORCA, AN, IN ENGLISH TRANSLATION WITH SPANISH ORIGINALS. AnSP
ANTHOLOGY OF SPANISH LITERATURE IN ENGLISH

TRANSLATION, AN. AnSpL 1-2
ANTHOLOGY OF SWEDISH LYRICS, FROM 1750 TO 1925.
   AnSL
ANTHOLOGY OF VICTORIAN POETRY. AVP
ANTHOLOGY OF WORLD POETRY, AN. AWP
ANTHOLOGY OF WORLD'S BEST POEMS. BAP, BCEP, BMEP, PYM
APPROVED SELECTIONS FOR READING AND MEMORIZING.
   ASR 1-2
APPROACHES TO POETRY. ATP
ARBOR DAY. ADAH
ARBOR DAY IN POETRY. ADP
ARBOR DAY IN THE PRIMARY ROOM. ADPR
ARBOR DAY MANUAL. AD
ARBOR DAY PROGRAM, No. 1. FOR MIXED GRADES. ADP *
ARMENIAN LEGENDS AND POEMS. ArmL
ARMISTICE DAY. AOAH
ART OF READING POETRY, THE. ArRePo
AS I WALKED OUT ONE EVENING. AIW
AS YOU WERE. AsYW
ATLANTIC BOOK OF BRITISH AND AMERICAN POETRY,
   THE. AtBAP
ATLANTIC PROSE AND POETRY. APP
AUTHORS' BIRTHDAYS. AB 1-2
BALLAD BOOK, THE. W. Allingham. BB
BALLAD BOOK, A. K.L. Bates. BB *
BALLAD BOOK, THE. M. Leach. BaBo
BALLADS AND FOLK SONGS OF THE SOUTHWEST. BFSS
BALLADS AND SEA SONGS FROM NOVA SCOTIA. BSNS
BALLADS AND SONGS. BaS
BALLADS AND SONGS FROM OHIO. BSO
BALLADS AND SONGS OF INDIANA. BaSoIn
BALLADS AND SONGS FROM SOUTHERN MICHIGAN.
   BaSoSo
BALLADS FOR LITTLE FOLKS. BLF
BALLADS MIGRANT IN NEW ENGLAND. BaMNE
BALLADS OF AMERICAN BRAVERY. BAB
BALLADS OF BOOKS. A. Lang. LBB
BALLADS OF BOOKS. B. Matthews. MBB
BARTON'S COMIC RECITATIONS. BC
BATTLE POEMS AND PATRIOTIC VERSES. BP
BEACON LIGHTS OF PATRIOTISM. BLP
BEASTLY BOYS AND GHASTLY GIRLS. BBGG

BEAUTIFUL POEMS ON JESUS. **BePJ**
BECAUSE I LOVE YOU. **BIL**
BEECHER'S RECITATIONS AND READINGS. **BeR**
BEFORE THE ROMANTICS. **BeR ***
BEGINNING WITH POEMS. **BWP**
BEING BORN AND GROWING OLDER. **BBGO**
BEST ENGLISH AND SCOTTISH BALLADS. **BESB**
BEST LOVED POEMS OF THE AMERICAN PEOPLE, THE. **BLPA**
BEST LOVED RELIGIOUS POEMS, THE. **BLRP**
BEST LOVED SONGS AND HYMNS. **BLSH**
BEST LOVED SONGS OF THE AMERICAN PEOPLE. **BLSo**
BEST LOVED STORY POEMS. **BeLS**
BEST OF MODERN EUROPEAN LITERATURE, THE, 1920-1940. **BeME**
BEST POEMS OF 1922, 1923, 1924 & 1926, THE. T. Moult. **MBP 22-26**
BEST POEMS OF 1923, 1924 & 1926, THE. L.A. Strong. **BP 3-6**
BEST POEMS OF 1930, 1931, 1932, 1933, 1934, 1935, 1936 & 1937, THE. **BPM 30-37**
BEST SHORT POEMS OF THE 19th CENTURY. **BSP**
BEST THINGS FROM BEST AUTHORS. **BTB 1-9**
BIRD-LOVERS' ANTHOLOGY, THE. **BLA**
BIRD SONGS. **BiS**
BIRTHDAY CANDLES BURNING BRIGHT. **BiCB**
BLACK AMERICAN LITERATURE: POETRY. **BALP**
BLACK FIRE. **BF**
BLACK OUT LOUD. **BOLo**
BLACK POETRY. **BP ***
BLACK POETS. **BPo**
BLUE AND THE GRAY, THE. **BlG**
BLUE POETRY BOOK, THE. **BPB**
BLUE LINES, THE. **BluL**
BOOK OF AMERICAN NEGRO POETRY, THE. **BANP**
BOOK OF AMERICAN NEGRO SPIRITUALS. **BoAN 1-2**
BOOK OF AMERICAN POETRY, THE. **BAP**
BOOK OF AMERICAN VERSE, A. **BAV**
BOOK OF ANIMAL POEMS, A. **BoAnP**
BOOK OF AUSTRALIAN VERSE, A. **BoAV**
BOOK OF AUSTRALIAN AND NEW ZEALAND VERSE, A. **BoAu**
BOOK OF POETRY, THE. **MBOP 1-2**

BOOK OF BABY VERSE, THE. BBV
BOOK OF BALLADS, THE. BoB
BOOK OF BRITISH BALLADS, A. BBB
BOOK OF CANADIAN POETRY, THE. BoCaPo
BOOK OF CHILDREN'S LITERATURE, A. BoChLi
BOOK OF CHRISTMAS, THE. BOC
BOOK OF CLASSIC ENGLISH POETRY, THE, 600-1830. BCEP
BOOK OF COMFORT, A. BoC
BOOK OF DANISH BALLADS, A. BoDaBa
BOOK OF EARTH. BEN
BOOK OF ENGLISH LITERATURE, A. BEL
BOOK OF FAMOUS VERSE, A. BFVR
BOOK OF FIRESIDE POEMS, A. BFP
BOOK OF FRIENDSHIP, THE. S. M. Crothers. BOF
BOOK OF FRIENDSHIP, THE. E. Selden. BoFr
BOOK OF FRIENDSHIP VERSE, THE. BFV
BOOK OF GEORGIAN VERSE, THE. BGV
BOOK OF HEROIC VERSE, A. BHV
BOOK OF HISTORICAL POEMS, A. BoHiPo
BOOK OF HUMOROUS POEMS, A. BHP
BOOK OF HUMOROUS VERSE, THE. BOHV
BOOK OF IRISH POETRY, THE. BIP
BOOK OF IRISH VERSE, THE. BIrV
BOOK OF JOYOUS CHILDREN. BJC
BOOK OF LIGHT VERSE, A. BLV
BOOK OF LIVELY VERSE, A. BoLV 1-3
BOOK OF LIVING POEMS, A. BLP *
BOOK OF LIVING VERSE, THE. BLV, BoLiVe
BOOK OF LOVE, THE. BOL
BOOK OF LOVE POEMS, A. BoLP
BOOK OF LOVE POETRY, A. BoLoP
BOOK OF LULLABIES, A. BOL *
BOOK OF MODERN CATHOLIC VERSE, THE. BMC
BOOK OF MODERN ENGLISH POETRY, THE. BMEP
BOOK OF MOTHER VERSE, THE. BMV
BOOK OF NATURE POEMS, A. BoNaP
BOOK OF NONSENSE, THE. BoN
BOOK OF PEACE, A. BoPe
BOOK OF PERSONAL POEMS, A. BPP
BOOK OF POEMS, A. BoPo
BOOK OF RELIGIOUS VERSE, A. BoReV
BOOK OF RUSSIAN VERSE, A. BoR

BOOK OF SCOTTISH VERSE, A. **BSV**
BOOK OF SOUTH AFRICAN VERSE, A. **BoSA**
BOOK OF TABLEAUX. **TDT**
BOOK OF A THOUSAND POEMS, THE. **BoTP**
BOOK OF THE WINTER, A. **BoW**
BOOK OF TREASURED POEMS, A. **BTP**
BOOK OF VERSES FOR CHILDREN, A. **BVC**
BOOKS OF AMERICAN NEGRO SPIRITUALS, THE. **BoAN 1-2**
BOY'S BOOK OF VERSE, THE. **BBV** *
BREATHES THERE THE MAN. **BTTM**
BRIDLED WITH RAINBOWS. **BrR**
BRIEF ANTHOLOGY OF POETRY, A. **BrAP**
BRIGHT SIDE, THE. **BS**
BRITISH POETRY 1880-1920. **BrPo**
BRITISH POETS OF THE NINETEENTH CENTURY. **BPN**
BRITISH POPULAR BALLADS. **BrPB**
BROADWAY BOOK OF ENGLISH VERSE, THE. **BrBE**
BUCK IN THE SNOW. **BIS**
BUGLE ECHOES. **BE**
BUNDLE OF BALLADS, A. **BuBa**
BURBANK'S RECITATIONS AND READINGS. **BRR**
BURDETT'S DUTCH DIALECT RECITATIONS AND
    HUMOROUS READINGS. **BDD**
BURNING THORN, THE. **BuTh**
CAMBRIDGE BOOK OF POETRY AND SONG, THE. **CBP**
CAMBRIDGE BOOK OF POETRY FOR CHILDREN, THE. **CBPC**
CANADIAN POETRY IN ENGLISH. **CaP**
CANADIAN POETS. **CPG**
CAP AND GOWN: 1st-4th series. **CAG, CG 1-3**
CAPE COD BALLADS. **CCB**
CAROLING DUSK. **CDC**
CARRIERS OF THE DREAM WHEEL. **CDW**
CASE FOR POETRY, THE. **CaFP**
CASSELL BOOK OF ENGLISH POETRY, THE. **CBEP**
CASSELL'S ANTHOLOGY OF ENGLISH POETRY. **CaAE**
CAT IN VERSE, THE. **CIV** *
CATCH YOUR BREATH. **CaYB**
CATHOLIC ANTHOLOGY, THE. **CAW**
CAVALIER POETS, THE. **CavP**
CENTURY OF HUMOROUS VERSE, A, 1850-1950. **CenHV**
CENTURY OF LYRICS, A, 1550-1650. **CenL**
CENTURY READINGS FOR A COURSE IN AMERICAN
    LITERATURE. **CRAL**

CENTURY READINGS IN ENGLISH LITERATURE. **CRE**
CERTAIN POETS OF IMPORTANCE. **CPOI**
CHATTO BOOK OF MODERN POETRY, THE, 1915-1955.
    ChMP
CHAUTAUQUA INSTRUCTOR OF ELOCUTION & DRAMATIC
    ART. **PS**
CHERRY-TREE, THE. **ChTr**
CHICAGO POEMS. **CPCS**
CHIEF AMERICAN POETS. THE. **CAP**
CHIEF MODERN POETS OF ENGLAND AND AMERICA.
    ChMo, CMoP, CMP
CHILD LIFE. **WCL**
CHILD WORLD, A. **CW**
CHILDHOOD SONGS. **LCS**
CHILDREN'S BOOK, THE. **CB**
CHILDREN'S BOOK OF BALLADS, THE. **CBB**
CHILDREN'S BOOK OF POETRY. **CBOP**
CHILDREN'S FIRST BOOK OF POETRY, THE. **CFBP**
CHILDREN'S GARLAND, THE. **CG**
CHILDREN'S GARLAND OF VERSE, THE. **CGOV**
CHILDREN'S POEMS THAT NEVER GROW OLD. **CPN**
CHILDREN'S SECOND BOOK OF POETRY, THE. **CSBP**
CHILDREN'S THIRD BOOK OF POETRY, THE. **CTBP**
CHILD'S CALENDAR BEAUTIFUL, THE. **CCB** *
CHILD'S GARDEN OF VERSE, THE. **CGV**
CHILD'S HARVEST OF VERSE, THE. **CHV**
CHILD'S OWN SPEAKER. **COS**
CHIMNEY CORNER POEMS. **CCP**
CHINESE LOVE POEMS. **ChLP**
CHISWELL BOOK OF ENGLISH POETRY, THE. **CBE**
CHOICE DIALECT AND OTHER CHARACTERIZATIONS. **CD**
CHOICE DIALECT AND VAUDEVILLE JOKES. **CDV**
CHOICE DIALOGUES. **CDS**
CHOICE ENGLISH LYRICS. **CEL**
CHOICE HUMOR FOR READING AND RECITATION. **CHS**
CHOICE HUMOR OF ENGLISH ROMANTIC POETRY. **ChER**
CHOICE PIECES FOR LITTLE PEOPLE. **CPL**
CHOICE POEMS FOR ELEMENTARY GRADES. **ChPo**
CHOICE READINGS. **CCR**
CHOICE READINGS FROM STANDARD AND POPULAR
    AUTHORS. **FTR**
CHORAL SPEAKING ARRANGEMENTS FOR THE LOWER
    GRADES. **CSL**
CHORAL SPEAKING ARRANGEMENTS FOR THE UPPER

GRADES. CSU
CHORIC INTERLUDES. ChIn
CHRIST IN POETRY. ChIP
CHRISTMAS. A. Dalgliesh. CAD
CHRISTMAS. R.H. Schauffler. COAH
CHRISTMAS ANTHOLOGY OF POETRY AND PAINTING, A. ChAP
CHRISTMAS BELLS ARE RINGING. ChBR
CHRISTMAS BOOK OF LEGENDS AND STORIES, THE. ChrBoLe
CHRISTMAS ENTERTAINMENTS. CE
CHRISTMAS HOLIDAY BOOK, A. CHB
CHRISTMAS IN LEGEND AND STORY. CLS
CHRISTMAS IN POETRY: 1st & 2d series. CP 1-2
CHRISTMAS RECITATIONS FOR YOUNG AND OLD. CRYO
CHRISTMAS SELECTIONS FOR READING AND RECITATIONS. CS
CITY IN ALL DIRECTIONS. CAD *
CLASSIC DIALOGUES AND DRAMAS. CDD
COAL DUST ON THE FIDDLE. CoDuFi
COLLECTED ENGLISH VERSE. CoEV
COLLECTED POEMS. R.Brooke. CPB
COLLECTED POEMS. V.Lindsay. CPL *
COLLECTED POEMS. A.Noyes. CPAN 1-3
COLLECTED VERSE. E.Guest. CVG
COLLECTION OF ENGLISH POEMS, A, 1660-1800. CEP *
COLLEGE ANTHOLOGY OF BRITISH AND AMERICAN VERSE, THE. CABA
COLLEGE BOOK OF AMERICAN LITERATURE, A. CoBA
COLLEGE BOOK OF ENGLISH LITERATURE. CoBE
COLLEGE BOOK OF MODERN VERSE, A. CoBMV
COLLEGE BOOK OF VERSE, THE, 1250-1925. CBOV
COLLEGE BOOK OF VERSE, A. C.F.Main. CBV
COLLEGE READINGS IN POETRY. CRP
COLLINS ALBATROSS BOOK OF LONGER POEMS. CABL
COLONIAL PLAYS FOR THE SCHOOL-ROOM. CPs
COME HITHER. CH
COME LIVE WITH ME. CLWM
COMIC SPEECHES. MCS
COMMENCEMENT PARTS. CPD
COMIC RECITATIONS AND READINGS. CRR
COMMON MUSE, THE. CoMu

COMPLETE GEORGE WASHINGTON ANNIVERSARY PROGRAMS. **CWAP**
COMPLETE HOLIDAY PROGRAM FOR THE FIRST GRADE, A. **CHP**
COMPLETE POEMS. R. Service. **CPS**
COMPLETE POETICAL WORKS OF JAMES WHITCOMB RILEY. **CPWR**
COMPREHENSIVE ANTHOLOGY OF AMERICAN POETRY, A. **CoAnAm**
CONFUCIUS TO CUMMINGS. **CTC**
CONSCIOUS VOICE, THE. **CoV**
CONTEMPORARY AMERICAN AND AUSTRALIAN POETRY. **CAAP**
CONTEMPORARY AMERICAN POETRY. D. Hall. **ConAP**
CONTEMPORARY AMERICAN POETRY. A. Poulin, Jr. **CAPP**
CONTEMPORARY AMERICAN POETS, THE. **CoAP**
CONTEMPORARY FRENCH POETRY. **CoFP**
CONTEMPORARY GERMAN POETRY. **CGP**
CONTEMPORARY ITALIAN POETRY. **CoIP**
CONTEMPORARY POETRY. **CP**
CONTEMPORARY POETRY IN AMERICA. **CoPAm**
CONTEMPORARY SPANISH POETRY. **CoSP**
CONTEMPORARY VERSE. **CV**
CONTROVERSY OF POETS, A. **CoPo**
CONVERSATION AT MIDNIGHT. **CMM**
COPELAND READER, THE. **CR** *
CORNHUSKERS, THE. **CCS**
COWBOY SONGS AND OTHER FRONTIER BALLADS. **CoSo, CSF**
CRADLE BOOK OF VERSE, THE. **CBV** *
CRAZY TO BE ALIVE IN SUCH A STRANGE WORLD. **CTBA**
CRITERION BOOK OF MODERN AMERICAN VERSE, THE. **CrMA**
CUMNOCK'S SCHOOL SPEAKER. **CSS**
DAFFODIL POETRY BOOK, THE. **DaB**
DARK OF THE MOON. **DaM**
DARK TOWER, THE. **DTo**
DAWN AND DUSK. **DaDu**
DAYS AND DEEDS. **DD**
DAYS WE CELEBRATE, THE. **DWC**
DELSARTE RECITATION BOOK. **DRB**
DELSARTE SPEAKER, THE. **DS**

DESK DRAWER ANTHOLOGY. **DDA**
DIALECT READINGS. **SDR**
DIALOGUES AND DRAMAS. **MPD**
DIALOGUES FOR YOUNG FOLKS. **FDY**
DICK TURPIN'S RIDE AND OTHER POEMS. **DTRN**
DICK'S CHOICE PIECES FOR LITTLE CHILDREN. **DCP**
DICK'S COMIC AND DIALECT RECITATIONS. **DCR**
DICK'S COMIC DIALOGUES. **DCD**
DICK'S DIALOGUES AND MONOLOGUES. **DDM**
DICK'S DIVERTING DIALOGUES. **DDD**
DICK'S DRAMATIC RECITER. **DDR**
DICK'S DUTCH, FRENCH, AND YANKEE RECITATIONS. **DFY**
DICK'S ETHIOPIAN SCENES, VARIETY SKETCHES AND STUMP SPEECHES. **DE**
DICK'S FESTIVAL RECITER. **DFR**
DICK'S IRISH DIALECT AND RECITATIONS. **DI** *
DICK'S JUVENILE SPEAKER FOR BOYS AND GIRLS. **DJS**
DICK'S LITTLE DIALOGUES FOR LITTLE PEOPLE. **DLD**
DICK'S LITTLE FOLKS' RECITER. **DLF**
DICK'S LITTLE SPEECHES FOR LITTLE SPEAKERS. **DLS**
DICK'S SPEECHES FOR TINY TOTS. **DST**
DICK'S STUMP SPEECHES AND MINSTREL JOKES. **DSS**
DIMENSIONS OF POETRY,THE. **DiPo**
DISTAFF MUSE, THE. **DiM**
DRAWING ROOM THEATRICALS. **DT**
DREAMS AND IMAGES. **DI**
DRILLS AND MARCHES. **DM**
DRINK FROM THE ROCK. **DrRo**
DUBLIN BOOK OF IRISH VERSE, THE, 1728-1909. **DB**
DUTCH DIALECT. **DRR**
DYLAN THOMAS'S CHOICE. **DTC**
EARLY AMERICAN ORATIONS. **EAO**
EARLY AMERICAN POETS. **EaAmPo**
EARLY MOON. **EMS**
EARTH IS THE LORD'S, THE. **EaLo**
EASTER. **EOAH**
EASTER IN POETRY. **EP**
EASY ENTERTAINMENTS FOR YOUNG PEOPLE. **EE**
EBONY RHYTHM. **EbR**
ECHOING GREEN, THE. **EcGr 1-3**
EDINBURGH BOOK OF SCOTTISH VERSE, THE, 1300-1900. **EBSV**

EIGHT LINES AND UNDER. ELU
EIGHTEENTH CENTURY ENGLISH LITERATURE. EiCL
EIGHTEENTH-CENTURY POETRY. EiCP
EIGHTEENTH CENTURY POETRY AND PROSE. EiPP
ELIZABETHAN AND SEVENTEENTH-CENTURY LYRICS.
　　ElSeCe
ELIZABETHAN LYRICS. ElL
ELIZABETHAN LYRICS; a critical anthology. ElLy
ELIZABETHAN SONGS. ES
ELOCUTION AND ACTION. EA
ELOCUTIONARY STUDIES. DES
EMINENT BRITISH POETS OF THE NINETEENTH CENTURY.
　　EmBrPo
ENCHANTED YEARS, THE. EY
ENGLISH AND SCOTTISH BALLADS. EnSB
ENGLISH AND SCOTTISH POPULAR BALLADS. ESPB
ENGLISH ANTHOLOGY OF PROSE AND POETRY, AN. EA *
ENGLISH GALAXY OF SHORTER POEMS, THE. EG
ENGLISH HEART, THE. EnH
ENGLISH HISTORY AS TOLD BY ENGLISH POETS. EHT
ENGLISH LITERATURE; a college anthology. EnL
ENGLISH LITERATURE; a period anthology. EnLit
ENGLISH LITERATURE AND ITS BACKGROUNDS. EnLi 1-2
ENGLISH LOVE POEMS. EnLoPo
ENGLISH LYRIC POEMS, 1500-1900. ELP
ENGLISH LYRIC POETRY. EnLP
ENGLISH LYRIC POETRY, 1500-1700. ELP *
ENGLISH MASTERPIECES, 700-1900. EM 1-2
ENGLISH PASTORAL POETRY. EnPP
ENGLISH PASTORALS. EP *
ENGLISH POEMS. EhP
ENGLISH POEMS: The Elizabethan age & the Puritan period.
　　EPEP
ENGLISH POEMS: The Nineteenth century. EPNC
ENGLISH POEMS: Old English & middle English periods. EPOM
ENGLISH POEMS: The Restoration & the Eighteenth century. EPRE
ENGLISH POEMS FROM CHAUCER TO KIPLING. EPC
ENGLISH POETRY (1170-1892). EP ***
ENGLISH POETRY 1550-1660. EP **
ENGLISH POETRY 1400-1580. EnPo
ENGLISH POETRY OF THE MID AND LATE EIGHTEENTH
　　CENTURY. EnPE
ENGLISH POETRY OF THE NINETEENTH CENTURY. EPN

ENGLISH POETRY OF THE SEVENTEENTH CENTURY. **EPS**
ENGLISH POETS, THE. **EPW 1-5**
ENGLISH PROSE AND POETRY. **EPP**
ENGLISH RENAISSANCE POETRY. **EnRePo**
ENGLISH ROMANTIC POETRY. **ERoP 1-2**
ENGLISH ROMANTIC POETRY AND PROSE. **EnRP**
ENGLISH ROMANTIC POETS. **ERP**
ENGLISH SATIRES. **ESs**
ENGLISH SATIRIC POETRY. **ESaP**
ENGLISH, SCOTTISH, AND WELSH LANDSCAPE, 1700-c. 1860. **EnSW**
ENGLISH SONNETS. **ES ***
ENGLISH VERSE. **EV 1-5**
ENTERTAINMENT SPEAKER, THE. **OFPE**
ENTERTAINMENTS AND AMUSEMENTS. **PS**
ENTERTAINMENTS FOR ALL THE YEAR. **EFY**
EPISODES IN FIVE POETIC TRADITIONS. **Epi**
EROTIC POETRY. **ErPo**
ETERNAL PASSION IN ENGLISH POETRY. **EtPaEn**
ETERNAL SEA, THE. **EtS**
EUGENE FIELD BOOK, THE. **EF**
EUREKA ENTERTAINMENTS. **EuE**
EVERY CHILD'S BOOK OF VERSE. **ECBV**
EVERY DAY IN THE YEAR. **EDY**
EVERY SOUL IS A CIRCUS. **ESCL**
EVERYBODY OUGHT TO KNOW. **EvOK**
EXCELSIOR DIALOGUES. **ED**
EXPLORING POETRY. **ExPo**
F.T. PALGRAVE'S THE GOLDEN TREASURY OF THE BEST SONGS AND LYRICAL POEMS. O. Williams. **GTBS-W**
FABER BOOK OF CHILDREN'S VERSE, THE. **FaBoCh**
FABER BOOK OF COMIC VERSE, THE. **FaBoCo**
FABER BOOK OF ENGLISH VERSE, THE. **FaBoEn**
FABER BOOK OF IRISH VERSE, THE. **BIrV**
FABER BOOK OF LOVE POEMS, THE. **GBL**
FABER BOOK OF MODERN VERSE, THE. **FaBoMo**
FABER BOOK OF POPULAR VERSE, THE. **GBP**
FABER BOOK OF RELIGIOUS VERSE, THE. **BoReV**
FABER BOOK OF TWENTIETH CENTURY VERSE, THE. **FaBoTw**
FACING FORWARD. **FF**
FAMILY ALBUM OF FAVORITE POEMS, THE. **FaFP**
FAMILY BOOK OF BEST LOVED POEMS, THE. **FaBoBe**

FAMILY BOOK OF VERSE, THE. FaBV
FAMOUS POEMS AND THE LITTLE-KNOWN STORIES
    BEHIND THEM. FaPL
FAMOUS POEMS EXPLAINED. FPE
FATAL INTERVIEW. FIM
FATHER. FAOV
FAVORITE CHRISTIAN POEMS. FaChP
FAVORITE POEMS; selected from English & American authors.
    FP
FAVORITE POEMS OF FAITH AND COMFORT. FaPoFa
FAVORITE POEMS OLD AND NEW. FaPON
FAVORITE SONGS OF THE NINETIES. FSN
FAVORITE SPEAKER, THE. FS
FEW FIGS FROM THISTLES, A. FFTM
FIFTEEN MODERN AMERICAN POETS. FiMAP
FIFTEEN POETS. FiP
FIFTEEN YEARS FROM THE LANTERN. FiYeLa
FIFTY CHRISTMAS POEMS FOR CHILDREN. CPC
FIFTY CONTEMPORARY POETS. FiCP
FIFTY POETS. FP *
FIRE AND SLEET. FiSC
FIRESIDE BOOK OF HUMOROUS POETRY, THE. FiBHP
FIRESIDE ENCYCLOPEDIA OF POETRY. FEP
FIRESIDE POEMS. FPH
FIRST READER OF CONTEMPORARY AMERICAN POETRY,
    A. FRC
FIVE COURTIER POETS OF THE ENGLISH RENAISSANCE.
    FCP
FIVE MINUTE DECLAMATIONS. FD 1-2
FIVE MINUTE READINGS. FMR
FIVE MINUTE RECITATIONS. FR
FLAG DAY. FOAH
FLOCK OF WORDS, A. FlW
FLOWERING AFTER FROST. FAF
FLYING COLOURS. FlCo
FOR HIS SAKE. FHS
FOR LOVE'S SWEET SAKE. FLS
FOR THEE ALONE. FTA
FORM OF POETRY, THE. ForPo
FORMAL SPRING. FoS
FORMS OF POETRY. FosPo
FOUR & TWENTY BLACKBIRDS. FTB

FOUR SEASONS FIVE SENSES. FSFS
FOUR WINDS. FoW 1-3
FOURTEEN BRITISH AND AMERICAN POETS. FoBA
FROM OTHER LANDS. FOL
FRIDAY AFTERNOON SERIES OF DIALOGUES. FAD
FRIDAY AFTERNOON SPEAKER, THE. FAS
FRIENDLY TOWN, THE. FT
FROM BEOWULF TO THOMAS HARDY. BTH [1]-2
FROM ONE WORD. FrOW
FROM TOTS TO TEENS. FTT
FUN IN AMERICAN FOLK RHYMES. FuAF
GAILY WE PARADE. GaP
GAMBIT BOOK OF POPULAR VERSE, THE. GBP
GAMBIT BOOK OF LOVE POEMS, THE. GBL
GARDEN BOOK OF VERSE, THE. GBOV
GARLAND OF CHILDHOOD, THE. GC
GATEWAY TO POETRY, A. GatP
GEORGIAN POETRY, 1911-1912. GnP-1
GEORGIAN POETRY, 1913-1915. GnP-2
GIRL'S BOOK OF VERSE, THE. GBV
GOLDEN BOOK OF CATHOLIC POETRY, THE. GoBC
GOLDEN BOOK OF POETRY, THE. GoBP
GOLDEN FLUTE, THE. GFA
GOLDEN GLEAMS OF THOUGHT. GG
GOLDEN JOURNEY, THE. GoJo
GOLDEN NUMBERS. GN
GOLDEN POEMS BY BRITISH AND AMERICAN AUTHORS. GP
GOLDEN SLIPPERS. GoSl
GOLDEN SONGS OF THE GOLDEN STATE. GS
GOLDEN STAIRCASE, THE. GS *
GOLDEN TREASURY. F.T. Palgrave. GTSE
GOLDEN TREASURY OF AMERICAN SONGS AND LYRICS. ASL
GOLDEN TREASURY OF IRISH VERSE, A. GTIV
GOLDEN TREASURY OF LONGER POEMS, THE. GoTL
GOLDEN TREASURY OF MODERN LYRICS, THE. GTML
GOLDEN TREASURY OF POETRY, THE. GoTP
GOLDEN TREASURY OF SCOTTISH POETRY, THE. GoTS
GOLDEN TREASURY OF SONGS AND LYRICS, THE. F.T. Palgrave. GTSL
GOLDEN TREASURY OF THE BEST SONGS AND LYRICAL POEMS IN THE ENGLISH LANGUAGE. F.T. Palgrave. GTBS

GOLDEN TREASURY OF THE BEST SONGS AND LYRICAL POEMS IN THE ENGLISH LANGUAGE, THE. F.T. Palgrave & C. Day Lewis. **GTBS-D**
GOLDEN TREASURY OF THE BEST SONGS AND LYRICAL POEMS IN THE ENGLISH LANGUAGE, THE. F.T. Palgrave & J. Press. **GTBS-P**
GOLDEN YEAR, THE. **GoYe**
GOOD HUMOR FOR READING AND RECITATION. **GH**
GOOD MORNING, AMERICA. **GMAS**
GOOD READINGS FOR HIGH SCHOOLS. **GR 1-2, Gr-a, Gr-e**
GOOD THINGS FOR WASHINGTON AND LINCOLN BIRTHDAYS. **GTWL**
GRACE MARIE STANISTREET'S RECITATIONS FOR CHILDREN. **GSRC**
GRADED MEMORY SELECTIONS. **GMs**
GRADUATION DAY. **GDAH**
GRAHAM'S SCHOOL DIALOGUES FOR YOUNG PEOPLE. **GS ****
GRANDFATHER ROCK. **GrRo**
GREAT AMERICANS AS SEEN BY THE POETS. **GA**
GREAT COMPANIONS. **GrCo 1-2**
GREAT ENGLISH POETS. **GEPC**
GREAT POEMS OF THE ENGLISH LANGUAGE. **GPE**
GREAT POEMS OF THE WORLD WAR. **GPWW**
GREAT STORY-POEMS. **GSP**
GREEK LITERATURE IN TRANSLATION. **GrL**
GREEK POETRY FOR EVERYMAN. **GrPE**
GREEK POETS, THE. **GrPo**
GREEK READER, THE. **GrR**
GYPSY TRAIL, THE. **GT, GT-2**
HALLOWE'EN. **HOAH**
HANDBOOK OF BEST READINGS. **HBR**
HARP-WEAVERS, THE. **HWM**
HARPER'S ANTHOLOGY FOR COLLEGE COURSES IN COMPOSITION & LITERATURE: Vol. 2. Poetry. **HAP**
HARPER'S SCHOOL SPEAKER. **HSS 1-3**
HARRAP BOOK OF MODERN VERSE, THE. **HaMV**
HARRAP BOOK OF SEA VERSE, THE. **HaSV**
HARVEST OF GERMAN VERSE, A. **HGV**
HEART OF EUROPE. **BeMe**
HEART THROBS. **HT**

HEARTLAND II. **HeS**
HEATH INTRODUCTION TO POETRY, THE. **HeIP**
HEAVEN'S DISTANT LAMPS. **HDL**
HERE AND THERE. **HT ***
HERE WE COME A' PIPING. **HWC**
HEROIC BALLADS. **HB**
HEROIC TALES IN VERSE. **HeT**
HIGH LIGHTS IN AMERICAN LITERATURE. **HiLiAm**
HIGH LIGHTS IN ENGLISH LITERATURE. **HiLiEn**
HIGH SCHOOL PRIZE SPEAKER, THE. **HSPS**
HIGH TIDE. **HTR**
HIGH WEDLOCK THEN BE HONOURED. **HW**
HIGHDAYS AND HOLIDAYS. **HH**
HISTORIC POEMS AND BALLADS. **HPB**
HOLDING YOUR EIGHT HANDS. **HYE**
HOLIDAY ENTERTAINMENTS. **HE**
HOLIDAY SELECTIONS FOR READING AND RECITATION. **HS**
HOLMES'S VERY LITTLE DIALOGUES FOR VERY LITTLE FOLKS. **HYD**
HOLYROOD. **HMSP**
HOME BOOK OF MODERN VERSE, THE. **HBMV**
HOME BOOK OF VERSE, THE. **HBV**
HOME BOOK OF VERSE FOR YOUNG FOLKS, THE. **HBVY**
HOMESPUN. **HB ***
HOUSEHOLD BOOK OF POETRY, THE. **HBP**
HOW DOES A POEM MEAN? **HoPM**
HOW TO CELEBRATE THANKSGIVING AND CHRISTMAS. **HCTC**
HOWARD'S RECITATIONS. **HR**
HUMBLER POETS, THE, 1870-1885. **HP-1**
HUMBLER POETS, THE, 1885-1910: 2d series. **HP-2**
HUMOROUS AND EXHIBITION DIALOGUES. **FHE**
HUMOROUS DIALOGUES. **MHD**
HUMOROUS DIALOGUES AND DRAMAS. **HD**
HUMOROUS HITS AND HOW TO HOLD AN AUDIENCE. **HHHA**
HUMOROUS POETRY OF THE ENGLISH LANGUAGE, FROM CHAUCER TO SAXE. **HPE**
HUMOROUS SPEAKER, THE. **HSP**
HUNDRED GREAT POEMS, A. **HGP**
HUNDRED NAMES, THE. **PoHN**

I AM THE DARKER BROTHER. IDB
I HEAR AMERICA SINGING. IHA
I HEAR MY SISTERS SAYING. IHMS
I SING OF A MAIDEN. ISi
ICELANDIC POEMS AND STORIES. IcP
IDEAL DRILLS. ID
IMAGINATION'S OTHER PLACE. ImOP
IN PRAISE OF NUNS. PraNu
INDEPENDENCE DAY. IDAH
INNOCENT MERRIMENT. InMe
INTERPRETIVE READING. IR
INTRODUCING POEMS. IPWM
INTRODUCTION TO AMERICAN POETRY, AN. IAP
INTRODUCTION TO LITERATURE: POEMS. ILP
INTRODUCTION TO POETRY, AN. J. Hubbell & J. Beaty. InP
INTRODUCTION TO POETRY, AN. X. Kennedy. InPK
INTRODUCTION TO POETRY, AN. L. Simpson. InPS
INTRODUCTION TO POETRY. M. Van Doren. InPo
INTRODUCTION TO THE STUDY OF POETRY, AN. ISP
INVITATION TO POETRY. InvP
INVITATION TO VERSE. InV
IRISH POEMS OF TODAY. IrP
IRISH POETS OF THE NINETEENTH CENTURY. IrPN
IRON MEN AND WOODEN SHIPS. AmSS
IT CAN BE DONE. ICBD
JOYCE KILMER. JK 1-2
JOYCE KILMER'S ANTHOLOGY OF CATHOLIC POETS. JKCP
JUMP BAD. JB
JUNIOR ANTHOLOGY OF WORLD POETRY, A. JAWP
JUNIOR HIGH SCHOOL POETRY. JHP
JUNIOR POETRY CURE, THE. JPC
KALEIDOSCOPE. Kal
KAVANAUGH'S COMIC DIALOGUES & PIECES FOR LITTLE CHILDREN. KC
KAVANAUGH'S EXHIBITION RECITER FOR VERY LITTLE CHILDREN. KER
KAVANAUGH'S HUMOROUS DRAMAS. KH
KAVANAUGH'S JUVENILE SPEAKER. KJ
KAVANAUGH'S NEW SPEECHES & DIALOGUES. KNS
KIDD'S NEW ELOCUTION. KNE

KINGS, LORDS, & COMMONS. **KiLC**
KNAPSACK, THE. **KN**
LAMB'S POETRY FOR CHILDREN. **LPC**
LAND OF SONG, THE. **LOS 1-3**
LAST VOYAGE, THE. **LVN**
LATE AUGUSTAN POETRY. **LAuP**
LATE AUGUSTANS, THE. **LaA**
LATEST DIALOGUES. **MBD**
LATIN POETRY IN VERSE TRANSLATION. **LaP**
LAUGHING VERSE. **LauV**
LAYS OF THE NEW LAND. **LaNeLa**
LE GALLIENNE BOOK OF ENGLISH AND AMERICAN POETRY, THE. **LEAP**
LEAN OUT OF THE WINDOW. **LOW**
LIBRARY OF POETRY & SONG. **LPS 1-3**
LIGHT OF THE WORLD. **LOW** *
LIMITS OF ART. **LiA**
LINCOLN AND THE POETS. **LiPo**
LINCOLN LITERARY COLLECTION. **LLC**
LINCOLN'S BIRTHDAY. **LBAH**
LISTEN, CHILDREN, LISTEN. **LCL**
LISTENING CHILD, THE. **LC**
LITERATURE AND LIFE. **LL 1-4**
LITTLE ANTHOLOGY OF CANADIAN POETS, A. **LiAnCa**
LITTLE BOOK OF AMERICAN HUMOROUS VERSE, A. **LHV**
LITTLE BOOK OF AMERICAN POETS, THE, 1787-1900. **LBAP**
LITTLE BOOK OF LIMERICKS, THE. **LiBL**
LITTLE BOOK OF MODERN BRITISH VERSE, THE. **LBBV**
LITTLE BOOK OF MODERN VERSE, THE. **LBMV**
LITTLE BOOK OF NECESSARY NONSENSE, A. **LBN**
LITTLE-FOLK LYRICS. **LFL**
LITTLE FOLKS SPEAKER. **LFS**
LITTLE LAUGHTER, A. **LiL**
LITTLE LINES FOR LITTLE SPEAKERS. **LL**
LITTLE PEOPLE'S DIALOGUES. **LPD**
LITTLE PEOPLE'S SPEAKER. **LPS**
LITTLE PRIMARY PIECES FOR WEE FOLKS TO SPEAK. **LPP**
LITTLE TREASURY OF AMERICAN POETRY, A. **LiTA**
LITTLE TREASURY OF BRITISH POETRY, A. **LiTB**
LITTLE TREASURY OF GREAT POETRY, A. **LiTG**
LITTLE TREASURY OF LOVE POEMS, A. **LiTL**
LITTLE TREASURY OF MODERN POETRY, A, ENGLISH & AMERICAN. **LiTM**

LITTLE TREASURY OF WORLD POETRY, A. **LiTW**
LIVING POETRY. **PoMa**
LIVING POETS. **LP**
LONDON BOOK OF ENGLISH VERSE, THE. **LoBV**
LOOK TO THIS DAY. **LoDa**
LOOKING GLASS BOOK OF VERSE, THE. **LoGBV**
LOVE. **LO**
LOVE POEMS. **LoP**
LOVE POEMS OF SIX CENTURIES. **LoPS**
LOVE POEMS, OLD AND NEW. **LoPo**
LOVE SONGS OF CHILDHOOD. **LS**
LOVER'S TREASURY OF VERSE. **LTV**
LOVE'S ASPECTS. **LoAs**
LOVE'S ENCHANTMENT. **LoEn**
LOVE'S HIGH WAY. **LHW**
LYRA HEROICA. **LH**
LYRA HISTORICA. **LHT**
LYRIC AMERICA. **LA**
LYRIC MODERNS. **LyMo**
LYRIC POETRY OF THE ITALIAN RENAISSANCE. **LyPI**
LYRIC SOUTH, THE. **LS ***
LYRIC VERSE. **LV**
LYRIC YEAR. **LY**
LYRICS OF THE MIDDLE AGES. **LyMA**
McBRIDE'S CHOICE DIALECTS. **MC**
McBRIDE'S COMIC DIALOGUES. **MCD**
McBRIDE'S FUNNY DIALOGUES. **MFD**
McBRIDE'S NEW DIALOGUES. **MND**
MADE IN SCOTLAND. **MIS**
MAGIC CARPET, THE. **MCT**
MAGIC CASEMENTS. **MCCG**
MAGIC CIRCLE, THE. **MaC**
MAGIC OF BOOKS, THE. **MOB**
MAGIC WORLD, A. **MW**
MAJOR AMERICAN POETS TO 1914. **MAmP**
MAJOR BRITISH POETS OF THE ROMANTIC PERIOD. **MBPR**
MAJOR BRITISH WRITERS. **MBW 1-2**
MAJOR ENGLISH ROMANTIC POETS, THE. **MERP**
MAJOR METAPHYSICAL POETS OF THE SEVENTEENTH
    CENTURY, THE. **MaMe**
MAJOR POETS, THE. **MaPo**
MAJOR VICTORIAN POETS, THE. **MaVP**
MAJOR WRITERS OF AMERICA. **MWA 1-2**

MAN ANSWERS DEATH. MaAnDe
MANY VOICES. MV 1-2
MAP OF AUSTRALIAN VERSE, A. MAuV
MARK IN TIME. MIT
MARTINE'S DROLL DIALOGUES & LAUGHABLE RECITA-
    TIONS. MDD
MARVELOUS LIGHT, THE. ML
MASTER OF MEN, THE. MOM
MASTER POEMS OF THE ENGLISH LANGUAGE. MasP
MASTERPIECES OF AMERICAN LITERATURE. MAL
MASTERPIECES OF AMERICAN POETS. MOAP
MASTERPIECES OF BRITISH LITERATURE. MBL
MASTERPIECES OF MODERN VERSE. MMV
MASTERPIECES OF RELIGIOUS VERSE. MaRV
MEDITATIVE POEM, THE. MeP
MEDIEVAL ENGLISH LYRICS. MeEL
MEDIEVAL ENGLISH VERSE AND PROSE, IN MODERN-
    IZED VERSIONS. MeEV
MELODY OF EARTH, THE. ME
MEMORABLE POETRY. MemP
MEMORIAL DAY. MDAH
MEMORIAL DAY IN POETRY. MDIP
MEN AND WOMEN. MeWo
MEN WHO MARCHED AWAY. MMA
MENTOR BOOK OF RELIGIOUS VERSE, THE. MeRV
MERRY MEET AGAIN. MeMeAg
MESSAGES. MAT
METAPHYSICAL LYRICS & POEMS OF THE SEVENTEENTH
    CENTURY. MeLP
METAPHYSICAL POETS, THE. H. Gardner. MePo
METAPHYSICAL POETS, THE. M. Willy. MetP
MID-CENTURY AMERICAN POETS. MiAP
MID-CENTURY FRENCH POETS. MiCF
MINDSCAPES. MiP
MINNESOTA SKYLINE. MiSk
MINSTRELS OF THE MINE PATCH. MiMiPa
MIRROR FOR FRENCH POETRY, A, 1840-1940. MiFP
MISCELLANY OF AMERICAN POETRY, A, 1927. AMA
MISCELLANEOUS READINGS. MMR
MODEL DIALOGUES. MD
MODERN AMERICAN & MODERN BRITISH POETRY. MoAB
MODERN AMERICAN LYRICS. MAL *

MODERN AMERICAN POETRY. MAP, MoAmPo, UAP
MODERN AMERICAN POETS. MAPA
MODERN AUSTRALIAN POETRY. MoAuPo
MODERN BALLADS AND STORY POEMS. MoBS
MODERN BRITISH LYRICS. MBL *
MODERN BRITISH POETRY. MBP, MoBoPo, UBP
MODERN CANADIAN VERSE. MoCV
MODERN FRENCH POETRY. MFP
MODERN GERMAN POETRY, 1910-1960. MGP
MODERN GREEK POETRY. MoGP
MODERN LOVE POEMS. MoLP
MODERN LYRIC POETRY. MLP
MODERN MUSE, THE. MM
MODERN POET, THE. MoP
MODERN POETRY; American & British. MoPo
MODERN POETRY; a selection. MPo
MODERN POETRY FOR CHILDREN. MPC 1-14
MODERN POETS, THE. MP
MODERN POETS' WORLD, THE. MoPW
MODERN READER AND SPEAKER, A. MRS
MODERN RELIGIOUS POEMS. MoRP
MODERN RELIGIOUS VERSE AND PROSE. MRV
MODERN VERSE IN ENGLISH, 1900-1950. MoVE
MODERN WELSH POETRY. MoWP
MONOLOGUES AND NOVELTIES. MN
MOON IS SHINING BRIGHT AS DAY, THE. MoShBr
MOONSTRUCK. Moon
MOORISH POETRY. MooP
MORE HEART THROBS. MHT
MORE SILVER PENNIES. MoSiPe
MOTHER GOOSE. W.R. Benet. MoGo
MOTHER GOOSE NURSERY RHYMES. MG
MOTHER GOOSE ON THE RIO GRANDE. MoGoRi
MOTHER GOOSE RHYMES. MoGoRh
MOTHERS' ANTHOLOGY, THE. MotAn
MOTHERS' DAY. MOAH
MOTHER'S DAY IN POETRY. MDP
MOUNTAIN MOVING DAY. MMD
MUSK & SWEET POETRY. MuSP
MUSIC MAKERS, THE. MuM
MUSIC OF POETRY, THE. MuP
MY CARAVAN. MCG

MY COUNTRY. MC *
MY FAVOURITE ENGLISH POEMS. MyFE
MY POETRY BOOK. MPB
MY RECITATIONS. MR
NAKED POETRY. NaP
NARRATIVE AND LYRIC POETRY. NAL
NARRATIVE ENGLISH POEMS. PCN
NARRATIVE POEMS. NPH
NATIONAL EPICS. NE
NATURE IN VERSE. NV
NATURE LOVER'S KNAPSACK, THE. NLK
NEGRO CARAVAN, THE. NeCa
NEGRO MINSTRELS, A COMPLETE GUIDE TO NEGRO MINSTRELSY. NM
NEW AMERICAN AND CANADIAN POETRY. NeAC
NEW AMERICAN POETRY, THE, 1945-1960. NeAP
NEW ANTHOLOGY OF MODERN POETRY, A. NAMP
NEW ARBOR DAY EXERCISES. NAE
NEW BLACK POETRY, THE. NBP
NEW BOOK OF DIALOGUES. FND
NEW BOOK OF ENGLISH VERSE, THE. NBE
NEW BRITISH POETS, THE. NeBP
NEW CANON OF ENGLISH POETRY, A. NCEP
NEW CENTURY SPEAKER, THE. NC
NEW COASTS AND STRANGE HARBORS. NCSH
NEW DIALOGUES AND PLAYS. NDP
NEW GOLDEN TREASURY OF SONGS AND LYRICS, THE. NT
NEW HOME BOOK OF BEST LOVED POEMS, THE. NeHB
NEW IRISH POETS. NeIP
NEW LAND, NEW LANGUAGE. NeLNL
NEW LIBRARY OF POETRY AND SONG, A. BNL
NEW MICHIGAN VERSE. NeMiVE
NEW MODERN AMERICAN & BRITISH POETRY, THE. NeMA
NEW MODERN POETRY, THE. NMP
NEW NEGRO POETS: U.S.A. NNP
NEW OXFORD BOOK OF AMERICAN VERSE, THE. NOBA
NEW OXFORD BOOK OF ENGLISH VERSE, THE, 1250-1950. NOBE
NEW PATRIOTISM, THE. TNP
NEW PIECES THAT WILL TAKE PRIZES IN SPEAKING CONTESTS. NPTP

NEW PLAYS FOR CHRISTMAS. NPC
NEW POCKET ANTHOLOGY OF AMERICAN VERSE FROM
    COLONIAL DAYS TO THE PRESENT, THE. NePA
NEW POEMS, 1942. NePo
NEW POEMS BY AMERICAN POETS. NePoAm
NEW POEMS BY AMERICAN POETS #2. NePoAM-2
NEW POEMS THAT WILL TAKE PRIZES IN SPEAKING CON-
    TESTS. NPSC
NEW POETRY, THE. NP *
NEW POETS OF ENGLAND AND AMERICA. NePoEA
NEW POETS OF ENGLAND AND AMERICA: 2d selection.
    NePoEA-2
NEW POETS: WOMEN. NPW
NEW POPULAR SPEAKER. NPS
NEW SCIENCE OF ELOCUTION. HNS
NEW TREASURY OF WAR POETRY, THE. NeTW
NEW VOICES. NV *
NEW VOICES IN AMERICAN POETRY. NVAP
NEW YEAR AND MIDWINTER EXERCISES. NYM
NEW YORK TIMES BOOK OF VERSE, THE. NYTB
NEW YORKER BOOK OF POEMS, THE. NYBP
NEW YORKER BOOK OF VERSE, THE. NYBV
19th CENTURY MINOR BRITISH POETS. NBM
NO MORE MASKS! NMM
NONSENSE ANTHOLOGY, A. NA
NORTH CAROLINA POETRY. PoNC
NORTON ANTHOLOGY OF MODERN POETRY, THE. NoAM
NORTON ANTHOLOGY OF POETRY, THE. NoP
NEW VOICES, THE. NowV
O FRABJOUS DAY! OFD
O! SING ME YOUR SONG. SiMeYo
OF POETRY AND POWER. **OPP**
OFF THE GROUND. OFG 1-4
OFF TO ARCADY. OTA
OKLAHOMA ANTHOLOGY FOR 1929, THE. OA
OLD ENGLISH BALLADS. OEB
OLD ENGLISH LOVE SONGS. OEL
OLD ENGLISH SONGS. OES
OLD FAVORITE SONGS AND HYMNS. OlF
OLD POEMS AND NEW VERSE. OlPN
ON CITY STREETS. OCS

ON THIS DAY. OTD
100 AMERICAN POEMS. OnAP
ONE HUNDRED AND ONE FAMOUS POEMS. OHFP
ONE HUNDRED AND TEN FAVORITE CHILDREN'S POEMS. OnHT
100 BRITISH POETS. OBP
ONE HUNDRED CHOICE SELECTIONS. OHCS 1-40
100 GREAT RELIGIOUS POEMS. OnGR
100 MODERN POEMS. OnHM
100 MORE STORY POEMS. OnMSP
ONE HUNDRED NARRATIVE POEMS. OHNP
100 POEMS. OnP
100 POEMS ABOUT PEOPLE. OnPP
ONE HUNDRED POEMS FROM THE CHINESE. OnPC
ONE HUNDRED POEMS FROM THE JAPANESE. OnPJ
ONE HUNDRED POEMS OF IMMORTALITY. OHPI
ONE HUNDRED POEMS OF PEACE. OHPP
100 POSTWAR POEMS. OPoP
100 STORY POEMS. OnSP
ONE LITTLE ROOM, AN EVERYWHERE. OLR
ONE THOUSAND AND ONE POEMS OF MANKIND. OnPM
ONE THOUSAND POEMS FOR CHILDREN. OTPC
1000 QUOTABLE POEMS. OQP
1000 YEARS OF IRISH POETRY. OnYI
ONIONS AND CUCUMBERS AND PLUMS. OnCuPl
OPEN DOOR TO POETRY, THE. ODP
OPEN GATES. OG
OPEN ROAD, THE. OR
OPEN SESAME. OS 1-3
ORATOR'S MANUAL, THE. OM
ORIGINAL RECITATIONS WITH LESSON TALKS. BR
OTHER MEN'S FLOWERS. OtMeF
OUR CANADIAN LITERATURE. OCL
OUR COUNTRY IN POEM AND PROSE. OCP
OUR HERITAGE OF WORLD LITERATURE. OuHeWo
OUR HOLIDAYS IN POETRY. OHIP
OUR MOTHERS. OrM
OUR SINGING COUNTRY. OuSiCo
OUT OF THE ARK. OA *
OUT OF THE HEART. OH
OVER ONE HUNDRED FAMOUS POEMS & THE ENTERTAINMENT SPEAKER. OFPE

OXFORD ANTHOLOGY OF ENGLISH POETRY, AN. **OAEP**
OXFORD BOOK OF AMERICAN VERSE, THE. B. Carman. **OBAV**
OXFORD BOOK OF AMERICAN VERSE, THE. F. Matthiessen. **OxBA**
OXFORD BOOK OF AUSTRALASIAN VERSE, THE. **BoAu**
OXFORD BOOK OF BALLADS, THE. J. Kinsley. **OxBB**
OXFORD BOOK OF BALLADS, THE, A. Quiller-Couch. **OBB**
OXFORD BOOK OF CANADIAN VERSE, THE. **OCV**
OXFORD BOOK OF CANADIAN VERSE IN ENGLISH & FRENCH, THE. **OBCV**
OXFORD BOOK OF CHILDREN'S VERSE, THE. **OxBChV**
OXFORD BOOK OF CHRISTIAN VERSE, THE. **OxBoCh**
OXFORD BOOK OF EIGHTEENTH CENTURY VERSE, THE. **OBEC**
OXFORD BOOK OF ENGLISH VERSE, THE. A. Quiller-Couch. **OBEV**
OXFORD BOOK OF ENGLISH VERSE OF THE ROMANTIC PERIOD, THE. **OBRV**
OXFORD BOOK OF GREEK VERSE IN TRANSLATION, THE. **OxBG**
OXFORD BOOK OF IRISH VERSE, THE. **OxBI**
OXFORD BOOK OF LIGHT VERSE, THE. W.H. Auden. **OxBoLi**
OXFORD BOOK OF MEDIEVAL ENGLISH VERSE, THE. **OxBM**
OXFORD BOOK OF MODERN VERSE, THE, 1892-1935. **OBMV**
OXFORD BOOK OF NINETEENTH-CENTURY VERSE, THE. **OBNC**
OXFORD BOOK OF REGENCY VERSE, THE, 1798-1837. **OBRV**
OXFORD BOOK OF SCOTTISH VERSE, THE. **OxBS**
OXFORD BOOK OF SEVENTEENTH CENTURY VERSE, THE. **OBS**
OXFORD BOOK OF SIXTEENTH CENTURY VERSE, THE. **OBSC**
OXFORD BOOK OF TWENTIETH-CENTURY ENGLISH VERSE, THE. **OxBTC**
OXFORD BOOK OF VICTORIAN VERSE, THE. **OBVV**
OXFORD NURSERY RHYME BOOK, THE. **OxNR**
PAGEANT OF OLD SCANDINAVIA, THE. **PaOS**
PARLOUR POETRY. **PaPo**

PARNASSUS. EPs
PARNASSUS EN ROUTE. PER
PARODIES. Par
PARODY ANTHOLOGY, A. PA
PATRICIAN RHYMES. PR *
PATRIOTIC ANTHOLOGY, A. PaAn
PATRIOTIC ANTHOLOGY, THE. C. Van Doren. PaA
PATRIOTIC PIECES OF THE GREAT WAR. PPGW
PATRIOTIC POEMS AMERICA LOVES. PAL
PATRIOTIC READINGS AND RECITATIONS. PRR
PEERLESS RECITER. PR
PENGUIN BOOK OF BALLADS, THE. PeBB
PENGUIN BOOK OF CANADIAN VERSE, THE. PeCV
PENGUIN BOOK OF ENGLISH ROMANTIC VERSE, THE.
    PeER
PENGUIN BOOK OF RESTORATION VERSE, THE. PeRV
PENGUIN BOOK OF SONNETS, THE. PeBoSo
PENGUIN BOOK OF SOUTH AFRICAN VERSE, THE. PeSA
PENGUIN BOOK OF VICTORIAN VERSE, THE. PeVV
PEOPLE, YES, THE. PYS
PERSIAN POEMS. PeP
PIECES FOR EVERY DAY THE SCHOOLS CELEBRATE.
    PEDC
PIECES FOR EVERY MONTH OF THE YEAR. PEM
PIECES FOR EVERY OCCASION. PEOR
PIECES FOR PRIZE SPEAKING. PPSC
PIECES FOR PRIZE SPEAKING CONTESTS. PPSC
PIECES THAT HAVE WON PRIZES. PTWP
PIECES TO SPEAK. PTS
PINAFORE PALACE. PPL
PINK BOOK OF VERSE FOR VERY LITTLE CHILDREN, THE.
    PBV
PIPE AND DRUM. PiDr
PIPE AND POUCH. PPh
PIPING DOWN THE VALLEYS WILD. PDV
PITH AND VINEGAR. PV
PLEASURES OF POETRY, THE. PPoe
POCKET BOOK OF AMERICA, THE. PoBoAm
POCKET BOOK OF VERSE, THE. PoBoVe
POCKET COMPANION, THE. PoCo
POCKET MYSTERY READER, THE. PoMyRe
POCKET READER, THE. PoRe

Pocketful of Rhymes

POCKETFUL OF RHYMES, A. PoRh
POEM, THE; an anthology. PoAn
POEM, THE; a critical anthology. Po
POEMS. J. Masefield. PM
POEMS AND POETS. PoPo
POEMS BY CONTEMPORARY WOMEN. PCW
POEMS BY GRADES: Vol. 1. PBGP
POEMS BY GRADES: Vol. 2. PBGG
POEMS, CHIEFLY NARRATIVE. PCN
POEMS CHILDREN LOVE. PCL
POEMS EVERY CHILD SHOULD KNOW. PECK
POEMS FOR A MACHINE AGE. PoMa
POEMS FOR DAILY NEEDS. PDN
POEMS FOR ENJOYMENT. PFE
POEMS FOR MODERN YOUTH. PoeMoYo
POEMS FOR RED LETTER DAYS. PoRL
POEMS FOR SEASONS AND CELEBRATIONS. PoSC
POEMS FOR SPECIAL DAYS AND OCCASIONS. PSO
POEMS FOR STUDY. PoFS
POEMS FOR THE CHILDREN'S HOUR. PCH
POEMS FOR THE GREAT DAYS. PGD
POEMS FOR YOUTH. PFY
POEMS FROM BLACK AFRICA. PBA
POEMS FROM ICELAND. PFIc
POEMS I REMEMBER. PIR
POEMS IN ENGLISH, 1530-1940. PoE
POEMS-1940 FROM "THE LANTERN." PoNiLa
POEMS OF ACTION. POA
POEMS OF AMERICAN HISTORY. PAH
POEMS OF AMERICAN PATRIOTISM. B. Matthews. PAP
POEMS OF AMERICAN PATRIOTISM, 1776-1898. PAPm
POEMS OF DEATH. PoD
POEMS OF DOUBT AND BELIEF. PoDB
POEMS OF EUGENE FIELD, THE. PEF
POEMS OF FAITH AND DOUBT. PFD
POEMS OF HENRY VAN DYKE. PVD
POEMS OF INSPIRATION. POI
POEMS OF MAGIC AND SPELLS. PoMS
POEMS OF OUR TIME. POTE
POEMS OF PROTEST OLD AND NEW. PPON
POEMS OF THE ENGLISH RACE. PTER
POEMS OF THE GREAT WAR. PGW

POEMS OF THE HUNDRED NAMES. PoHN
POEMS OF THE OLD WEST. PoOW
POEMS OF TO-DAY. English Association. PoeT
POEMS OF TODAY. A. Cooper. POT, PoTo
POEMS OF YOUTH. POY
POEMS ON POETRY. PP
POEMS ONE LINE AND LONGER. POL
POEMS SINCE 1900. PSN
POEMS TEACHERS ASK FOR. PTA 1-2
POEMS THAT LIVE FOREVER. PoLF
POEMS THAT TOUCH THE HEART. PoToHe
POEMS TO READ ALOUD. PoRA
POEMS TO REMEMBER. PoTR
POEMS WORTH KNOWING. PoWorKn
POEMS YOU OUGHT TO KNOW. PYO
POETS IN AMERICA, THE. PiAm
POET PHYSICIANS. PoP
POET TO POET. PtP
POETIC NEW-WORLD, THE. PNW
POETIC OLD-WORLD, THE. POW
POETICAL FAVORITES—YOURS AND MINE. PF
POETICAL WORKS OF ROBERT BRIDGES. PWB
POETRY; an introductory anthology. PIA
POETRY: ITS APPRECIATION AND ENJOYMENT. PIAE
POETRY: PAST AND PRESENT. PPP
POETRY: POINTS OF DEPARTURE. PPoD
POETRY AND ITS CONVENTIONS. PAIC
POETRY AND LIFE; an introduction to poetry. PoeLi
POETRY AND LIFE; an anthology of English Catholic poetry. PoLi
POETRY ANTHOLOGY, A. PAn
POETRY ARRANGED FOR THE SPEAKING CHOIR. PASC
POETRY AS EXPERIENCE. PoEx
POETRY BOOK, THE. PB 1-9
POETRY CURE, THE. PC *
POETRY FOR CHILDREN. PC
POETRY FOR HOME AND SCHOOL. PHS
POETRY FOR JUNIOR HIGH SCHOOLS. PJH 1-2
POETRY FOR MEN TO SPEAK CHORALLY. PoMeSp
POETRY FOR PLEASURE. PoPl
POETRY FOR SCHOOL READINGS. PSR
POETRY FOR SENIOR STUDENTS. PoSS

POETRY FOR WOMEN TO SPEAK CHORALLY. PoWoSp
POETRY FROM LITERATURE FOR OUR TIME. PoLFOT
POETRY IN AUSTRALIA. PoAu 1-2
POETRY IN ENGLISH. PoIE
POETRY NOW. PoN
POETRY OF AMERICAN WIT AND HUMOR, THE. AWH
POETRY OF BLACK AMERICA, THE. PoBA
POETRY OF CATS, THE. PCat
POETRY OF FLIGHT, THE. PoF
POETRY OF FREEDOM, THE. PoFr
POETRY OF LIVING JAPAN, THE. PoLJ
POETRY OF OUR TIMES. POOT
POETRY OF THE ENGLISH RENAISSANCE. TuPP
POETRY OF THE NEGRO, THE, 1746-1970. PoNe
POETRY OF THE NINETIES. PON
POETRY OF THE SEASONS. POS
POETRY OF THE TRANSITION, 1850-1914. POTT
POETRY OF THE VICTORIAN PERIOD. PoVP
POETRY OF TO-DAY. PT
POETRY OF YOUTH. PYM
POETRY SAMPLER, A. PoSa
POETRY SOCIETY OF AMERICA ANTHOLOGY, THE. PSA
POETRY TO KNOW. PTK
POETRY'S PLEA FOR ANIMALS. PPA
POETS & POEMS. PoeP
POET'S CAT, THE. PoC
POET'S CHOICE. PoCH
POET'S CRAFT, THE. PCD
POET'S GARDEN, THE. PoG
POET'S GOLD. PG
POETS LAUREATE, THE. PoLa
POETS OF NORTH CAROLINA. PoNC
POETS OF OUR TIME. F. Finn. POTi
POETS OF OUR TIME. E. Gillett. PtOT
POETS OF THE ENGLISH LANGUAGE. PoEL 1-5
POETS OF THE PACIFIC: 2d series. PtPa
POETS OF THE SOUTH. PSh
POETS OF TODAY. PtTo
POETS SPEAK, THE, 1943. PoSp
POET'S TALES, THE. PoTa
POINT LACE AND DIAMONDS. PLD
POP/ROCK SONGS OF THE EARTH. PoRo

POPULAR DIALOGUES. PD
POPULAR ENGLISH BALLADS. PEB 1-4
POPULAR PLATFORM PIECES. PPP *
POPULAR SONGS OF NINETEENTH-CENTURY AMERICA.
    PSoN
POSY RING, THE. PRWS
PRACTICAL DIALOGUES. PDK
PRACTICAL ELOCUTION. PE
PRACTICAL PUBLIC SPEAKING. PPS
PRACTICAL RECITATIONS. PRK
PRAISE OF LINCOLN, THE. POL
PRAYER POEMS. PraP
PREFACE TO POETRY. PreP
PREFERENCES. Prf
PREMIER BOOK OF MAJOR POETS, THE. PBMP
PRE-RAPHAELITES IN LITERATURE AND ART, THE. PrRL
PRESENTING WELSH POETRY. PrWP
PRIMARY RECITATIONS. PyR
PRIMARY SPEAKER. PyS
PRINCETON VERSE BETWEEN TWO WARS. PriVe
PRINCIPLES OF ORAL INTERPRETATION, THE. POOI
PRIZE POEMS, 1913-1919. PP *
PRIZE POETICAL SPEAKER, THE. PPSr
PRO PATRIA, A BOOK OF PATRIOTIC VERSE. PPV
PROGRESSIVE SPEAKER, THE. PS
PROSE AND POETRY FOR YOUNG PEOPLE. PPYP
PROSE AND POETRY OF THE CONTINENTAL RENAIS-
    SANCE IN TRANSLATION. PrPoTo
PROSE AND POETRY OF TODAY. PrPoTo
PROSE AND VERSE FOR SPEAKING AND READING. PVS
PROSE, POETRY, AND DRAMA FOR ORAL INTERPRETA-
    TION. PPD 1-2
PSYCHE. Psy
PULITZER PRIZE POEMS. PuPrPo
QUEST FOR REALITY. QFR
QUESTING SPIRIT, THE. QS
QUICKLY AGING HERE. QAH
QUIET HOUR, THE. QH
QUIZ KIDS' BOOK, THE. QKB
QUOTABLE POEMS. QP 1-2
RADIANT TREE, THE. RT
RAINBOW GOLD. RG

Rainbow in the Sky 152

RAINBOW IN THE SKY. RIS
READING MODERN POETRY. ReMP
READING OF POETRY, THE. RePo
READING POEMS. ReaPo
READINGS AND MONOLOGUES OF DISTINCTION. RM
READINGS FROM THE NEW POETS. RNP
READINGS IN ENGLISH AND AMERICAN LITERATURE. REAL
READINGS IN EUROPEAN LITERATURE. REL
REAL MOTHER GOOSE, THE. ReMoGo
RECITATIONS FOR ASSEMBLY AND CLASSROOM. RAC
RECITATIONS FOR YOUNGER CHILDREN. RYC
RECITATIONS, OLD AND NEW, FOR BOYS AND GIRLS. RON
RECITER'S TREASURY OF IRISH VERSE AND PROSE, THE. RTI
RECITER'S TREASURY OF SCENES AND POEMS, THE. ReTS
RECITER'S TREASURY OF VERSE, SERIOUS & HUMOROUS. RTV
RED HARVEST, THE. RH
RED LETTER POEMS. RLP
RENAISSANCE AND BAROQUE LYRICS. RBL
RENAISSANCE IN ENGLAND, THE. ReIE
RENAISSANCE ENGLAND. ReEn
RENASCENCE AND OTHER POEMS. RM *
RESTORATION CARNIVAL. ReC
RICHARD DYER-BENNET FOLK SONG BOOK, THE. RDB
RILEY CHILD RHYMES. RCR
RINEHART BOOK OF VERSE, THE. RiBV
RING-A-ROUND. RAR
RISING EARLY. MoBS
RISING TIDES. RiTi
RIVERSIDE BOOK OF VERSE, THE. RBV
ROAD TO TEXAS, THE. RoTe
ROMAN LITERATURE IN TRANSLATION. RoL
ROMANTICS, THE. RO
ROOFS OF GOLD, RoGo
ROOM FOR ME AND A MOUNTAIN LION. RFM
ROOSEVELT DAY. RHAD
ROSES RACE AROUND HER NAME. RRA
ROUND ABOUT EIGHT. RAE

RUDYARD KIPLING'S VERSE (1885-1932). RKV
RUSSIAN POETRY, 1917-1955. RuPo
SACRED FIRE, THE. BrBE
SAILOR'S GARLAND, THE. SG
SAINT FRANCIS AND THE POET. SaFP
SALAMANDER. SaL
SALT AND BITTER AND GOOD. SBG
SARA SHRINER'S SELECTIONS. SSS
SATIRE ANTHOLOGY, A. SAy
SAUCY SAILOR AND OTHER DRAMATIZED BALLADS, THE. SaSa
SCHOOL AND COLLEGE SPEAKER. SC
SCHOOL AND PARLOR COMEDIES. SPC *
SCHOOL SPEAKER AND READER. SSR
SCHOOLDAY DIALOGUES. SDD
SCHOOL ELOCUTION. SE
SCIENCE AND THE ART OF ELOCUTION. SA
SCOTTISH LOVE POEMS. SLP
SCRAP-BOOK RECITATIONS. SR 1-15
SEALED UNTO THE DAY. SeUD
SECOND APRIL. SAM
SECOND BOOK OF DANISH VERSE, A. BoDS
SECOND BOOK OF MODERN VERSE, THE. SBMV
SECOND BOOK OF NEGRO SPIRITUALS, THE. BoAN 1-2
SECOND BOOK OF RUSSIAN VERSE, A. BoRS
SECOND DAFFODIL POETRY BOOK, THE. DaBS
SECOND TREASURY OF THE FAMILIAR, A. TreFS
SELECT SPEECHES FOR DECLAMATION. SSD
SELECTED MEMORY GEMS. SMG
SELECTED READINGS. SR
SELECTION FROM THE GREAT ENGLISH POETS, A. GEPM
SELECTIONS FOR CHORAL SPEAKING. SFC
SELECTIONS FOR MEMORIZING. L. Foster. SM
SELECTIONS FOR MEMORIZING. A. Skinner. SFM
SELECTIONS FOR PUBLIC SPEAKING. SPS
SETTLING AMERICA. SA *
SEVEN CENTURIES OF POETRY. SeCePo
SEVEN CENTURIES OF VERSE, ENGLISH & AMERICAN. SeCeV
SEVEN POETS IN SEARCH OF AN ANSWER. SePoSe
SEVENTEENTH-CENTURY AMERICAN POETRY. SCAP
SEVENTEENTH-CENTURY ENGLISH POETRY. SeEP

17th CENTURY ENGLISH POETRY. SCEP 1-2
SEVENTEENTH CENTURY LYRICS. SeCL
SEVENTEENTH CENTURY POETRY. SeCP
SEVENTEENTH CENTURY SONGS AND LYRICS. SeCSL
SEVENTEENTH-CENTURY VERSE AND PROSE. SeCV 1-2
SHANTYMEN AND SHANTYBOYS. ShS
SHELDON BOOK OF VERSE, THE. ShBV 1-4
SHOEMAKER'S BEST SELECTIONS. BS 1-27
SHORTER GOLDEN BOOK OF NARRATIVE VERSE, THE.
   ShGoBo
SHORTER MODERN POEMS, 1900-1931. SMP
SHRIEKS AT MIDNIGHT. ShM
SIGNET CLASSIC POETS OF THE 17th CENTURY. SCP 1-2
SILVER BRANCH, THE. SiB
SILVER LININGS. SL
SILVER PENNIES. SP
SILVER POETS OF THE SIXTEENTH CENTURY. SiPS
SILVER SWAN, THE. SiSw
SILVER TREASURY, THE. ST
SILVER TREASURY OF LIGHT VERSE, THE. SiTL
SINCE FEELING IS FIRST. SFF
SING A SONG OF SEASONS. SiSoSe
SINGING AND THE GOLD, THE. SiGo
SINGING WORDS. SiWo
SIXTEENTH-CENTURY ENGLISH POETRY. SiCE
SMILES. SL *
SMILES YOKED WITH SIGHS. SYS
SMOKE AND STEEL AND SLABS OF THE SUNBURNT WEST.
   SASS
SOLDIERS' VERSE. SoV
SONGS AND BALLADS FROM OVER THE SEA. SBOS
SONGS AND BALLADS OF GREATER BRITAIN. SGB
SONGS FROM THE LAND OF DAWN. SoLD
SONGS OF AMERICAN FOLKS. SoAF
SONGS OF AMERICAN SAILORMEN. SoAmSa
SONGS OF CHILDHOOD. SOC
SONGS OF NATURE. SN
SONGS OF THE CATTLE TRAIL AND COW CAMP. SCC
SONGS OF THE GOLD RUSH, THE. SGR
SONGS OF THE SEA AND SAILORS' CHANTEYS. SSSC
SONGS OF THREE CENTURIES. STC
SONNET, THE. Sonn

SOUND AND SENSE. SoSe
SOUND OF POETRY, THE. SoPo
SOUNDS AND SILENCES. SS
SOURCEBOOK OF POETRY. SoP
SOUTHERN POETS. SPP
SPEAK ROUGHLY TO YOUR LITTLE BOY. SpRo
SPEAKER, THE. SPE 1-8
SPEAKER'S GARLAND, THE. OHCS 1-40
SPEAKER'S TREASURY OF 400 QUOTABLE POEMS, THE. STF
SPECIAL DAY EXERCISES. SDE
SPEECH CHOIR, THE. SC *
SPENCER'S COMIC SPEECHES. SCS
SPORTS POEMS. SPo
SPRING AND SUMMER SCHOOL CELEBRATIONS. SSSC *
SPRINTS AND DISTANCES. SD
STANDARD BOOK OF BRITISH AND AMERICAN VERSE, THE. SBA
STANDARD DIALOGUES. SD *
STANDARD ENGLISH POEMS. SEP
STANDARD SELECTIONS. StS
STANDARD SPEAKER, THE. SS *
STAR-POINTS. SPT
STARDUST AND HOLLY. SDH
STARS TO STEER BY. StaSt
STEAMBOATIN' DAYS. StDa
STEELE'S EXHIBITION DIALOGUES. SED
STEPS TO ORATORY. SO
STERLING DIALOGUES. SDC
STORIES AND POEMS FOR CHILDREN. SAP
STORIES IN VERSE. SIV
STORY AND VERSE FOR CHILDREN. StVeCh
STORY OF JESUS IN THE WORLD'S LITERATURE, THE. StJW
STORY POEMS, NEW AND OLD. StPo
STORY-TELLING BALLADS. STB
STORY-TELLING POEMS. STP *
STUDYING POETRY. StP
SUBTREASURY OF AMERICAN HUMOR, A. SuAmHu
SUGAR AND SPICE. SAS
SUNDAY SCHOOL ENTERTAINMENTS. SSE
SUNDAY SCHOOL SELECTIONS. SSS *

SUNFLOWERS. S
SUNG UNDER THE SILVER UMBRELLA. SUS
SYMBOLIST POEM, THE. SyP
TABLEAUX, CHARADES AND PANTOMIMES. TCP
TAKE HOLD! TH
TAKEN FROM LIFE. TL
TALKS. TK
TALL BOOK OF MOTHER GOOSE, THE. TaBoMg
TEMPERANCE DIALOGUES. MTD
TEMPERANCE SELECTIONS. TS
TEN CENTURIES OF SPANISH POETRY. TeCS
THANKSGIVING. TOAH
THANKSGIVING IN POETRY. TP
THESE I HAVE LOVED. TIHL
THIRD BOOK OF MODERN VERSE, THE. TBM
THIRD TREASURY OF THE FAMILIAR, THE. TreFT
31 NEW AMERICAN POETS. ThO
THIS HAPPY HOME. ThHaHo
THIS IS FOR YOU. TFY
THIS LAND IS MINE. ThLM
THIS SINGING WORLD. TSW
THIS SINGING WORLD FOR YOUNGER CHILDREN. TSWC
THIS WAY, DELIGHT. ThWaDe
THREAD OF GOLD, A. ThGo
THREE CENTURIES OF AMERICAN POETRY AND PROSE.
    TCAP
THREE DIMENSIONS OF POETRY. TDP
THREE MINUTE DECLAMATIONS FOR COLLEGE MEN.
    TMD
THREE MINUTE READINGS FOR COLLEGE GIRLS. TMR
THREE RUSSIAN POETS. ThRuPo
3000 YEARS OF BLACK POETRY. TTY
THREE YEARS WITH THE POETS. TYP
THROUGH ITALY WITH THE POETS. TIWP
THROUGH MAGIC CASEMENTS. TMC
THUDDING DRUMS. ThDr
TIME FOR POETRY. TiPo
TINY TOTS SPEAKER. TT
TO MOTHER. TM
TO PLAY MAN NUMBER ONE. TPM
TO SEE THE WORLD AFRESH. TSWA
TODAY'S LITERATURE. TL *

TODAY'S NEGRO VOICES. TNV
TODAY'S POETS. ToPo
TOMMY'S FIRST SPEAKER. TFS
TOMMY'S SECOND SPEAKER. TSS
TORCH-BEARERS, THE. BEN, LVN, WSN
TRANSLATIONS FROM THE CHINESE. TrCh
TRAVELER'S BOOK OF VERSE, THE. TBV
TREASURY OF AMERICAN BALLADS, A. TrAB
TREASURY OF AMERICAN SACRED SONG. TAS
TREASURY OF AMERICAN SONG, A. TrAS
TREASURY OF AMERICAN VERSE. TAV *
TREASURY OF BRITISH HUMOR, A. TrBrHu
TREASURY OF CANADIAN VERSE. TCV
TREASURY OF ENGLISH VERSE, NEW AND OLD. TrEV
TREASURY OF FRENCH POETRY, A. TrFP
TREASURY OF GREAT POEMS, ENGLISH AND AMERICAN, A. TrGrPo
TREASURY OF HELPFUL VERSE, A. THV
TREASURY OF HUMOROUS POETRY, A. THP
TREASURY OF IRISH POETRY, A. TIP
TREASURY OF JEWISH POETRY, A. TrJP
TREASURY OF MIDDLE ENGLISH VERSE. TMEV
TREASURY OF NEW ENGLAND FOLKLORE, A. TrNE
TREASURY OF POEMS FOR WORSHIP AND DEVOTION, A. TrPWD
TREASURY OF RELIGIOUS VERSE, THE. TRV
TREASURY OF RUSSIAN LITERATURE, A. TrRuLi
TREASURY OF RUSSIAN VERSE, A. TrRV
TREASURY OF SATIRE, A. TrS
TREASURY OF THE FAMILIAR, A. TreF
TREASURY OF VERSE FOR LITTLE CHILDREN, A. TVC
TREASURY OF VERSE FOR SCHOOL AND HOME, A. TVSH
TREASURY OF WAR POETRY, A. TWP 1-2
TRIAL BALANCES. TB
TRIUMPH OF LIFE, THE. TriL
TUDOR POETRY AND PROSE. TuPP
TUDOR VERSE SATIRE. TVS
TWELVE CENTURIES OF ENGLISH POETRY AND PROSE. TCEP
12 POETS. TwP
12 SPANISH AMERICAN POETS. TwSpPo
TWENTIETH-CENTURY AMERICAN POETRY. TwAmPo

TWENTIETH CENTURY CANADIAN POETRY. TwCaPo
TWENTIETH-CENTURY GERMAN VERSE. TwGV
TWENTIETH-CENTURY POETRY. TCPD
TWENTIETH CENTURY POETRY. TCP *
TWENTIETH CENTURY POETRY; American and British. TwCP
TWENTIETH CENTURY VERSE. TwCV
TWENTY GERMAN POETS. TwGP
TWENTY-THREE MODERN BRITISH POETS. TwMBP
TWO CREATIVE TRADITIONS IN ENGLISH POETRY. TwCrTr
TWO HUNDRED POEMS. TwHP
TYPES OF ENGLISH POETRY. TyEnPo
TYPES OF POETRY. H. Hall. TPH
TYPES OF POETRY. J. Zeitlin. TOP
UNDER THE TENT OF THE SKY. UTS
UNDERSTANDING POETRY. UnPo
UNINHIBITED TREASURY OF EROTIC POETRY, AN. UnTE
UNSEEN WINGS. UnW
UNTUNE THE SKY. UnS
UP FROM THE EARTH. UFE
VALIANT MUSE, THE. VM
VARIETY OF POETRY, THE. VaPo
VERMONT CHAP BOOK. VeChBo
VERS DE SOCIETE ANTHOLOGY, A. VSA
VERSE FOR PATRIOTS. VP
VERSE OF OUR DAY. VOD
VERSE OF VALOUR. VeV
VERSES I LIKE. VIL
VICTORIAN AND LATER ENGLISH POETS. VLEP
VICTORIAN ANTHOLOGY, A, 1837-1895. VA
VICTORIAN POETRY. E. Brown. ViPo
VICTORIAN POETRY; Clough to Kipling. ViP
VICTORIAN POETRY; ten major poets. VP *
VICTORIAN POETRY: "THE CITY OF DREADFUL NIGHT
    AND OTHER POEMS. VPC
VICTORIAN POETRY AND POETICS. ViPP
VICTORIAN SONGS. VS
VIKING BOOK OF FOLK BALLADS OF THE ENGLISH-
    SPEAKING WORLD, THE. ViBoFo
VIKING BOOK OF POETRY OF THE ENGLISH-SPEAKING
    WORLD, THE. ViBoPo
VINTAGE VERSE. ViV
VISTA OF ENGLISH VERSE. VE

VOICE, SPEECH, AND GESTURE. VSG
VOICE THAT IS GREAT WITHIN US, THE. VGW
VOICES FROM THE FIELDS. VF
VOICES FROM THE PAST. VoFP
VOICES FROM WAH'KON-TAH. VW
VOICES OF POETRY. VoPo
WAGGON OF LIFE, THE, AND OTHER LYRICS BY RUSSIAN POETS OF THE NINETEENTH CENTURY. WaL
WAR AND THE POET... FROM ANCIENT TIMES TO THE PRESENT. WaaP
WAR POETS, THE. WaP
WASHINGTON'S BIRTHDAY. WOAH
WATCHERS OF THE SKY. WSN
WAY OF KNOWING, A. WaKn
WAY OF POETRY. WP
WAYSIDE POEMS OF THE EARLY EIGHTEENTH CENTURY. WaPE
WE BECOME NEW. WBN
WE SPEAK AS LIBERATORS. WSL
WEALTH OF POETRY, A. WePo
WELCOME CHRISTMAS! WeCh
WELSH POEMS AND BALLADS. WPB
WERNER'S READINGS AND RECITATIONS. WRR 1-18
WHAT CHEER. WhC
WHAT I LIKE IN POETRY. WLIP
WHEN THE LESSONS ARE OVER. WLO
WHERE BIRDS SING. WhBS
WHIMSEY ANTHOLOGY, A. WA
WHITE HOUSE HANDBOOK OF ORATORY. WHO
WHITE PONY, THE. WhP
WILLIAMS'S CHOICE LITERATURE... FOR GRAMMAR GRADES. WCLG 1-2
WILLIAMS'S CHOICE LITERATURE... FOR INTERMEDIATE GRADES. WCLI 1-2
WILSON'S DRILLS AND MARCHES FOR YOUNG PEOPLE AND SMALL CHILDREN. WDM
WILSON'S RECITATIONS AND DIALOGUES. WRD
WIND AND THE RAIN, THE. WiR
WIND HAS WINGS, THE. WHW
WIND IS ROUND, THE. WIRo
WINE FROM THESE GRAPES. WFG
WINGED HORSE ANTHOLOGY, THE. WHA

WINKS. **WN**
WITH HARP AND LUTE. **WHL**
WITH TRUMPET AND DRUM. **WTD**
WOMEN POETS IN ENGLISH, THE. **WPE**
WORDS IN FLIGHT. **WIF**
WORLD LITERATURE. **WoL**
WORLDLY MUSE, THE. **WoMu**
WORLD'S BEST-LOVED POEMS, THE. **WBLP**
WORLD'S BEST POEMS, THE. **WBP**
WORLD'S GREATEST RELIGIOUS POETRY, THE. **WGRP**
WORLD'S GREATEST SHORT STORIES, THE. **WGS**
WORLD'S ONE THOUSAND BEST POEMS, THE. **WTP 1-10**
WREATH OF CANADIAN SONG, A. **WCS**
WREATH OF CHRISTMAS POEMS, A. **WrChPo**
WRITING ON THE WALL. **WOW**
YALE BOOK OF AMERICAN VERSE. **YBV**
YALE CAROL BOOK, THE. **YaCaBo**
YANKEE DOODLES. **YaD**
YEAR AROUND, THE. **YeAr**
YEAR BOOK OF FAMOUS LYRICS. **YBF**
YEAR OF BEAUTIFUL THOUGHTS FOR BOYS AND GIRLS. **YBT**
YESTERDAY AND TODAY. **YT**
YOUNG AMERICAN POETS, THE. **YAP**
YOUNG AMERICAN'S SPEAKER. **YA**
YOUNG AMERICAN'S TREASURY OF ENGLISH POETRY, A. **YAT**
YOUNG FOLKS' BOOK OF MIRTH, THE. **BOM**
YOUNG FOLKS' DIALOGUES. **YFD**
YOUNG FOLKS' ENTERTAINMENTS. **YFE**
YOUNG FOLKS' READINGS. **MYF**
YOUNG FOLKS' RECITATIONS. **YFR**
YOUNG PEOPLE'S SPEAKER. H. Northrup. **YP**
YOUNG PEOPLE'S SPEAKER. E. Rook. **YPS**
YULE FIRE. **YF**
YULE TIDE CHEER. **YC**
YULETIDE ENTERTAINMENTS. **YTE**

AUTHOR LIST

Directions for Use. All works are listed alphabetically by author ("author" being used generically to include editor, compiler, and, when no other attribution is possible, translator, illustrator, or publisher).

Co-authors are included in the listing. The author entry gives: (i) the primary title of the work and (ii) its Granger Symbol. By reference to the Granger Symbol List, variant titles, primacy of authorship, and other details of the work can be found.

The form of the author's name used as the main entry generally is the name which appears on the title page of the work (which is consistent with the usage established in the early editions of *Granger's*). Cross-references from other names under which the author may appear or may conceivably be found are also given (to provide consistency with the usage adopted in the Third Edition of *Granger's* where writers are listed under best-known writing names).

When the form of the author's name in the main entry is a pseudonym, the author's legal name is cited; the legal name is also listed with a cross-reference to the main entry name. When the name used as the main entry is a legal name, but the other works of the author are indexed under a pseudonym, cross-reference to the pseudonym is given.

The names of married women are given main entry in this list under the name utilized in *Granger's*. In the earlier editions of *Granger's*, this was the married name; in later editions, this is the writing-name. In either case, the author's full name is provided in the main entry, and the alternate name is listed with cross-reference to the main entry.

Abcarian, Richard. WORDS IN FLIGHT. **WIF**
Abdul, Raoul. 3000 YEARS OF BLACK POETRY. **TTY**
Abney, Louise. CHORAL SPEAKING FOR THE LOWER GRADES. **CSL**

Abney, Louise

———. CHORAL SPEAKING FOR THE UPPER GRADES. **CSU**
Adams, Elizabeth. PIECES FOR EVERY MONTH OF THE YEAR. **PEM**
Adams, Florence. HIGHDAYS AND HOLIDAYS. **HH**
Adams, Franklin P. INNOCENT MERRIMENT. **InMe**
Adams, Hazard. POETRY; AN INTRODUCTORY ANTHOLOGY. **PIA**
Adams, St. Clair. BOOK OF BABY VERSE, THE. **BBV**
———. BOOK OF FRIENDSHIP VERSE, THE. **BFV**
———. BOOK OF MOTHER VERSE, THE. **BMV**
———. FACING FORWARD. **FF**
———. IT CAN BE DONE. **ICBD**
———. LIGHT OF THE WORLD. **LOW** *
———. POEMS OF INSPIRATION. **POI**
———. SILVER LININGS. **SL**
Adamson, Margot Robert. TREASURY OF MIDDLE ENGLISH VERSE. **TMEV**
Adoff, Arnold. BLACK OUT LOUD. **BOLo**
———. CITY IN ALL DIRECTIONS. **CAD**
———. I AM THE DARKER BROTHER. **IDB**
———. POETRY OF BLACK AMERICA, THE. **PoBA**
Agay, Denes. BEST LOVED SONGS OF THE AMERICAN PEOPLE. **BLSo**
Aiken, Conrad. AMERICAN POETRY, 1671-1928. **APA**
———. ANTHOLOGY OF FAMOUS ENGLISH & AMERICAN POETRY, AN. **AnFE**
———. COMPREHENSIVE ANTHOLOGY OF AMERICAN POETRY, A. **CoAnAm**
———. MODERN AMERICAN POETS. **MAPA**
———. TWENTIETH-CENTURY AMERICAN POETRY. **TwAmPo**
Alden, Raymond MacDonald. POEMS OF THE ENGLISH RACE. **PTER**
Aldington, Richard. VIKING BOOK OF POETRY OF THE ENGLISH-SPEAKING WORLD, THE. **ViBoPo**
Alexander, A. L. POEMS THAT TOUCH THE HEART. **PoToHe**
Alexander, Frances. MOTHER GOOSE ON THE RIO GRANDE. **MoGoRi**
Allen, Donald M. NEW AMERICAN POETRY, THE, 1945-1960. **NeAP**
Allen, Gay Wilson. AMERICAN POETRY. **AP** **
Allingham, William. BALLAD BOOK, THE. **BB**
Aloian, David. POEMS AND POETS. **PoPo**

Altenbernd, Lynn. INTRODUCTION TO LITERATURE: POEMS. ILP
Ames, Mary Clemmer. BALLADS FOR LITTLE FOLKS. BLF
Anderson, Wallace L. POETRY AS EXPERIENCE. PoEx
Andrews, Alice E. THREE CENTURIES OF AMERICAN POETRY & PROSE. TCAP
———. TWELVE CENTURIES OF ENGLISH POETRY & PROSE. TCEP
Andrews, C. E. POETRY OF THE NINETIES. PON
Arberry, A. J. MOORISH POETRY. MooP
———. PERSIAN POEMS. PeP
Arbuthnot, May Hill. TIME FOR POETRY. TiPo
Armstrong, Helen. PRAYER POEMS. PraP
Armstrong, O. V. PRAYER POEMS. PraP
Arp, Thomas R. FORM OF POETRY, THE. ForPo
Aspel, Alexander. CONTEMPORARY FRENCH POETRY. CoFP
Association for Childhood Education. SUNG UNDER THE SILVER UMBRELLA. SUS
Atkinson, Benjamin P. POETRY FROM LITERATURE FOR OUR TIME. PoLFOT
Auden, W. H. CRITERION BOOK OF MODERN AMERICAN VERSE, THE. CrMA
———. 19th CENTURY MINOR BRITISH POETS. NBM
———. OXFORD BOOK OF LIGHT VERSE, THE. OxBoLi
———. POETS OF THE ENGLISH LANGUAGE. PoEL 1-5
Ault, Norman. ELIZABETHAN LYRICS. ElL
———. SEVENTEENTH CENTURY LYRICS. SeCL
Auslander, Joseph. WINGED HORSE ANTHOLOGY, THE. WHA
Austin, Margot. MOTHER GOOSE RYHMES. MoGoRh
Austin, Mary C. SOUND OF POETRY, THE. SoPo
Ausubel, Maryann. TREASURY OF JEWISH POETRY, A. TrJP
Ausubel, Nathan. TREASURY OF JEWISH POETRY, A. TrJP
Ayer, Mary Allette. OUR MOTHERS. OrM
Babbitt, Adeline. GOLDEN FLUTE, THE. GFA
Bachelor, Joseph Morris. See Morris, Joseph (pseud.)
Bailey, J. O. VICTORIAN POETRY. ViPo
Baker, Emilie Kip. CHILDREN'S FIRST BOOK OF POETRY, THE. CFBP
———. CHILDREN'S SECOND BOOK OF POETYR, THE. CSBP
———. CHILDREN'S THIRD BOOK OF POETRY, THE. CTBP
Baker, George A. Jr. POINT LACE AND DIAMONDS. PLD
Baker, Herschel. RENAISSANCE IN ENGLAND, THE. ReIE

Baker, Stewart A. ANCIENTS AND MODERNS. **AnMo**
Bald, R. C. SEVENTEENTH-CENTURY ENGLISH POETRY. **SeEP**
Baldwin, Edward Chauncey. ENGLISH POEMS. **EhP**
Baldwin, James. CHOICE ENGLISH LYRICS. **CEL**
——. HARPER'S SCHOOL SPEAKER. **HSS 1-3**
Ballard, Harlan H. PIECES TO SPEAK. **PTS**
Banks, Emma Dunning. ORIGINAL RECITATIONS. **BR**
Barba, Sharon. RISING TIDES. **RiTi**
Barbe, Waitman. FAMOUS POEMS EXPLAINED. **FPE**
Barnes, R. G. EPISODES IN FIVE POETIC TRADITIONS. **Epi**
Barnes, Ruth. I HEAR AMERICA SINGING. **IHA**
Barrows, Marjorie. PULITZER PRIZE POEMS. **PuPrPo**
Barton, Jerome. BARTON'S COMIC RECITATIONS. **BC**
Bass, Ellen. NO MORE MASKS! **NMM**
Bates, Charlotte Fiske. See Rogé, C. F.
Bates, Herbert. MODERN LYRIC POETRY. **MLP**
Bates, Katharine Lee. BALLAD BOOK, A. **BB** *
——. ENGLISH HISTORY AS TOLD BY ENGLISH POETS. **EHT**
Baugh, Albert C. ENGLISH LITERATURE. **EnLit**
Bax, Clifford. DISTAFF MUSE, THE. **DiM**
——. VINTAGE VERSE. **ViV**
Bayliss, A. E. M. INVITATION TO VERSE. **InV**
Beaty, John O. INTRODUCTION TO POETRY, AN. **InP**
Bechtel, John H. SELECT SPEECHES FOR DECLAMATION. **SSD**
——. SUNDAY SCHOOL SELECTIONS. **SSS** *
——. TEMPERANCE SELECTIONS. **TS**
Beck, Edwin. ENGLISH ROMANTIC POETS. **ERP**
——. VICTORIAN & LATER ENGLISH POETS. **VLEP**
Beck, Richard. ICELANDIC POEMS AND STORIES. **IcP**
Beeson, Rebecca Katherine. CHILD'S CALENDAR BEAUTIFUL, THE. **CCB** *
Belden, H. M. BALLADS AND SONGS. **BaS**
Bellamy, Blanche W. OPEN SESAME. **OS 1-3**
Bemis, Katharine I. PIECES FOR EVERY DAY THE SCHOOLS CELEBRATE. **PEDC**
Bender, Robert M. FIVE COURTIER POETS OF THE ENGLISH RENAISSANCE. **FCP**
——. SONNET, THE. **Sonn**
Benét, William Rose. ANTHOLOGY OF FAMOUS ENGLISH & AMERICAN POETRY, AN. **AnFE**
——. FIFTY POETS. **FP** *
——. GREAT POEMS OF THE ENGLISH LANGUAGE. **GPE**

———. MOTHER GOOSE. **MoGo**
———. POEMS FOR MODERN YOUTH. **PoeMoYo**
———. POEMS FOR YOUTH. **PFY**
———. POETRY OF FREEDOM, THE. **PoFr**
———. TWENTIETH CENTURY POETRY. **TCPD**
Bennett, Jonathan. ANTHOLOGY OF NEW ZEALAND VERSE, AN. **AnNZ**
Benoit, Clement F. CHILDREN'S POEMS THAT NEVER GROW OLD. **CPN**
Berg, Stephen. NAKED POETRY. **NaP**
Best, Susie M. ARBOR DAY IN THE PRIMARY ROOM. **ADPR**
Bethurum, Dorothy. AMERICAN POETRY. **AmPo**
———. ENGLISH LYRIC POETRY. **EnLP**
Betjeman, John. ENGLISH LOVE POEMS. **EnLoPo**
———. ENGLISH, SCOTTISH, & WELSH LANDSCAPE, 1700-c. 1860. **EnSW**
———. WEALTH OF POETRY, A. **WePo**
Betsky, Sarah. ONIONS AND CUCUMBERS AND PLUMS. **OnCuPl**
Betts, Otsie Vernona. HIGH LIGHTS OF ENGLISH LITERATURE. **HiLiEn**
Betts, William W., Jr. LINCOLN AND THE POETS. **LiPo**
Binyon, Laurence. GOLDEN TREASURY OF MODERN LYRICS, THE. **GTML**
Birney, Earle. TWENTIETH CENTURY CANADIAN POETRY. **TwCaPo**
Bishop, John. MUSIC & SWEET POETRY. **MuSP**
Bishop, Morris. TREASURY OF BRITISH HUMOR, A. **TrBrHu**
Black Matthew W. ELIZABETHAN & SEVENTEENTH-CENTURY LYRICS. **ElSeCe**
Blackstone, Harriet. NEW PIECES THAT WILL TAKE PRIZES IN SPEAKING CONTESTS. **NPTP**
Blair, Walter. APPROACHES TO POETRY. **ATP**
Blanchard, Frederic M. PRACTICAL PUBLIC SPEAKING. **PPS**
Blanchard, Harold Hooper. PROSE & POETRY OF THE CONTINENTAL RENAISSANCE IN TRANSLATION. **PrPoCR**
Blistein, Elmer M. VARIETY OF POETRY, THE. **VaPo**
Bloom, Edward A. VARIETY OF POETRY, THE. **VaPo**
Bloom, Harold. ENGLISH ROMANTIC POETRY, THE. **ERoP 1-2**
———. WIND & THE RAIN, THE. **WiR**
Blunden, Edmund. WAYSIDE POEMS OF THE EARLY EIGHTEENTH CENTURY. **WaPE**
Body, Alfred H. MUSIC OF POETRY, THE. **MuP**

Bogan, Louise. GOLDEN JOURNEY, THE. **GoJo**
Boggs, Tom. AMERICAN DECADE. **AmD**
———. LYRIC MODERNS. **LyMo**
Bonner, Amy. POETRY SOCIETY OF AMERICA ANTHOLOGY, THE. **PSA**
Bontemps, Arna. AMERICAN NEGRO POETRY. **AmNP**
———. GOLDEN SLIPPERS. **GoSl**
———. POETRY OF THE NEGRO, THE. **PoNe**
Book of Knowledge, Editors of. POETRY TO KNOW. **PTK**
Borrow, George Henry. WELSH POEMS AND BALLADS. **WPB**
Botkin, B. A. TREASURY OF NEW ENGLAND FOLKLORE, A. **TrNE**
Bottrall, Margaret. COLLECTED ENGLISH VERSE. **CoEV**
Bottrall, Ronald. COLLECTED ENGLISH VERSE. **CoEV**
Boulton, James T. ENGLISH SATIRIC POETRY. **ESaP**
Bouton, Josephine. POEMS FOR THE CHILDREN'S HOUR. **PCH**
Bowes, Major Edward. VERSES I LIKE. **VIL**
Bowlin, William R. BOOK OF FIRESIDE POEMS, A. **BFP**
———. BOOK OF HISTORICAL POEMS, A. **BoHiPo**
———. BOOK OF LIVING POEMS, A. **BLP** *
———. BOOK OF PERSONAL POEMS, A. **BPP**
———. BOOK OF TREASURED POEMS, A. **BTP**
Bowra, C. M. BOOK OF RUSSIAN VERSE, A. **BoR**
———. OXFORD BOOK OF GREEK VERSE IN TRANSLATION, THE. **OxBG**
———. SECOND BOOK OF RUSSIAN VERSE, A. **BoRS**
Boyajian, Zabelle C. ARMENIAN LEGENDS AND POEMS. **ArmLP**
Boynton, Percy H. AMERICAN POETRY. **APB**
Boynton, Robert W. SOUNDS AND SILENCES. **SS**
Bozman, M. M. POEMS OF OUR TIME. **POTE**
Bozyan, H. Frank. YALE CAROL BOOK, THE. **YaCaBo**
Brackett, Anna C. POETRY FOR HOME AND SCHOOL. **PHS**
Braddy, Nella. STANDARD BOOK OF BRITISH & AMERICAN VERSE, THE. **SBA**
Brady, Frank. POETRY: PAST AND PRESENT. **PPP**
Braithwaite, William Stanley. ANTHOLOGY OF MAGAZINE VERSE FOR: 1913, 1914, 1915, 1916, 1924, 1925, 1926. **AMV 1-4, AMV 24-26**
———. BOOK OF GEORGIAN VERSE, THE. **BGV**
Braley, Berton. WORLD'S ONE THOUSAND BEST POEMS, THE. **WTP 1-10**

Bredvold, Louis I. EIGHTEENTH CENTURY POETRY AND PROSE. **EiPP**
Bregman, Adolph. SONGS OF AMERICAN FOLKS. **SoAF**
Brentano, Frances. QUESTING SPIRIT, THE. **QS**
Brett, R. L. POEMS OF FAITH AND DOUBT. **PFD**
Brewer, Hugh. VOICE, SPEECH, AND GESTURE. **VSG**
Brewster, Paul G. BALLADS AND SONGS OF INDIANA. **BaSoIn**
Brewton, John E. AMERICA FOREVER NEW. **AmFN**
———. BIRTHDAY CANDLES BURNING BRIGHT. **BiCB**
———. BRIDLED WITH RAINBOWS. **BrR**
———. CHRISTMAS BELLS ARE RINGING. **ChBR**
———. GAILY WE PARADE. **GaP**
———. SHRIEKS AT MIDNIGHT. **ShM**
———. SING A SONG OF SEASONS. **SiSoSe**
———. UNDER THE TENT OF THE SKY. **UTS**
Brewton, Sara. AMERICA FOREVER NEW. **AmFN**
———. BIRTHDAY CANDLES BURNING BRIGHT. **BiCB**
———. BRIDLED WITH RAINBOWS. **BrR**
———. CHRISTMAS BELLS ARE RINGING. **ChBR**
———. SHRIEKS AT MIDNIGHT. **ShM**
———. SING A SONG OF SEASONS. **SiSoSe**
Bridgeman, John C. THREE MINUTE DECLAMATIONS FOR COLLEGE MEN. **TMD**
Bridges, Robert. CHISWELL BOOK OF ENGLISH POETRY, THE. **CBE**
———. POETICAL WORKS OF ROBERT BRIDGES. **PWB**
Briggs, Wallace Alvin. GREAT POEMS OF THE ENGLISH LANGUAGE. **GPE**
Brinkley, Roberta Florence. ENGLISH POETRY OF THE SEVENTEENTH CENTURY. **EPS**
Brinnin, John Malcolm. MODERN POETRY. **MoPo**
———. MODERN POETS, THE. **MP**
———. TWENTIETH CENTURY POETS. **TwCP**
Broadbent, John. SIGNET CLASSIC POETS OF THE 17th CENTURY. **SCP 1-2**
Broadhurst, Jean. VERSE FOR PATRIOTS. **VP**
Brock, H. I. LITTLE BOOK OF LIMERICKS, THE. **LiBL**
Bronson, Walter C. AMERICAN POEMS (1625-1892). **AP**
———. ENGLISH POEMS:
    Vol. 1. Old English & Middle English periods. **EPOM**
    Vol. 2. The Elizabethan age & the Puritan period. **EPEP**
    Vol. 3. The Restoration & the 18th century. **EPRE**
    Vol. 4. The 19th century. **EPNC**

Brooke, Rupert. COLLECTED POEMS. **CPB**
Brooke, Stopford A. TREASURY OF IRISH POETRY, A. **TIP**
Brooks, Cleanth. UNDERSTANDING POETRY. **UnPo**
Brooks, Gwendolyn. JUMP BAD. **JB**
Brosius, Rudolph F. READINGS IN EUROPEAN LITERATURE. **REL**
Brower, Reuben A. BEGINNING WITH POEMS. **BWP**
Brown, Charles Walter. AMERICAN STAR SPEAKER, THE. **AmSS ***
―――. COMIC RECITATIONS AND READINGS. **CRR**
―――. LITTLE FOLKS SPEAKER. **LFS**
Brown, Edward K. VICTORIAN POETRY. **ViPo**
Brown, Sharon. POETRY OF OUR TIMES. **POOT**
Brown, Sterling A. NEGRO CARAVAN, THE. **NeCa**
Brown, Stuart Gerry. READING POEMS. **ReaPo**
Browne, Anita. HOMESPUN. **HB ***
Browne, Francis F. BUGLE ECHOES. **BE**
―――. GOLDEN POEMS BY BRITISH & AMERICAN AUTHORS. **GP**
Bruner, Herbert. POETRY BOOK, THE. **PB 1-9**
Brunini, John Gilland. DRINK FROM THE ROCK. **DrRo**
―――. FROM ONE WORD. **FrOW**
―――. SEALED UNTO THE DAY. **SeUD**
Bryant, Al. SOURCEBOOK OF POETRY. **SoP**
Bryant, Edward Andem. BEST ENGLISH AND SCOTTISH BALLADS. **BESB**
―――. YULE TIDE CHEER. **YC**
Bryant, William Cullen. LIBRARY OF POETRY AND SONG. **LPS 1-3**
―――. NEW LIBRARY OF POETRY AND SONG, A. **BNL**
Buckley, Jerome Hamilton. POETRY OF THE VICTORIAN PERIOD. **PoVP**
Bullen, Keith. SALAMANDER. **SaL**
Bullett, Gerald. ENGLISH GALAXY OF SHORTER POEMS, THE. **EG**
―――. SILVER POETS OF THE SIXTEENTH CENTURY. **SiPS**
Bullough, G. OXFORD BOOK OF SEVENTEENTH CENTURY VERSE, THE. **OBS**
Burbank, Alfred P. BURBANK'S RECITATIONS AND READINGS. **BRR**
Burdett, James S. BURDETT'S DUTCH DIALECT RECITATIONS. **BDD**
Burdette, Robert Jones. SMILES YOKED WITH SIGHS. **SYS**

Burkland, Carl Edwin. NEW MICHIGAN VERSE. **NeMiVe**
Burnett, Frances (Hodgson). CHILDREN'S BOOK, THE. **CB**
Burns, Dana Thurlow. PRINCIPLES OF ORAL INTERPRE-
 TATION, THE. **POOI**
Burns, Nancy May. COMPLETE HOLIDAY BOOK, A. **CHP**
Burns, Vincent Godgrey. RED HARVEST, THE. **RH**
Burrell, Arthur. BOOK OF HEROIC VERSE, A. **BHV**
Burroughs, John. SONGS OF NATURE. **SN**
Burt, Mary Elizabeth. EUGENE FIELD BOOK, THE. **EF**
———. POEMS EVERY CHILD SHOULD KNOW. **PECK**
Burtis, Edwin. ALL THE BEST DOG POEMS. **AlBD**
Butler, Guy. BOOK OF SOUTH AFRICAN VERSE, A. **BoSA**
Cable, Mary B. EUGENE FIELD BOOK, THE. **EF**
Cady, Edwin H. AMERICAN POETS, THE, 1800-1900. **AmePo**
Cairns, Huntington. LIMITS OF ART, THE. **LiA**
Calderwood, James L. FORMS OF POETRY. **FosPo**
Calverton, V. F. ANTHOLOGY OF AMERICAN NEGRO
 LITERATURE. **ANL**
Campbell, Hugh. VOICE, SPEECH, AND GESTURE. **VSG**
Campbell, Kathleen. ANTHOLOGY OF ENGLISH POETRY,
 AN: DRYDEN TO BLAKE. **AEP-D**
———. ANTHOLOGY OF ENGLISH POETRY, AN. WYATT TO
 DRYDEN. **AEP-W**
Campbell, Oscar James. GREAT ENGLISH POETS. **GEPC**
Campbell, Vivian. CHRISTMAS ANTHOLOGY OF POETRY
 & PAINTING, A. **ChAP**
Campbell, William Wilfred. OXFORD BOOK OF CANADIAN
 VERSE, THE. **OCV**
Canby, Henry Seidel. TWENTIETH CENTURY POETRY. **TCPD**
Cane, Melville. GOLDEN YEAR, THE. **GoYe**
Capps, Claudius Meade. BLUE AND THE GRAY, THE. **BlG**
Carhart, George S. MAGIC CASEMENTS. **MCCG**
———. THROUGH MAGIC CASEMENTS. **TMC**
Carli, Angelo. NOW VOICES, THE. **NowV**
Carlisle, Laura Mae. MY POETRY BOOK. **MPB**
Carman, Bliss. CANADIAN POETRY IN ENGLISH. **CaP**
———. OUR CANADIAN POETRY. **OCL**
———. OXFORD BOOK OF AMERICAN VERSE, THE. **OBAV**
Carnegie Library School Assn. ARBOR DAY IN POETRY. **ADP**
———. CHRISTMAS IN POETRY. **CP 1-2**
———. EASTER IN POETRY. **EP**
———. MEMORIAL DAY IN POETRY. **MDIP**

Carnegie Library School Association (cont.)

———. MOTHER'S DAY IN POETRY. **MDP**
———. THANKSGIVING IN POETRY. **TP**
Carpenter, Frederic Ives. ENGLISH LYRIC POETRY, 1500-1700. **ELP** *
Carr, Arthur J. VICTORIAN POETRY. **ViP**
Carr, Samuel. POETRY OF CATS, THE. **PCat**
Carrier, Warren. READING MODERN POETRY. **ReMP**
Carrington, FitzRoy. QUIET HOUR, THE. **QH**
Carrington, Henry Beebee. BEACON LIGHTS OF PATRIOTISM. **BLP**
———. ANTHOLOGY OF FRENCH POETRY. **AFP**
Carroll, Paul. YOUNG AMERICAN POETS, THE. **YAP**
Carruth, Hayden. VOICE THAT IS GREAT WITHIN US, THE. **VGW**
Cary, Alice. BALLADS FOR LITTLE FOLKS. **BLF**
Cary, Phoebe. BALLADS FOR LITTLE FOLKS. **BLF**
Causley, Charles. DAWN AND DUSK. **DaDu**
———. MODERN BALLADS AND STORY POEMS. **MoBS**
Cawein, Madison. BOOK OF LOVE, THE. **BOL**
Cecil, David. MODERN VERSE IN ENGLISH, 1900-1950. **MoVE**
———. OXFORD BOOK OF CHRISTIAN VERSE, THE. **OxBoCh**
Chabannes La Palice, Cecily de. See Mackworth, Cecily (pseud.)
Chadman, Charles. WHITE HOUSE HANDBOOK OF ORATORY. **WHO**
Chadwick, Annie Hathaway. LOVER'S TREASURY OF VERSE. **LTV**
———. OUT OF THE HEART. **OH**
———. TREASURY OF HELPFUL VERSE, A. **THV**
Chadwick, John White. LOVER'S TREASURY OF VERSE. **LTV**
———. OUT OF THE HEART. **OH**
———. TREASURY OF HELPFUL VERSE, A. **THV**
Chambers, Edmund Kerchever. ENGLISH PASTORALS. **EP** *
———. OXFORD BOOK OF SIXTEENTH CENTURY VERSE, THE. **OBSC**
Chandler, W.K. APPROACHES TO POETRY. **ATP**
Chapman, Robert, ANTHOLOGY OF NEW ZEALAND VERSE, AN. **AnNZ**
Chapple, Joseph Mitchell. HEART THROBS. **HT**
———. MORE HEART THROBS. **MHT**
Charvot, William. POEMS IN ENGLISH, 1530-1940. **PoE**
Chase, John Terry. TO PLAY MAN NUMBER ONE. **TPM**

———. WIND IS ROUND, THE. WIRo
Chester, Laura. RISING TIDES. RiTi
Chickering, Geraldine Jencks. BALLADS & SONGS OF SOUTHERN MICHIGAN. BaSoSo
Child, Francis James. ENGLISH AND SCOTTISH POPULAR BALLADS. ESPB
Chilman, Eric. TREASURY OF VERSE FOR SCHOOL AND HOME, A. TVSH
Chisholm, Louey. GOLDEN STAIRCASE, THE. GS *
Christy, Arthur E. WORLD LITERATURE. WoL
Church, Richard. POEMS OF OUR TIME. POTE
Ciardi, John. HOW DOES A POEM MEAN? HoPM
———. MID-CENTURY AMERICAN POETS. MiAP
Clark, Alexander. SCHOOLDAY DIALOGUES. SDD
———. STANDARD DIALOGUES. SD *
Clark, Donald B. ENGLISH LITERATURE. EnL
Clark, Robert Earle. POEMS FOR THE GREAT DAYS. PGD
Clark, Solomon Henry. HANDBOOK OF BEST READINGS. HBR
———. PRACTICAL PUBLIC SPEAKING. PPS
Clark, Thomas Curtis. CHRIST IN POETRY. ChIP
———. MASTER OF MEN, THE. MOM
———. NEW PATRIOTISM, THE. TNP
———. ONE HUNDRED POEMS OF IMMORTALITY. OHPI
———. ONE HUNDRED POEMS OF PEACE. OHPP
———. 1000 QUOTABLE POEMS. OQP
———. POEMS FOR DAILY NEEDS. PDN
———. POEMS FOR THE GREAT DAYS. PGD
———. POEMS FOR SPECIAL DAYS AND OCCASIONS. PSO
———. QUOTABLE POEMS. QP 1-2
Clark, William M. MODEL DIALOGUES. MD
———. STERLING DIALOGUES. SDC
Clarke, Frances E. POETRY'S PLEA FOR ANIMALS. PPA
Clarke, George Herbert. NEW TREASURY OF WAR POETRY, THE. NeTW
———. TREASURY OF WAR POETRY, A. TWP 1-2
Clipson, Ellis. POPULAR PLATFORM PIECES. PPP *
Coates, Henry Troth. CHILDREN'S BOOK OF POETRY. CBOP
———. FIRESIDE ENCYCLOPEDIA OF POETRY. FEP
Coblentz, Stanton A. MODERN AMERICAN LYRICS. MAL *
———. MODERN BRITISH LYRICS. MBL *
———. MUSIC MAKERS, THE. MuM

Coblentz, Stanton A. (cont.)

———. UNSEEN WINGS. UnW
Cody, Sherwin. SELECTION FROM THE GREAT ENGLISH POETS, A. GEPM
———. WORLD'S GREATEST SHORT STORIES, THE. WGS
Coffey, Dairine. DARK TOWER, THE. DTo
Coffin, Charles M. MAJOR POETS, THE. MaPo
Colcord, Joanna C. SONGS OF AMERICAN SAILORMEN. SoAmSa
Cole, William. BEASTLY BOYS AND GHASTLY GIRLS. BBGG
———. BOOK OF ANIMAL POEMS, A. BoAnP
———. BOOK OF LOVE POEMS, A. BoLP
———. BOOK OF NATURE POEMS, A. BoNaP
———. EIGHT LINES AND UNDER. ELU
———. EROTIC POETRY. ErPo
———. FIRESIDE BOOK OF HUMOROUS POETRY, THE. FiBHP
———. PITH AND VINEGAR. PV
———. POEMS FOR SEASONS AND CELEBRATIONS. PoSC
———. POEMS FROM IRELAND. PFIr
———. POEMS OF MAGIC AND SPELLS. PoMS
———. POEMS ONE LINE AND LONGER. POL
———. POET'S TALES, THE. PoTa
———. STORY POEMS, NEW AND OLD. StPo
Coleman, Satis N. SONGS OF AMERICAN FOLKS. SoAF
Collins, A.S. TREASURY OF ENGLISH VERSE, NEW AND OLD. TrEV
Collins, Rowland L. FOURTEEN BRITISH & AMERICAN POETS. FoBA
Collins, Vere Henry. POEMS OF ACTION. POA
Colum, Padraic. ANTHOLOGY OF IRISH VERSE, AN. AnIV
———. ROOFS OF GOLD. RoGo
Coman, Katharine. ENGLISH HISTORY AS TOLD BY ENGLISH POETS. EHT
Condee, Ralph W. CASE FOR POETRY, THE. CaFP
Conder, Alan, TREASURY OF FRENCH POETRY, A. TrFP
Connell, Catharine. LOVE POEMS, OLD AND NEW. LoPo
Cook, Roy J. ONE HUNDRED AND ONE FAMOUS POEMS. OHFP
Cooke, John. DUBLIN BOOK OF IRISH VERSE, THE. DB
Coombs, Orde. WE SPEAK AS LIBERATORS. WSL
Cooper, Alice Cecilia. POEMS OF TODAY. POT, POTO
———. POEMS OF YOUTH. POY

Cooper, Charles W. PREFACE TO POETRY. PreP
Cope, Jack. PENGUIN BOOK OF SOUTH AFRICAN VERSE, THE. PeSA
Copeland, Charles Townsend. COPELAND READER, THE. CR *
Cott, Jonathan, ROSES RACE AROUND HER NAME, THE. RRA
Cousins, Norman. POETRY OF FREEDOM, THE. PoFr
Coussens, Penrhyn W. POEMS CHILDREN LOVE. PCL
Craig, Asa H. PIECES FOR PRIZE SPEAKING. PPSC
Crane, Ronald S. COLLECTION OF ENGLISH POEMS, A. 1660-1800. CEP *
Creekmore, Hubert. LITTLE TREASURY OF WORLD POETRY, A. LiTW
———. LYRICS OF THE MIDDLE AGES. LyMA
Cromer, John. SALAMANDER. Sal
Cross, Richard James. HUNDRED GREAT POEMS, A. HGP
Cross, Tom Peete. GOOD READINGS FOR HIGH SCHOOLS. GR 1-2; GR-a; GR-b
Crossland, John R. BOOK OF BALLADS, THE. BoB
Crothers, Samuel McChord. BOOK OF FRIENDSHIP, THE. BOF
Crowell, Thomas Young. FAVORITE POEMS. FP
———. RED LETTER POEMS. RLP
Cullen, Countee. CAROLING DUSK. CDC
Cummings, Irving. POETS AND POEMS. PoeP
Cumnock, Robert McLean. CHOICE READINGS. CCR
———. CUMNOCK'S SCHOOL SPEAKER. CSS
Cunliffe, John W. CENTURY READINGS IN ENGLISH LITERATURE. CRE
———. POEMS OF THE GREAT WAR. PGW
Currey, R. N. FORMAL SPRING. FoS
Curry, Charles Madison. THE POETRY BOOK. PB 1-9
Cutts, John P. SEVENTEENTH CENTURY SONGS AND LYRICS. SeCSL
Daiches, David. POEMS IN ENGLISH, 1530-1940. PoE
Dalgliesh, Alice. CHRISTMAS. CAD
———. CHRISTMAS HOLIDAY BOOK, A. CHB
Dalven, Rae. MODERN GREEK POETRY. MoGP
Daly, T.A. LITTLE BOOK OF AMERICAN HUMOROUS VERSE, A. LHV
Dana, Charles A. HOUSEHOLD BOOK OF POETRY, A. HBP
Daniels, Earl. ART OF READING POETRY, THE. ArRePo
Danziger, Marlies K. POETRY ANTHOLOGY, A. PAn

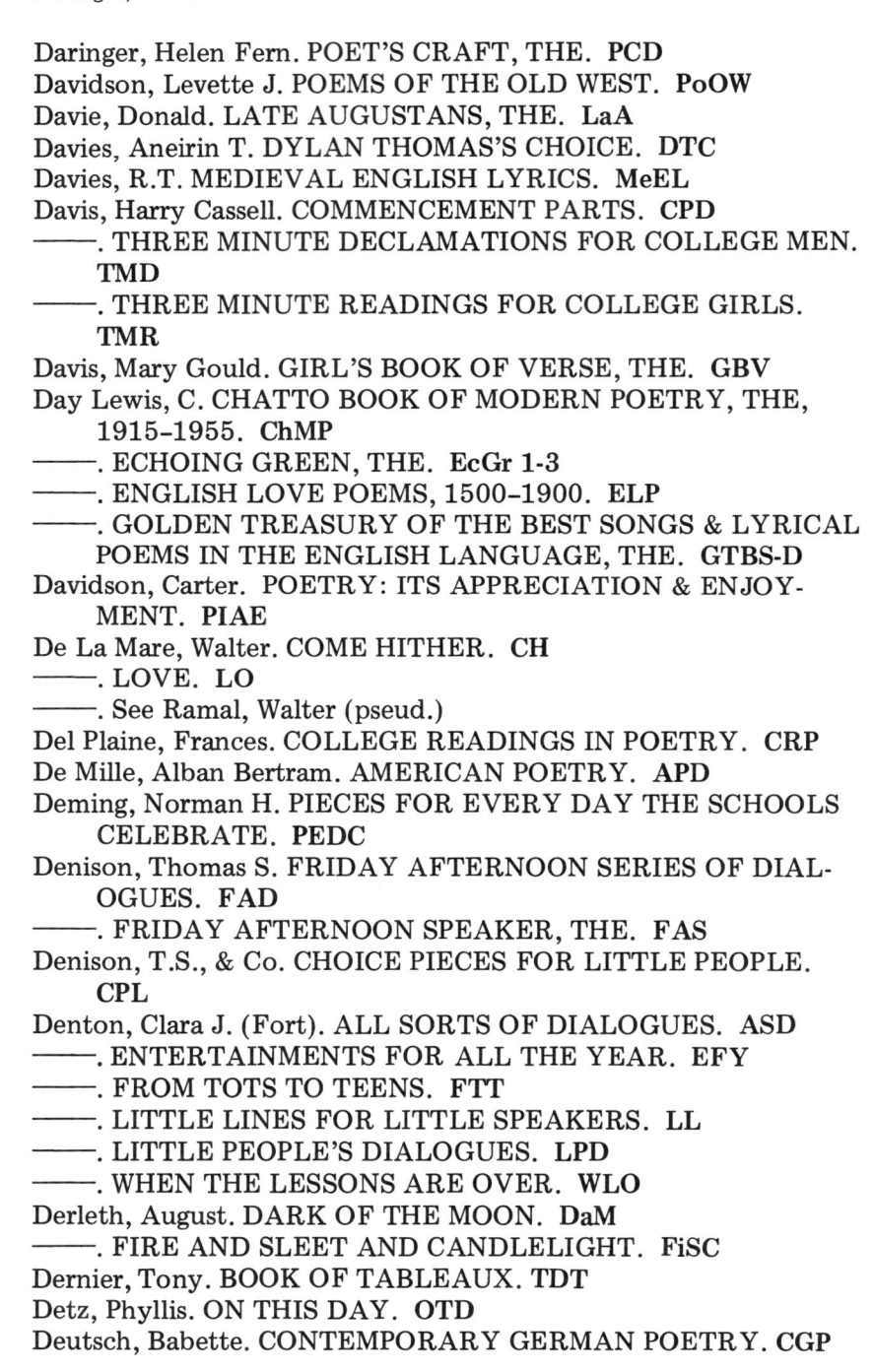

Daringer, Helen Fern. POET'S CRAFT, THE. PCD
Davidson, Levette J. POEMS OF THE OLD WEST. PoOW
Davie, Donald. LATE AUGUSTANS, THE. LaA
Davies, Aneirin T. DYLAN THOMAS'S CHOICE. DTC
Davies, R.T. MEDIEVAL ENGLISH LYRICS. MeEL
Davis, Harry Cassell. COMMENCEMENT PARTS. CPD
———. THREE MINUTE DECLAMATIONS FOR COLLEGE MEN. TMD
———. THREE MINUTE READINGS FOR COLLEGE GIRLS. TMR
Davis, Mary Gould. GIRL'S BOOK OF VERSE, THE. GBV
Day Lewis, C. CHATTO BOOK OF MODERN POETRY, THE, 1915-1955. ChMP
———. ECHOING GREEN, THE. EcGr 1-3
———. ENGLISH LOVE POEMS, 1500-1900. ELP
———. GOLDEN TREASURY OF THE BEST SONGS & LYRICAL POEMS IN THE ENGLISH LANGUAGE, THE. GTBS-D
Davidson, Carter. POETRY: ITS APPRECIATION & ENJOYMENT. PIAE
De La Mare, Walter. COME HITHER. CH
———. LOVE. LO
———. See Ramal, Walter (pseud.)
Del Plaine, Frances. COLLEGE READINGS IN POETRY. CRP
De Mille, Alban Bertram. AMERICAN POETRY. APD
Deming, Norman H. PIECES FOR EVERY DAY THE SCHOOLS CELEBRATE. PEDC
Denison, Thomas S. FRIDAY AFTERNOON SERIES OF DIALOGUES. FAD
———. FRIDAY AFTERNOON SPEAKER, THE. FAS
Denison, T.S., & Co. CHOICE PIECES FOR LITTLE PEOPLE. CPL
Denton, Clara J. (Fort). ALL SORTS OF DIALOGUES. ASD
———. ENTERTAINMENTS FOR ALL THE YEAR. EFY
———. FROM TOTS TO TEENS. FTT
———. LITTLE LINES FOR LITTLE SPEAKERS. LL
———. LITTLE PEOPLE'S DIALOGUES. LPD
———. WHEN THE LESSONS ARE OVER. WLO
Derleth, August. DARK OF THE MOON. DaM
———. FIRE AND SLEET AND CANDLELIGHT. FiSC
Dernier, Tony. BOOK OF TABLEAUX. TDT
Detz, Phyllis. ON THIS DAY. OTD
Deutsch, Babette. CONTEMPORARY GERMAN POETRY. CGP

Dick, Harris B. DICK'S CHOICE PIECES FOR LITTLE CHILDREN. DCP
——. DICK'S LITTLE DIALOGUES FOR LITTLE PEOPLE. DLD
——. DICK'S LITTLE SPEECHES FOR LITTLE SPEAKERS. DLS
Dick, William Brisbane. DICK'S COMIC & DIALECT RECITATIONS. DCR
——. DICK'S COMIC DIALOGUES. DCD
——. DICK'S DIALOGUES & MONOLOGUES. DDM
——. DICK'S DIVERTING DIALOGUES. DDD
——. DICK'S DUTCH, FRENCH, & YANKEE RECITATIONS. DFY
——. DICK'S ETHIOPIAN SCENES, VARIETY SPEECHES & STUMP SPEECHES. DE
——. DICK'S FESTIVAL RECITER. DFR
——. DICK'S IRISH DIALECT & RECITATIONS. DI *
——. DICK'S JUVENILE SPEAKER FOR BOYS & GIRLS. DJs
——. DICK'S LITTLE FOLKS' RECITER. DLF
——. DICK'S SPEECHES FOR TINY TOTS. DST
——. DICK'S STUMP SPEECHES & MINSTREL JOKES. DSS
Dick & Fitzgerald Co. DICK'S DRAMATIC RECITER. DDR
——. DRAWING ROOM THEATRICALS. DT
——. SPENCER'S COMIC SPEECHES. SCC
Dickerman, H.A., & Son (Publisher). PRIZE POETICAL SPEAKER, THE. PPSr
Dickinson, Leon T. ENGLISH LITERATURE; A COLLEGE ANTHOLOGY. EnL
Dickinson, Patric. SOLDIERS' VERSE. SoV
Diehl, Anna T. (Randall). ELOCUTIONARY STUDIES. DES
Dilworth, Ira. TWENTIETH CENTURY VERSE. TwCV
Dixon, W. Macneile. EDINBURGH BOOK OF SCOTTISH VERSE, THE, 1300–1900. EBSV
Dobrée, Bonamy. LONDON BOOK OF ENGLISH VERSE, THE. LoBV
Dobson, Austin. OLD ENGLISH SONGS. OES
Dodge, Robert K. VOICES FROM WAH'KON-TAH. VW
Doerflinger, William Main. SHANTYMEN AND SHANTYBOYS. ShS
Dore, Anita. PREMIER BOOK OF MAJOR POETS, THE. **PBMP**
Doubleday, Page & Co. TAKEN FROM LIFE. TL
Doud, Margery. FATHER. **FAOV**

Downes, Olin. TREASURY OF AMERICAN SONG, A. TrAS
Downey, Fairfax. LAUGHING VERSE. LauV
Downie, Mary Alice. WIND HAS WINGS, THE. WHW
Drake, A.J., & Co. CHOICE DIALECT & VAUDEVILLE STAGE JOKES. CDV
———. DUTCH DIALECT. DRR
Drinkwater, John. ANTHOLOGY OF ENGLISH VERSE, AN. AEV
———. TWENTIETH-CENTURY POETRY. TCPD
———. WAY OF POETRY. WP
Driver, Tom F. POEMS OF DOUBT AND BELIEF. PoDB
Dudek, Louis. ALL KINDS OF EVERYTHING. AKE
Dunton, Larkin. LAND OF SONG, THE. LOS 1-3
Dwyer, Richard A. SONGS OF THE GOLD RUSH, THE. SGR
Dyer-Bennet, Richard. RICHARD DYER-BENNET FOLK SONG BOOK, THE. RDB
Earle, Ferdinand. LYRIC YEAR. LY
Eastman, Arthur M. NORTON ANTHOLOGY OF POETRY, THE. NoP
Eastman, Max. ANTHOLOGY FOR THE ENJOYMENT OF POETRY. AnEnPo
Eaton, Anne Thaxter. POET'S CRAFT, THE. PCD
———. WELCOME CHRISTMAS! WeCh
Eaton, William Dunseath. GREAT POEMS OF THE GREAT WAR. GPWW
Ebert, P.K. SPORTS POEMS. SPo
Eberhart, Richard. WAR AND THE POET. WaaP
Eddy, Lefa Morse. FIFTEEN YEARS FROM THE LANTERN. FiYeLa
Eddy, Mary O. BALLADS AND SONGS FROM OHIO. BSO
Edgar, M.G. TREASURY OF VERSE FOR LITTLE CHILDREN, A. TVC
———. TREASURY OF VERSE FOR SCHOOL AND HOME, A. TVSH
Edwards, Jean. FOUR WINDS. FoW 1-4
Eggleston, George Cary. AMERICAN WAR BALLADS & LYRICS. AWB
Eliot, Ida M. POETRY FOR HOME AND SCHOOL. PHS
Eliot, Samuel. POETRY FOR CHILDREN. PC
Elliott, G. R. ENGLISH POETRY OF THE NINETEENTH CENTURY. EPN
Elliott, George P. FIFTEEN MODERN AMERICAN POETS. FiMAP

Ellis, Milton. COLLEGE BOOK OF AMERICAN LITERATURE, A. **CoBA**
Ellmann, Richard. NEW OXFORD BOOK OF AMERICAN VERSE, THE. **NOBA**
———. NORTON ANTHOLOGY OF MODERN POETRY, THE. **NoAM**
Ellsworth, William Webster. READINGS FROM THE NEW POETS. **RNP**
Elsea, Matilda Mahaffey. CHOICE POEMS FOR ELEMENTARY GRADES. **ChPo**
Elson, William. LITERATURE AND LIFE. **LL 1-4**
Emerson, Ralph Waldo. PARNASSUS. **EPs**
Emmons, Frederick E. TRAVELER'S BOOK OF VERSE, THE. **TBV**
Emrich, Duncan. AMERICAN FOLK POETRY. **AmFP**
Engelberg, Edward. SYMBOLIST POEM, THE. **SyP**
Engle, Paul. POET'S CHOICE. **PoCH**
———. READING MODERN POETRY. **ReMP**
English Association. MODERN MUSE, THE. **MM**
———. POEMS OF TO-DAY. **PoeT**
Enright, Dennis J. POETRY OF LIVING JAPAN, THE. **PoLJ**
Erickson, Lois J. SONGS FROM THE LAND OF DAWN. **SoLD**
Ernest, P. Edward. FAMILY ALBUM OF FAVORITE POEMS, THE. **FaFP**
Evans, David Allen. NEW VOICES IN AMERICAN POETRY. **NVAP**
Everett, Louella D. CAT IN VERSE, THE. **CIV** *
Falck, Colin. POEMS SINCE 1900. **PSN**
Farma, William J. PROSE, POETRY, & DRAMA FOR ORAL INTERPRETATION. **PPD 1-2**
Farrar, John. GOLDEN YEAR, THE. **GoYe**
Felleman, Hazel. BEST LOVED POEMS OF THE AMERICAN PEOPLE, THE. **BLPA**
———. POEMS THAT LIVE FOREVER. **PoLF**
Fenno, Frank H. SCIENCE AND ART OF ELOCUTION. **SA**
Ferris, Helen. FAVORITE POEMS OLD AND NEW. **FaPON**
———. LOVE'S ENCHANTMENT. **LoEn**
———. MY POETRY BOOK. **MPB**
Ferry, Anne D. BEGINNING WITH POEMS. **BWP**
Field, Eugene. LOVE SONGS OF CHILDHOOD. **LS**
———. POEMS OF EUGENE FIELDS, THE. **PEF**
———. WITH TRUMPET AND DRUM. **WTD**

Fields, Kenneth. QUEST FOR REALITY. **QFR**
Finn, F. E. S. POETS OF OUR TIME. **POTi**
Fish, Helen Dean. BOY'S BOOK OF VERSE, THE. **BBV** *
———. FOUR & TWENTY BLACKBIRDS. **FTB**
Fitts, Dudley. ANTHOLOGY OF CONTEMPORARY LATIN-AMERICAN POETRY. **AnCL**
Flanders, Helen Hartness. BALLADS MIGRANT IN NEW ENGLAND. **BaMNE**
———. VERMONT CHAP BOOK. **VeChBo**
Fleming, Alice. AMERICA IS NOT ALL TRAFFIC LIGHTS. **ANTL**
Flores, Angel. ANTHOLOGY OF FRENCH POETRY FROM NERVAL TO VALERY IN ENGLISH TRANSLATION, AN. **AnFP**
———. ANTHOLOGY OF GERMAN POETRY FROM HOLDERLIN TO RILKE IN ENGLISH TRANSLATION, AN. **AnGP**
———. ANTHOLOGY OF MEDIEVAL LYRICS, AN. **AnML**
———. ANTHOLOGY OF SPANISH LYRICS FROM GARCILASO TO GARCIA LORCA IN ENGLISH TRANSLATION WITH SPANISH ORIGINALS, AN. **AnSP**
Flower, Margaret. CASSELL'S ANTHOLOGY OF ENGLISH POETRY. **CaAE**
Fobes, Walter K. FIVE MINUTE DECLAMATIONS. **FD 1-2**
———. FIVE MINUTE READINGS. **FMR**
———. FIVE MINUTE RECITATIONS. **FR**
Foerster, Norman. AMERICAN POETRY AND PROSE. **AmPP**
———. ENGLISH POETRY OF THE NINETEENTH CENTURY. **EPN**
Fogle, Stephen F. BRIEF ANTHOLOGY OF POETRY, A. **BrAP**
Ford, James Lauren. EVERY DAY IN THE YEAR. **EDY**
Ford, Mary K. EVERY DAY IN THE YEAR. **EDY**
Foster, Luther Clark. SELECTIONS FOR MEMORIZING. **SM**
Fowler, Ethel L. DAFFODIL POETRY BOOK, THE. **DaB**
———. SECOND DAFFODIL POETRY BOOK, THE. **DaBS**
Fowlie, Wallace. MID-CENTURY FRENCH POETS. **MiCF**
Frankenberg, Lloyd. INVITATION TO POETRY. **SLP**
Fraser, Antonia. SCOTTISH LOVE POEMS. **SLP**
Fraser, G. S. POETRY NOW. **PoN**
Fremont, Robert A. FAVORITE SONGS OF THE NINETIES. **FSN**
Friar, Kimon. MODERN POETRY. **MoPo**
Friedman, Albert B. VIKING BOOK OF FOLK BALLADS OF

THE ENGLISH-SPEAKING WORLD, THE. **ViBoPo**
Frink, Henry A. NEW CENTURY SPEAKER, THE. **NC**
Frost, S. A. [Sarah Annie Shields]. DIALOGUES FOR YOUNG FOLKS. **FDY**
———. HUMOROUS & EXHIBITION DIALOGUES. **FHE**
———. NEW BOOK OF DIALOGUES. **FND**
Frothingham, Robert. SONGS OF THE SEA & SAILORS' CHANTEYS. **SSSC**
Fulton, Robert Irwin. CHOICE READINGS. **FTR**
———. STANDARD SELECTIONS. **StS**
Fussell, Paul, Jr., EIGHTEENTH CENTURY ENGLISH LITERATURE. **EiCL**
Fyleman, Rose. HERE WE COME A' PIPING. **HWC**
———. PIPE AND DRUM. **PiDr**
Gaige, Grace. RECITATIONS FOR YOUNGER CHILDREN. **RYC**
———. RECITATIONS, OLD AND NEW, FOR BOYS AND GIRLS. **RON**
Gannett, Lewis. FAMILY BOOK OF VERSE, THE. **FaBV**
Gardner, Emelyn Elizabeth. BALLADS AND SONGS OF SOUTHERN MICHIGAN. **BaSoSo**
Gardner, Helen. BOOK OF RELIGIOUS VERSE, A. **BoReV**
———. METAPHYSICAL POETS, THE. **MePo**
———. NEW OXFORD BOOK OF ENGLISH VERSE, THE, 1250-1950. **NOBE**
Garioch, Robert. MADE IN SCOTLAND. **MIS**
Garrett, Edmund Henry. ELIZABETHAN SONGS. **ES**
———. VICTORIAN SONGS. **VS**
Garrett, Phineas. EXCELSIOR DIALOGUES. **ED**
———. ONE HUNDRED CHOICE SELECTIONS IN POETRY & PROSE. **OHCS 1-40**
———. POPULAR DIALOGUES. **PD**
Garrigue, Jean. LOVE'S ASPECTS. **LoAs**
Garrison, Winifred Ernest. ONE HUNDRED POEMS OF IMMORTALITY. **OHPI**
———. ONE HUNDRED POEMS OF PEACE. **OHPP**
Garrity, Devin A. NEW IRISH POETS. **NeIP**
Garvin, John W. CANADIAN POETS. **CPG**
Gassner, John. OUR HERITAGE OF WORLD LITERATURE. **OuHeWo**
Gay, Robert M. COLLEGE BOOK OF VERSE, THE, 1250-1925. **CHOV**
———. RIVERSIDE BOOK OF VERSE. **RBV**
Gelpi, Albert. POET IN AMERICA, THE. **PiAm**

George, David L. FAMILY BOOK OF BEST LOVED POEMS, THE. **FaBoBe**
Gibbons, Oliphant. BOOK OF POEMS, A. **BoPo**
Giese, William P. HARPER'S ANTHOLOGY. **HAP**
Gilbert, Charles B. POEMS BY GRADES. **PBGP, PBGG**
Gilder, Joseph B. AMERICAN IDEA, THE. **AI**
Gill, Elaine. MOUNTAIN MOVING DAY. **MMD**
Gill, J. L. POETRY FOR SENIOR STUDENTS. **PoSS**
Gill, John. NEW AMERICAN AND CANADIAN POETRY. **NeAC**
Gillespie, Esther A. NEW PATRIOTISM, THE. **TNP**
———. QUOTABLE POEMS. **QP 1-2**
Gillett, Eric. POETS OF OUR TIME. **PtOT**
Gillis, Adolph. POEMS FOR MODERN YOUTH. **PoeMoYo**
Gleeson, Patrick. FIRST READER OF CONTEMPORARY AMERICAN POETRY, A. **FRC**
Glikes, Erwin A. OF POETRY AND POWER. **OPP**
Gode, Alexander. ANTHOLOGY OF GERMAN POETRY THROUGH THE 19th CENTURY. **AGP**
Goldmark, Pauline. GYPSY TRAIL. **GT, GT-2**
Goldstone, Herbert. POETS & POEMS. **PoeP**
Golino, Carlo L. CONTEMPORARY ITALIAN POETRY. **CoIP**
Goodchild, George G. BATTLE POEMS AND PATRIOTIC VERSES. **BP**
Gooden, Mona. POET'S CAT, THE. **PoC**
Goodfellow, E. J. H. TINY TOTS SPEAKER. **TT**
Goodsman, C. S. THIS HAPPY HOME. **ThHaHo**
Goodwin, Maud W. OPEN SESAME. **OS 1-3**
Gordon, Dudley Chadwick. TODAY'S LITERATURE. **TL ***
Gordon, Margery. MAGIC WORLD, A. **MW**
———. VERSE OF OUR DAY. **VOD**
Goudge, Elizabeth. BOOK OF COMFORT, A. **BoC**
———. BOOK OF PEACE, A. **BoPe**
Graham, Eleanor. THREAD OF GOLD, A. **ThGo**
Graham, George C. GRAHAM'S SCHOOL DIALOGUES. **GS ****
Grahame, Kenneth. CAMBRIDGE BOOK OF POETRY FOR CHILDREN, THE. **CBPC**
Grandy, Adah Georgina. COLLEGE READINGS IN POETRY. **CRP**
Grandsen, K. W. TUDOR VERSE SATIRE. **TVS**
Grant Duff, M. E. ANTHOLOGY OF VICTORIAN POETRY. **AVP**

Graves, Alfred Perceval. BOOK OF IRISH POETRY, THE. **BIP**
———. RECITER'S TREASURY OF IRISH VERSE & PROSE. **RTI**
Graves, Robert. ENGLISH AND SCOTTISH BALLADS. **EnSB**
Gray, Richard. AMERICAN VERSE OF THE NINETEENTH CENTURY. **AmVN**
Greaves, Griselda. BURNING THORN, THE. **BuTh**
Grebanier, Bernard D. N. ENGLISH LITERATURE AND ITS BACKGROUND. **EnLi 1-2**
Green, A. Wigfall. TUDOR POETRY AND PROSE. **TuPP**
Green, H. M. MODERN AUSTRALIAN POETRY. **MoAuPo**
Green, Roger Lancelyn. BOOK OF NONSENSE, THE. **BoN**
———. CENTURY OF HUMOROUS VERSE, A, 1850-1950. **CenHV**
Greene, David H. ANTHOLOGY OF IRISH LITERATURE, AN. **AnIL**
Greenfield, Stanley B. POEM, THE. **PoAn**
Greenlaw, Edwin A. LITERATURE AND LIFE. **LL 1-4**
Greenough, Jeanie A. B. YEAR OF BEAUTIFUL THOUGHTS FOR BOYS & GIRLS. **YBT**
Gregory, Horace. MENTOR BOOK OF RELIGIOUS VERSE, THE. **MeRV**
———. SILVER SWAN, THE. **SiSw**
———. TRIUMPH OF LIFE, THE. **TriL**
Grierson, Herbert J. C. METAPHYSICAL LYRICS & POEMS OF THE SEVENTEENTH CENTURY. **MeLP**
———. OXFORD BOOK OF SEVENTEENTH CENTURY VERSE, THE. **OBS**
Grieve, Christopher Murray. See MacDiarmid, Hugh (pseud.)
Griffin, Caroline Stearns. LITTLE PRIMARY PIECES. **LPP**
Griffith, Benjamin Lease Crozer. MONOLOGUES AND NOVELTIES. **MN**
———. SCHOOL AND PARLOR COMEDIES. **SPC** *
Griffith, William. GARDEN BOOK OF VERSE, THE. **GBOV**
Grigson, Geoffrey. BEFORE THE ROMANTICS. **BeR** *
———. CHERRY-TREE, THE. **ChTr**
———. GAMBIT BOOK OF LOVE POEMS, THE. **GBL**
———. GAMBIT BOOK OF POPULAR VERSE, THE. **GBP**
———. PENGUIN BOOK OF BALLADS, THE. **PeBB**
———. ROMANTICS, THE. **RO**
Gross, Sarah Chokla. EVERY CHILD'S BOOK OF VERSE. **ECBV**

Grover, Edwin Osgood. NATURE LOVER'S KNAPSACK, THE. NLK
Grover, Eulalie Osgood. MY CARAVAN. MCG
Guerney, Bernard Guilbert. TREASURY OF RUSSIAN LITERATURE, A. TrRuLi
Guest, Edgar A. ALL IN A LIFETIME. ALG
——. COLLECTED VERSE. CVG
Guindon, Frederick A. JUNIOR HIGH SCHOOL POETRY. JHP
Gullan, Marjorie. SPEECH CHOIR, THE. SC *
Gunnison, Binney. NEW DIALOGUES AND PLAYS. NDP
——. PIECES FOR PRIZE SPEAKING. PPSC
Gustafson, Ralph. ANTHOLOGY OF CANADIAN POETRY. AnCaPo
——.LITTLE ANTHOLOGY OF CANADIAN POETS, A. LiAnCa
——. PENGUIN BOOK OF CANADIAN VERSE, THE. PeCV
Gwynn, Frederick L. CASE FOR POETRY, THE. CaFP
Hadas, Moses. GREEK POETS, THE. GrPo
Hadow, Alexander. OFF THE GROUND. OFG 1-4
Hall Donald. CONTEMPORARY AMERICAN POETRY. ConAP
——. NEW POETS OF ENGLAND AND AMERICA. NePoEA
——. NEW POETS OF ENGLAND AND AMERICA: SECOND SELECTION. NePoEA-2
——. PLEASURES OF POETRY. PPoe
——. POETRY IN ENGLISH. PoIE
——. POETRY SAMPLER, A. PoSa
Hall, Howard Judson. THREE CENTURIES OF AMERICAN POETRY & PROSE. TCAP
——. TWELVE CENTURIES OF ENGLISH POETRY & PROSE. TCEP
——. TYPES OF POETRY. TPH
Halliday, Wilfrid Joseph. PRO PATRIA. PPV
Hallmark Greeting Card Co. POETRY FOR PLEASURE. PoPl
Halpern, Daniel. AMERICAN POETRY ANTHOLOGY, THE. AmPA
Hamburger, Michael. MODERN GERMAN POETRY, 1910-1960. MGP
Hamill, S. S. NEW SCIENCE OF ELOCUTION, THE. HNS
Hamilton, Ian. POEMS SINCE 1900. PSN
Hamilton, W. H. HOLYROOD. HMSP
Hamm, Agnes Curren. SELECTIONS FOR CHORAL SPEAKING. SFC

Handford, Thomas W. TOMMY'S FIRST SPEAKER. **TFS**
———. TOMMY'S SECOND SPEAKER. **TSS**
Hannum, Sara. LEAN OUT OF THE WINDOW. **LOW**
———. TO PLAY MAN NUMBER ONE. **TPM**
———. WIND IS ROUND, THE. **WIRo**
Harbinger House. AMERICAN VOICE. **AmVo**
Hardie, John L. VERSE OF VALOUR. **VeV**
Harrer, Gustave Adolphus. ROMAN LITERATURE IN TRANSLATION. **RoL**
Harrington, Mildred P. OUR HOLIDAYS IN POETRY. **OHIP**
———. RING-A-ROUND. **RAR**
Harris, Ada Van Stone. POEMS BY GRADES. **PBGP, PBGG**
Harrison, G. B. MAJOR BRITISH WRITERS. **MBW 1-2**
Harrison, Joseph Le Roy. CAP AND GOWN. **CG-1**
Hart, Henry H. POEMS OF THE HUNDRED NAMES. **PoHN**
Hartshorne, Grace. FOR THEE ALONE. **FTA**
Harvey, Nick. MARK IN TIME. **MIT**
Haverly, Jack. NEGRO MINSTRELS. **NM**
Hay, Gilbert. THESE I HAVE LOVED. **TIHL**
Hayden, Robert. KALEIDOSCOPE. **Kal**
Hayes, Albert M. WREATH OF CHRISTMAS POEMS, A. **WrChPo**
Hayes, James M. IN PRAISE OF NUNS. **PraNu**
Hays, H. R. 12 SPANISH AMERICAN POETS. **TwSpPo**
Hayward, John. FABER BOOK OF ENGLISH VERSE, THE. **FaBoEn**
———. OXFORD BOOK OF NINETEENTH-CENTURY ENGLISH VERSE, THE. **OBNC**
Hazard, Bertha. THREE YEARS WITH THE POETS. **TYP**
Hazeltine, Alice Isabel. CHRISTMAS BOOK OF LEGENDS & STORIES, THE. **ChrBoLe**
———. CHRISTMAS IN LEGEND AND STORY. **CLS**
———. YEAR AROUND, THE. **YeAr**
Heath, William. MAJOR BRITISH POETS OF THE ROMANTIC PERIOD. **MBRP**
Heath-Stubbs, John. FABER BOOK OF TWENTIETH CENTURY VERSE, THE. **FaBoTw**
Hebel, J. William. TUDOR POETRY AND PROSE. **TuPP**
Heller, Louie Regina. EARLY AMERICAN ORATIONS. **EAO**
Helps, E. A. SONGS AND BALLADS FROM OVER THE SEA. **SBOS**
———. SONGS AND BALLADS OF GREATER BRITAIN. **SGB**
Henderson, Alice Corbin. NEW POETRY, THE. **NP** *

Henley, William Ernest, LYRA HEROICA. **LH**
Henneberry Company. SUNDAY SCHOOL ENTERTAINMENTS. **SSE**
Herrington, H. W. ENGLISH MASTERPIECES, 700-1900. **EM 1-2**
Herzberg, Max J. NARRATIVE POEMS. **NPH**
———. OFF TO ARCADY. **OTA**
Hess, Frances Leedom. READINGS AND MONOLOGUES OF DISTINCTION. **RM**
Hewitt, Geof. QUICKLY AGING HERE. **QAH**
Hibbard, Addison. LYRIC SOUTH, THE. **LS ***
Hieatt, A. Kent. COLLEGE ANTHOLOGY OF BRITISH AND AMERICAN VERSE, THE. **CABA**
Higham, T. F. OXFORD BOOK OF GREEK VERSE IN TRANSLATION, THE. **OxBG**
Hill, Caroline Miles. WORLD'S GREAT RELIGIOUS POETRY, THE. **WGRP**
Hill, Frank Ernest. WINGED HORSE ANTHOLOGY, THE. **WHA**
Hill, Helen. NEW COASTS AND STRANGE HARBORS. **NCSH**
Hindley, Winifred. WEALTH OF POETRY, A. **WePo**
Hine, Al. FROM OTHER LANDS. **FOL**
———. THIS LAND IS MINE. **ThLM**
Hix, Melvin. APPROVED SELECTIONS FOR READING & MEMORIZING. **ASR 1-2**
Hoagland, Kathleen. 1000 YEARS OF IRISH POETRY. **OnYI**
Hodnett, Edward. POEMS TO READ ALOUD. **PoRA**
Hohn, Max T. STORIES IN VERSE. **SIV**
Holland, Rupert Sargent. HISTORIC POEMS AND BALLADS. **HPB**
Hollander, John. WIND AND THE RAIN, THE. **WiR**
Holliday, Robert Coates. JOYCE KILMER. **JK 1-2**
Hollowell, Lillian. BOOK OF CHILDREN'S LITERATURE, A. **BoChLi**
Holmes, Alice. HOLMES'S VERY LITTLE DIALOGUES. **HYD**
Holmes, John. LITTLE TREASURY OF LOVE POEMS, A. **LiTL**
Honey, William Bowyer. BROADWAY BOOK OF ENGLISH VERSE, THE. **BrBE**
Honig, Edwin. MAJOR METAPHYSICAL POETS OF THE NINETEENTH CENTURY, THE. **MaMe**
Hoopes, Robert. TUDOR POETRY AND PROSE. **TuPP**
Hope, Ronald. HARRAP BOOK OF SEA VERSE, THE. **HaSV**
Hopkins, Kenneth. POETS LAUREATE, THE. **PoLa**
Hopkins, Lee Bennett. TAKE HOLD! **TH**

Hopkins, Mary. GYPSY TRAIL. **GT, GT-2**
Horan, Mrs. Kenneth. PARNASSUS EN ROUTE. **PER**
Horder, W. Garrett. TREASURY OF AMERICAN SACRED SONG. **TAS**
Houghton, Walter E. VICTORIAN POETRY AND POETICS. **ViPP**
Housman, John E. BRITISH POPULAR BALLADS. **BrPB**
Hovde, Louise. CRADLE BOOK OF VERSE, THE. **CBV** *
Howard, Clarence J. HOWARD'S RECITATIONS. **HR**
Howe, Florence. NO MORE MASKS! **NMM**
Howe, George. ROMAN LITERATURE IN TRANSLATION. **RoL**
Hubbard, Alice. GOLDEN FLUTE, THE. **GFA**
Hubbell, Jay B. INTRODUCTION TO POETRY, AN. **InP**
Huber, Miriam Blanton. POETRY BOOK, THE. **PB 1-9**
———. STORY AND VERSE FOR CHILDREN. **StVeCh**
Hudson, Charles M. ENGLISH LITERATURE. **EnL**
Hudson, Hoyt H. TUDOR POETRY AND PROSE. **TuPP**
Huffard, Grace Thompson. MY POETRY BOOK. **MPB**
Hughes, C. C. GRADED MEMORY SELECTIONS. **GMs**
Hughes, Langston. NEW NEGRO POETS: U. S. A. **NNP**
———. POEMS FROM BLACK AFRICA. **PBA**
———. POETRY OF THE NEGRO, THE, 1746-1970. **PoNe**
Humphrey, Lucy H. POETIC NEW-WORLD, THE. **PNW**
———. POETIC OLD-WORLD, THE. **POW**
Humphries, Rolfe. NEW POEMS BY AMERICAN POETS. **NePoAm, NePoAm-2**
Hunter, Irene. AMERICAN MYSTICAL VERSE. **AMMV**
Huntington, T. W., Jr. TRAVELER'S BOOK OF VERSE, THE. **TBV**
Husted, Helen. LOVE POEMS OF SIX CENTURIES. **LoPS**
Hutchinson, Veronica S. CHIMNEY CORNER POEMS. **CCP**
———. FIRESIDE POEMS. **FPH**
Hyde, William DeWitt. SCHOOL SPEAKER AND READER. **SSR**
Hyett, Florence B. FIFTY CHRISTMAS POEMS FOR CHILDREN. **CPC**
Ibn Sa'id. MOORISH POETRY. **MooP**
Inglis, Fred. ENGLISH POETRY 1550-1660. **EP** **
Ingpen, Roger. ONE THOUSAND POEMS FOR CHILDREN. **OTPC**
Irish, Marie. DAYS WE CELEBRATE, THE. **DWC**
———. GOOD THINGS FOR WASHINGTON & LINCOLN BIRTHDAYS. **GTWL**
Iverson, Lucile. WE BECOME NEW. **WBN**

Jackson, Richard. POPULAR SONGS OF NINETEENTH-CENTURY AMERICA. **PSoN**
Jeffares, A. N. SEVEN CENTURIES OF POETRY. **SeCePo**
Johnson, Burges. LITTLE BOOK OF NECESSARY NONSENSE, A. **LBN**
Johnson, Edgar. TREASURY OF SATIRE, A. **TrS**
Johnson, Francis R. TUDOR POETRY AND PROSE. **TuPP**
Johnson, James Weldon. BOOK OF AMERICAN NEGRO POETRY, THE. **BANP**
———. BOOKS OF AMERICAN NEGRO SPIRITUALS, THE. **BoAN 1-2**
Johnson, Reginald Brimley. BOOK OF BRITISH BALLADS, A. **BBB**
———. POPULAR ENGLISH BALLADS. **PEB 1-4**
Johnson, Wendell Stacy. POETRY ANTHOLOGY, A. **PAn**
Jones, Edna D. PATRIOTIC PIECES OF THE GREAT WAR. **PPGW**
Jones, Frank. SHORTER GOLDEN BOOK OF NARRATIVE VERSE, THE. **ShGrBo**
Jones, LeRoi. BLACK FIRE. **BF**
Jones, Theodoric. GREAT STORY-POEMS. **GSP**
Justice, Donald. CONTEMPORARY FRENCH POETRY. **CoFP**
Kalstone, David. BEGINNING WITH POEMS. **BWP**
Kaplan, Cora. SALT AND BITTER AND GOOD. **SBG**
Kauffman, Donald T. FAVORITE CHRISTIAN POEMS. **FaChP**
———. TREASURY OF RELIGIOUS VERSE, THE. **TRV**
Kaufmann, Walter. TWENTY GERMAN POETS. **TwGP**
Kavanaugh, Mrs. Russell. KAVANAUGH'S COMIC DIALOGUES. **KC**
———. KAVANAUGH'S EXHIBITION RECITER FOR VERY LITTLE CHILDREN. **KER**
———. KAVANAUGH'S HUMOROUS DRAMAS. **KH**
———. KAVANAUGH'S JUVENILE SPEAKER. **KJ**
———. KAVANAUGH'S NEW SPEECHES & DIALOGUES. **KNS**
Keck, Christine M. LITERATURE AND LIFE. **LL 1-4**
Keefe, Mildred Jones. CHORIC INTERLUDES. **ChIn**
Kellogg, Alice M. ARBOR DAY PROGRAM. **ADP** *
———. AUTHOR'S BIRTHDAYS. **AB 1-2**
———. CHRISTMAS ENTERTAINMENTS. **CE**
———. HOW TO CELEBRATE THANKSGIVING & CHRISTMAS. **HCTC**
———. NEW ARBOR DAY EXERCISES. **NAE**

——. NEW YEAR AND MIDWINTER EXERCISES. **NYM**
——. SPRING AND SUMMER SCHOOL ENTERTAINMENTS. **SSSC** *
Kellogg, Amos M. PRACTICAL DIALOGUES. **PDK**
——. PRACTICAL RECITATIONS. **PRK**
——. PRIMARY RECITATIONS. **PyR**
——. PRIMARY SPEAKER. **PyS**
——. SPECIAL DAY EXERCISES. **SDE**
Kelly, Robert. CONTROVERSY OF POETS, A. **CoPo**
Kennedy, Charles O'Brien. TREASURY OF AMERICAN BALLADS, A. **TrAB**
Kennedy, Charles W. ANTHOLOGY OF OLD ENGLISH POETRY, AN. **AnOE**
Kennedy, X. J. INTRODUCTION TO POETRY, AN. **InPK**
——. MESSAGES. **MAT**
Kenner, Hugh. SEVENTEENTH CENTURY POETRY. **SeCP**
Kenseth, Arnold. POEMS OF PROTEST OLD AND NEW. **PPON**
Kermode, Frank. ENGLISH PASTORAL POETRY. **EnPP**
Kerr, William. OFF THE GROUND. **OFG 1-4**
Kessler, Jascha. AMERICAN POEMS. **AmPC**
Kesten, Hermann. BEST OF MODERN EUROPEAN LITERATURE, THE. **BeME**
Kheridan, David. SETTLING AMERICA. **SA** *
Kidd, Robert. KIDD'S NEW ELOCUTION & VOCAL CULTURE. **KNE**
Kieran, John. POEMS I REMEMBER. **PIR**
Kilby, Clyde S. POETRY AND LIFE. **PoeLi**
Kilman, Theodore. NOW VOICES, THE. **NowV**
Kilmer, Joyce. JOYCE KILMER. **JK 1-2**
——. JOYCE KILMER'S ANTHOLOGY OF CATHOLIC POETS. **JKCP**
King, Marie B. MAGIC WORLD, A. **MW**
——. VERSE OF OUR DAY. **VOD**
King, Vernon Rupert. TODAY'S LITERATURE. **TL** *
Kingston, E. F. OLD POEMS AND NEW VERSE. **OIPN**
——. POEMS TO REMEMBER. **PoTR**
Kinsley, James. ENGLISH SATIRIC POETRY. **ESaP**
——. OXFORD BOOK OF BALLADS, THE. **OxBB**
Kipling, Rudyard. RUDYARD KIPLING'S VERSE, 1885-1932. **RKV**
Kirk, Richard Ray. INTRODUCTION TO THE STUDY OF POETRY, AN. **ISP**

Kirk, Rudolf. TYPES OF ENGLISH POETRY. **TyEnPo**
Kirschner, Allen. VOICES OF POETRY. **VoPo**
Kisch, Sir Cecil. WAGGON OF LIFE, THE, & OTHER LYRICS BY RUSSIAN POETS OF THE NINETEENTH CENTURY. **WaL**
Kittredge, George Lyman. ENGLISH AND SCOTTISH POPULAR BALLADS. **ESPB**
Kleiser, Grenville. HUMOROUS HITS & HOW TO HOLD AN AUDIENCE. **HHHA**
Klemer, D. J. CHINESE LOVE POEMS. **ChLP**
———. MODERN LOVE POEMS. **MoLP**
Knight, Joseph. PIPE AND POUCH. **PPh**
Knowles, Frederic Lawrence. CAP AND GOWN; 2d series. **CG-2**
———. GOLDEN TREASURY OF AMERICAN SONGS & LYRICS. **ASL**
———. TREASURY OF HUMOROUS POETRY, A. **THP**
———. YEAR BOOK OF FAMOUS LYRICS. **YBF**
———. See Paget, R. L. (pseud.)
Knudson, R. R. SPORTS POEMS. **SPo**
Konek, Carol. I HEAR MY SISTERS SAYING. **IHMS**
Korson, George. COAL DUST ON THE FIDDLE. **CoDuFi**
———. MINSTRELS OF THE MINE PATCH. **MiMiPa**
Kreymborg, Alfred. ANTHOLOGY OF AMERICAN POETRY, AN. **AnAmPo**
———. LYRIC AMERICA. **LA**
Krige, Uys. PENGUIN BOOK OF SOUTH AFRICAN VERSE, THE. **PeSA**
Kroeber, Karl. STUDYING POETRY. **StP**
Kronenberger, Louis. ANTHOLOGY OF LIGHT VERSE, AN. **ALV**
La Moille, T. G. FAVORITE SPEAKER, THE. **FS**
La Palice, Cecily. See Mackworth, Cecily (pseud.)
Laird, Alma. COMPLETE GEORGE WASHINGTON ANNIVERSARY PROGRAMS. **CWAP**
Lamb, Charles. LAMB'S POETRY FOR CHILDREN. **LPC**
Lamb, Mary. LAMB'S POETRY FOR CHILDREN. **LPC**
Lamont, Corliss. MAN ANSWERS DEATH. **MaAnDe**
Lamson, Roy. RENAISSANCE ENGLAND. **ReEn**
Lang, Andrew. BALLADS OF BOOKS. **LBB**
———. BLUE POETRY BOOK. **BPB**
Langland, Joseph. POET'S CHOICE. **PoCH**
Lapides, Frederick. POETRY AND ITS CONVENTIONS. **PAIC**

Lapolla, Garibaldi M. JUNIOR ANTHOLOGY OF WORLD POETRY, A. **JAWP**
——. WORLD'S BEST POEMS, THE. **WBP**
Larcom, Lucy. CHILDHOOD SONGS. **LCS**
Larkin, Philip. OXFORD BOOK OF TWENTIETH-CENTURY ENGLISH VERSE, THE. **OxBTC**
Larrick, Nancy. CRAZY TO BE ALIVE IN SUCH A STRANGE WORLD. **CTBA**
——. ON CITY STREETS. **OCS**
——. PIPING DOWN THE VALLEYS WILD. **PDV**
——. ROOM FOR ME AND A MOUNTAIN LION. **RFM**
Lask, Thomas. NEW YORK TIMES BOOK OF VERSE, THE. **NYTB**
Laughlin, James. WREATH OF CHRISTMAS POEMS, A. **WrChPo**
Lawson, James Gilchrist. BEST LOVED RELIGIOUS POEMS, THE. **BLRP**
——. WORLD'S BEST-LOVED POEMS, THE. **WBLP**
Le Gallienne, Richard. LE GALLIENNE BOOK OF ENGLISH & AMERICAN POETRY, THE. **LEAP**
Le Row, Caroline B. PIECES FOR EVERY OCCASION. **PEOR**
Leach, Henry Goddard. PAGEANT OF OLD SCANDINAVIA, A. **PaOS**
Leach, MacEdward. BALLAD BOOK, THE. **BaBo**
Learned, Walter. TREASURY OF AMERICAN VERSE. **TAV** *
Leary, Paris. CONTROVERSY OF POETS, A. **CoPo**
Leavens, Mary Agnes. GREAT COMPANIONS. **GrCo 1-2**
Leavens, Robert French. GREAT COMPANIONS. **GrCo 1-2**
Leggett, Glenn. 12 POETS. **TwP**
Lehmann, John. CHATTO BOOK OF MODERN POETRY, THE, 1915-1955. **ChMP**
Leonard, Robert Maynard. BOOK OF LIGHT VERSE, A. **BLV**
Leslie, Shane. ANTHOLOGY OF CATHOLIC POETS, AN. **ACP**
Lewis, Arthur O., Jr. CASE FOR POETRY, THE. **CaFP**
Lewis, Claude E. POEMS WORTH KNOWING. **PoWorKn**
Lewis, Leslie L. INTRODUCTION TO LITERATURE: POETRY. **ILP**
Lieberman, Elias. POEMS FOR ENJOYMENT. **PFE**
——. POETRY FOR JUNIOR HIGH SCHOOLS. **PJH 1-2**
Lieder, Paul Robert. EMINENT BRITISH POETS OF THE NINETEENTH CENTURY. **EmBrPo**
Lincoln, Joseph Crosby. CAPE COD BALLADS. **CCB**
Lind, L. R. LATIN POETRY IN VERSE TRANSLATION. **LaP**
——. LYRIC POETRY OF THE ITALIAN RENAISSANCE. **LyPI**

Lindsay, Jack. RUSSIAN POETRY, 1917-1955. **RuPo**
Lindsay, Vachel. COLLECTED POEMS. **CPL** *
——. EVERY SOUL IS A CIRCUS. **ESCL**
Lingenfelter, Richard E. SONGS OF THE GOLD RUSH, THE. **SGR**
Linn, S. Pollock. GOLDEN GLEAMS OF THOUGHT. **GG**
Livingston, Myra Cohn. LISTEN, CHILDREN, LISTEN. **LCL**
——. O FRABJOUS DAY! **OFD**
——. ONE LTTLE ROOM, AN EVERYWHERE. **OLR**
——. SPEAK ROUGHLY TO YOUR LITTLE BOY. **SpRo**
Lloyd, Noel. ROUND ABOUT EIGHT. **RAE**
Lomax, Alan. AMERICAN BALLADS AND FOLK SONGS. **ABF**
——. COWBOY SONGS AND OTHER FRONTIER BALLADS. **CoSo**
——. OUR SINGING COUNTRY. **OuSiCo**
——. 3000 YEARS OF BLACK POETRY. **TTY**
Lomax, John A. AMERICAN BALLADS AND FOLK SONGS. **ABF**
——. COWBOY SONGS AND OTHER FRONTIER BALLADS. **CSF & CoSo**
——. OUR SINGING COUNTRY. **OuSiCo**
——. SONGS OF THE CATTLE TRAIL AND COW CAMP. **SCC**
Long, Augustus White. AMERICAN POEMS (1776-1922). **APL**
——. ENGLISH POEMS FROM CHAUCER TO KIPLING. **EPC**
Longworth, Alice Roosevelt. DESK DRAWER ANTHOLOGY, THE. **DDA**
Loomis, Roger Sherman. MEDIEVAL ENGLISH VERSE AND PROSE, IN MODERNIZED VERSIONS. **MeEV**
Lord, Russell. VOICES FROM THE FIELDS. **VF**
Lord, William Sinclair. BEST SHORT POEMS OF THE NINETEENTH CENTURY. **BSP**
——. THIS IS FOR YOU. **TFY**
Lounsbury, Thomas R. YALE BOOK OF AMERICAN VERSE. **YBV**
Love, Harold. PENGUIN BOOK OF RESTORATION VERSE, THE. **PeRV**
Love, Katherine. LITTLE LAUGHTER, A. **LiL**
——. POCKETFUL OF RHYMES, A. **PoRh**
Lovejoy, Mary I. NATURE IN VERSE. **NV**
——. PIECES FOR EVERY MONTH OF THE YEAR. **PEM**
——. POETRY OF THE SEASONS. **POS**
Lovett, Sidney. YALE CAROL BOOK, THE. **YaCaBo**

Lowenfels, Walter. POETS OF TODAY. **PtTo**
———. WRITING ON THE WALL, THE. **WOW**
Lowry, Howard Foster. OXFORD ANTHOLOGY OF ENGLISH POETRY, AN. **OAEP**
Lucas, Edward Verrall. ANOTHER BOOK OF VERSE FOR CHILDREN. **ABVC**
———. BOOK OF VERSES FOR CHILDREN, A. **BVC**
———. FRIENDLY TOWN, THE. **FT**
———. OPEN ROAD, THE. **OR**
Lucas, F. L. GREEK POETRY FOR EVERYMAN. **GrPE**
Lucas, Harriet Marcelia. PROSE AND POETRY OF TODAY. **PrPoTo**
Luccock, Halford E. QUESTING SPIRIT, THE. **QS**
Lucie-Smith, Edward. HOLDING YOUR EIGHT HANDS. **HYE**
Lyman, William Whittingham. TODAY'S LITERATURE. **TL** *
Lynch, William S. POET TO POET. **PtP**
Lyons, John O. STUDYING POETRY. **StP**
Lyons, Nellie. READING OF POETRY, THE. **RePo**
Mabie, Hamilton Wright. BOOK OF CHRISTMAS, THE. **BOC**
———. OLD ENGLISH BALLADS. **OEB**
———. OLD ENGLISH LOVE SONGS. **OEL**
McAllister, C. B. FIFTEEN YEARS FROM THE LANTERN. **FiYeLa**
———. POEMS–1940 FROM "THE LANTERN." **PoNiLa**
McAuley, James. MAP OF AUSTRALIAN VERSE, A. **MAuV**
MacBain, Jeannie Murray. BOOK OF A THOUSAND POEMS, THE. **BoTP**
MacBeth, George. PENGUIN BOOK OF VICTORIAN VERSE, THE. **PeVV**
McBride, H. Elliott. ALL KINDS OF DIALOGUES. **MAD**
———. COMIC SPEECHES AND RECITATIONS. **MCS**
———. HUMOROUS DIALOGUES. **MHD**
———. LATEST DIALOGUES. **MBD**
———. McBRIDE'S CHOICE DIALECTS. **MC**
———. McBRIDE'S COMIC DIALOGUES. **MCD**
———. McBRIDE'S FUNNY DIALOGUES. **MFD**
———. McBRIDE'S NEW DIALOGUES. **MND**
———. McBRIDE'S TEMPERANCE DIALOGUES. **MTD**
McCarrick, Elizabeth. HIGHDAYS AND HOLIDAYS. **HH**
McCaskey, John Piersol. LINCOLN LITERARY COLLECTION. **LLC**
McClelland, George William. ENGLISH LITERATURE. **EnLit**

McClure, Norman E. SIXTEENTH-CENTURY ENGLISH POETRY. SiCE
McClymonds, J. W. GRADED MEMORY SELECTIONS. GMs
McCord, David. WHAT CHEER. WhC
McCracken, Elizabeth. TO MOTHER. TM
McCullough, Joseph B. VOICES FROM WAH'KON-TAH. VW
McCutcheon, Roger Philip. INTRODUCTION TO THE STUDY OF POETRY, AN. ISP
MacDiarmid, Hugh, (pseud.) [i.e., Christopher Murray Grieve]. GOLDEN TREASURY OF SCOTTISH POETRY, THE. GoTS
MacDonagh, Donagh. OXFORD BOOK OF IRISH VERSE, THE. OxBI
MacDonald, Dwight. PARODIES. Par
McDonald, Gerald D. WAY OF KNOWING, A. WaKn
MacDonald, W. L. POEMS, CHIEFLY NARRATIVE. PCN
MacDonald, William. LAMB'S POETRY FOR CHILDREN. LPC
McDonough, Mary Lou. POET PHYSICIANS. PoP
McGhee, Paul A. MAGIC CASEMENTS. MCCG
———. THROUGH MAGIC CASEMENTS. TMC
McHale, Frank. PIECES THAT HAVE WON PRIZES. PTWP
Mack, Anna E. BECAUSE I LOVE YOU. BIL
———. FOR HIS SAKE. FHS
———. HEAVEN'S DISTANT LAMPS. HDL
Mack, Maynard. SOUNDS AND SILENCES. SS
Mackay, David. FLOCK OF WORDS, A. FlW
MacKenzie, Richard Charlton. NEW HOME BOOK OF BEST LOVED POEMS, THE. NeHB
———. OLD FAVORITE SONGS AND HYMNS. OlF
Mackenzie, W. Roy. BALLADS AND SEA SONGS FROM NOVA SCOTIA. BSNS
Mackie, R. L. BOOK OF SCOTTISH VERSE, A. BSV
McKillop, Alan D. EIGHTEENTH CENTURY POETRY AND PROSE. EiPP
Mackworth, Cecily, (pseud.) [i.e., Cecily De Chabannes La Palice]. MIRROR FOR FRENCH POETRY, A, 1840–1940. MiFP
McMahon, Michael. FLOWERING AFTER FROST. FAF
McNaught, Rosamond Livingstone. CHRISTMAS SELECTIONS FOR READING AND RECITATIONS. CS
McNeil, Horace J. POEMS FOR A MACHINE AGE. PoMa
MacQueen, John. OXFORD BOOK OF SCOTTISH VERSE, THE. OxBS

Main, C. F. COLLEGE BOOK OF VERSE, A. **CBV**
Major, Clarence. NEW BLACK POETRY, THE. **NBP**
Major, William Montgomery. OVER ONE HUNDRED FAMOUS POEMS & THE ENTERTAINMENT SPEAKER. **OFPE**
Malone, Ted, (pseud.) [i.e., F. A. Russell]. YANKEE DOODLES. **YaD**
Manchester, Frederick A. HARPER'S ANTHOLOGY: POETRY. **HAP**
Manly, John Matthews. ENGLISH POETRY (1170-1892). **EP *****
———. ENGLISH PROSE AND POETRY. **EPP**
Mann, Klaus. BEST OF MODERN EUROPEAN LITERATURE, THE, 1920-1940. **BeME**
Manner, Janet. SILVER TREASURY, THE. **ST**
Manning-Sanders, Ruth. BUNDLE OF BALLADS, A. **BuBa**
Markham, Edwin. BOOK OF AMERICAN POETRY, THE. **BAP**
———. BOOK OF CLASSIC ENGLISH POETRY, THE, 600-1830. **BCEP**
———. BOOK OF MODERN ENGLISH POETRY, THE. **BMEP**
———. BOOK OF POETRY, THE. **MBOP, MBOP-2**
———. POETRY OF YOUTH. **PYM**
Marsh, E. H. GEORGIAN POETRY, 1911-1912. **GnP-1**
———. GEORGIAN POETRY, 1913-1915. **GnP-2**
Marshall, Carol. TWENTIETH CENTURY POETRY. **TCP ***
Marshall, Shirley E. YOUNG AMERICAN'S TREASURY OF ENGLISH POETRY, A. **YAT**
Marshall, William H. MAJOR ENGLISH ROMANTIC POETS, THE. **MERP**
———. MAJOR VICTORIAN POETS, THE. **MaVP**
Marsland, Cora. INTERPRETIVE READING. **IR**
Martin, Robert Bernard. VICTORIAN POETRY. **VP ***
Martin, Robert Grant. BOOK OF ENGLISH LITERATURE, A. **BEL**
Martine, Arthur. MARTINE'S DROLL DIALOGUES & LAUGHABLE RECITATIONS. **MDD**
Martz, Louis L. ANCHOR ANTHOLOGY OF SEVENTEENTH CENTURY VERSE, THE. **AnAnS 1-2**
———. MEDITATIVE POEM, THE. **MeP**
Masefield, John. MY FAVOURITE ENGLISH POEMS. **MtFE**
———. POEMS. **PM**
———. SAILOR'S GARLAND, A. **SG**
Matthews, Brander. AMERICAN FAMILIAR VERSE. **AFV**
———. BALLADS OF BOOKS. **MBB**

Matthews, Brander (cont.)
——. POEMS OF AMERICAN PATRIOTISM. **PAP**
Matthias, John. TWENTY-THREE MODERN BRITISH POETS. **TwMBP**
Matthiessen, F. O. OXFORD BOOK OF AMERICAN VERSE, THE. **OxBA**
Maud, Ralph. DYLAN THOMAS'S CHOICE. **DTC**
Maynard, Theodore. BOOK OF MODERN CATHOLIC VERSE, THE. **BMC**
Mead, C. David. INTRODUCING POEMS. **IPWM**
Mecklenburger, James. SINCE FEELING IS FIRST. **SFF**
Mellor, Bernard. WAYSIDE POEMS OF THE EARLY EIGHTEENTH CENTURY. **WaPE**
Merrifield, Fred. MODERN RELIGIOUS VERSE AND PROSE. **MRV**
Merrill, A. Marion. CONTEMPORARY VERSE. **CV**
Meserole, Harrison T. SEVENTEENTH-CENTURY AMERICAN POETRY. **SCAP**
Messenger, N. P. VICTORIAN POETRY. **VPC**
Metcalf, John Calvin. ENCHANTED YEARS, THE. **EY**
Meyer, Frank S. BREATHES THERE THE MAN. **BTTM**
Meynell, Sir Francis. MEMORABLE POETRY. **MemP**
Mezey, Robert. NAKED POETRY. **NaP**
Middleton, Christopher. MODERN GERMAN POETRY, 1910-1960. **MGP**
Middlebrook, Samuel. ENGLISH LITERATURE AND ITS BACKGROUNDS. **EnLi 1-2**
Mikels, Rosa M. R. POETRY OF TO-DAY. **PT**
Miles, Dudley. LITERATURE AND LIFE. **LL 1-4**
Miles, Josephine. POEM, THE. **Po**
Milford, H. S. OXFORD BOOK OF REGENCY VERSE, THE, 1798-1837. **OBRV**
Millay, Edna St. Vincent. BUCK IN THE SNOW. **BIS**
——. CONVERSATION AT MIDNIGHT. **CMM**
——. FATAL INTERVIEW. **FIM**
——. FEW FIGS FROM THISTLES, A. **FFTM**
——. HARP-WEAVER, THE. **HWM**
——. RENASCENCE AND OTHER POEMS. **RM** *
——. SECOND APRIL. **SAM**
——. WINE FROM THESE GRAPES. **WFG**
Miller, Basil. BEAUTIFUL POEMS ON JESUS. **BePJ**
Miller, G. M. THUDDING DRUMS. **ThDr**
Miller, James E. DIMENSIONS OF POETRY, THE. **DiPo**

Miller, Perry. MAJOR WRITERS OF AMERICA. **MWA 1-2**
Mills, Queenie. SOUND OF POETRY, THE. **SoPo**
Mitchell, Wilmot Brookings. SCHOOL AND COLLEGE SPEAKER. **SC**
Mollenkott, Virginia R. ADAM AMONG THE TELEVISION TREES. **AATT**
Monroe, Harriet. NEW POETRY, THE. **NP** *
Monroe, Lewis B. DIALOGUES AND DRAMAS. **MPD**
——. HUMOROUS READINGS. **MHR**
——. MISCELLANEOUS READINGS. **MMR**
——. YOUNG FOLKS' READINGS. **MYF**
Montague, John. BOOK OF IRISH VERSE, THE. **BIrV**
Montheith, Augusta. PINK BOOK OF VERSE, THE. **PBV**
Montgomery, David Henry. HEROIC BALLADS. **HB**
Montgomery, Whitney. ROAD TO TEXAS, THE. **RoTe**
Moore, Chauncy O. BALLADS AND FOLK SONGS OF THE SOUTHWEST. **BFSS**
Moore, Ethel. BALLADS AND FOLK SONGS OF THE SOUTHWEST. **BFSS**
Moore, Lilian. CATCH YOUR BREATH. **CaYB**
——. TO SEE THE WORLD AFRESH. **TSWA**
Moore, T. Inglis. POETRY IN AUSTRALIA: Vol. 1. **PoAu-1**
Morehead, Albert. BEST LOVED SONGS AND HYMNS. **BLSH**
Morehead, James. BEST LOVED SONGS AND HYMNS. **BLSH**
Morgan, Anna. SELECTED READINGS. **SR**
Morgan, Edwin. COLLINS ALBATROSS BOOK OF LONGER POEMS. **CABL**
Morpurgo, Michael. LIVING POETS. **LP**
Morris, Joseph, (pseud.) [i.e., Joseph Morris Bachelor]. BOOK OF BABY VERSE, THE. **BBV**
——. BOOK OF FRIENDSHIP VERSE, THE. **BFV**
——. BOOK OF MOTHER VERSE, THE. **BMV**
——. FACING FORWARD. **FF**
——. IT CAN BE DONE. **ICBD**
——. LIGHT OF THE WORLD. **LOW** *
——. POEMS OF INSPIRATION. **POI**
——. SILVER LININGS. **SL**
Morrison, James Dalton. MASTERPIECES OF RELIGIOUS VERSE. **MaRV**
Morrison, Lillian. SPRINTS AND DISTANCES. **SD**
Morse, David. GRANDFATHER ROCK. **GrRo**
Morton, David. SHORTER MODERN POEMS, 1900-1931. **SMP**

Morton, Marguerite W. IDEAL DRILLS. **ID**
Moult, Thomas. BEST POEMS OF 1922, 1923, 1924, 1926, 1930, 1931, 1932, 1933, 1934, 1935, 1936, 1937. **MBP 22-26, BPM 30-37**
Muir, Kenneth. ELIZABETHAN LYRICS. **ElLy**
Munsterberg, Margarete. HARVEST OF GERMAN VERSE, A. **HGV**
Murdoch, Walter. BOOK OF AUSTRALIAN & NEW ZEALAND VERSE, A. **BoAu**
Murdock, James Edward. ANALYTICAL ELOCUTION. **AE ***
Murphy, Beatrice M. EBONY RHYTHM. **EbR**
———. TODAY'S NEGRO VOICES. **TNV**
Murphy, Charles Theophilus. GREEK LITERATURE IN TRANSLATION. **GrL**
Murphy, Francis. MAJOR AMERICAN POETS TO 1914. **MAmP**
Murphy, Gwendolen. MODERN POET, THE. **MoP**
Nabokov, Vladimir. THREE RUSSIAN POETS. **ThRuPo**
Nash, Ogden. EVERYBODY OUGHT TO KNOW. **EvOK**
———. MOON IS SHINING BRIGHT AS DAY. **MoShBr**
National Publishing Co. PROGRESSIVE SPEAKER, THE. **PS**
Neal, Larry. BLACK FIRE. **BF**
Nelson, John Herbert. CHIEF MODERN POETS OF ENGLAND & AMERICA. **ChMO, CMoP, CMP**
Neville, Henry G. VOICE, SPEECH, & GESTURE. **VSG**
New Yorker, The (periodical). NEW YORKER BOOK OF POEMS, THE. **NYBP**
———. NEW YORKER BOOK OF VERSE, THE. **NYBV**
Newbolt, Henry. ENGLISH ANTHOLOGY OF PROSE AND POETRY, AN. **EA ***
Newcomer, Alphonso Gerald. THREE CENTURIES OF AMERICAN POETRY & PROSE. **TCAP**
———. TWELVE CENTURIES OF ENGLISH POETRY & PROSE. **TCEP**
Newell, L. H. POETRY FOR SENIOR STUDENTS. **PoSS**
Niatum, Duane. CARRIERS OF THE DREAM WHEEL. **CDW**
Nicholl, Louise Townsend. GOLDEN YEAR, THE. **GoYe**
Ninomiya, Takamichi. POETRY OF LIVING JAPAN, THE. **PoLJ**
Norman, Charles. COME LIVE WITH ME. **CLWM**
Northrop, Henry Davenport. DELSARTE SPEAKER, THE. **DS**
———. NEW POPULAR SPEAKER. **NPS**
———. PEERLESS RECITER. **PR**
———. YOUNG AMERICAN'S SPEAKER. **YA**

―――. YOUNG PEOPLE'S SPEAKER. **YP**
Norton, Robert. ETERNAL PASSION IN ENGLISH POETRY. **EtPaEn**
Noyes, Alfred. BOOK OF EARTH. **BEN**
―――. COLLECTED POEMS. **CPAN 1-3**
―――. DICK TURPIN'S RIDE AND OTHER POEMS. **DTRN**
―――. GOLDEN BOOK OF CATHOLIC POETRY, THE. **GoBC**
―――. LAST VOYAGE, THE. **LVN**
―――. WATCHERS OF THE SKY. **WSN**
Noyes, Russell. ENGLISH ROMANTIC POETRY AND PROSE. **EnRP**
Nunney, May Gertrude. COMPLETE HOLIDAY PROGRAM, A. **CHP**
Oates, Whitney Jennings. GREEK LITERATURE IN TRANSLATION. **GrL**
O'Clair, Robert. NORTON ANTHOLOGY OF MODERN POETRY, THE. **NoAM**
O'Connor, Frank, (pseud.) [i.e., Michael O'Donovan]. KINGS, LORDS, & COMMONS. **KiLC**
O'Connor, William Van. POEMS FOR STUDY. **PoFS**
O'Donnell, Margaret J. ANTHOLOGY OF COMMONWEALTH VERSE, AN. **ACV**
―――. ANTHOLOGY OF CONTEMPORARY VERSE, AN. **AnCV**
O'Faolain, Sean. SILVER BRANCH, THE. **SiB**
O'Keefe, John A. JUNIOR HIGH SCHOOL POETRY. **JHP**
Olcott, Frances Jenkins. STORY-TELLING BALLADS. **STB**
―――. STORY-TELLING POEMS. **STP** *
Olds, Barbara Moses. FAVORITE POEMS OF FAITH AND COMFORT. **FaPoFa**
Olney, Marguerite. BALLADS MIGRANT IN NEW ENGLAND. **BaMNE**
Olrik, Axel. BOOK OF DANISH BALLADS, A. **BoDaBa**
Olson, Elder. AMERICAN LYRIC POEMS. **AmLP**
O'Neill, Anna Theodora Lee. RECITATIONS FOR ASSEMBLY & CLASSROOM. **RAC**
Opie, Iona. OXFORD BOOK OF CHILDREN'S VERSE, THE. **OxBChV**
―――. OXFORD NURSERY RHYME BOOK, THE. **OxNR**
Opie, Peter. OXFORD BOOK OF CHILDREN'S VERSE, THE. **OxBChV**
―――. OXFORD NURSERY RHYME BOOK, THE. **OxNR**
Orel, Harold. BRITISH POETRY 1880-1920. **BrPo**

F. A. Owen Publishing Company. POEMS TEACHERS ASK FOR. **PTA 1-2**
Pace, George B. ENGLISH LITERATURE. **EnL**
Pack, Robert. NEW POETS OF ENGLAND AND AMERICA. **NEPoEA, NePoEA-2**
——. POEMS OF DOUBT AND BELIEF. **PoDB**
Padgett, Ron. ANTHOLOGY OF NEW YORK POETS, AN. **ANYP**
Page, Charles Hidden. BRITISH POETS OF THE NINETEENTH CENTURY. **BPN**
——. CHIEF AMERICAN POETS, THE. **CAP**
Paget, R. L., (pseud.) [i.e., Frederic Lawrence Knowles]. CAP & GOWN; 3d series. **CG-3**
——. CAP & GOWN; 4th series. **CAG**
——. POEMS OF AMERICAN PATRIOTISM. **PAPm**
——. POETRY OF AMERICAN WIT & HUMOR, THE. **AWH**
——. See Knowles, Frederic Lawrence for additional works.
Painter, Franklin V. N. POETS OF THE SOUTH. **PSh**
Palgrave, Francis Turner. GOLDEN TREASURY OF THE BEST SONGS & LYRICAL POEMS IN THE ENGLISH LANGUAGE, THE. **GTBS-D, GTBS-P, GTSE, GTBS**
——. GOLDEN TREASURY OF SONGS & LYRICS, THE. **GTSL**
Palmer, Geoffrey. ROUND ABOUT EIGHT. **RAE**
Pancoast, Henry S. STANDARD ENGLISH POEMS. **SEP**
——. VISTA OF ENGLISH VERSE. **VE**
Paris, Mrs. John Walton. GARDEN BOOK OF VERSE, THE. **GBOV**
Park, William. COLLEGE ANTHOLOGY OF BRITISH & AMERICAN VERSE, THE. **CABA**
Parker, Elinor. FOUR SEASONS FIVE SENSES. **FSFS**
——. HERE AND THERE. **HT** *
——. 100 MORE STORY POEMS. **MSP**
——. 100 POEMS ABOUT PEOPLE. **OnPP**
——. 100 STORY POEMS. **OnSP**
——. SINGING AND THE GOLD, THE. **SiGo**
Parker, Kathleen B. HARRAP BOOK OF MODERN VERSE, THE. **HaMV**
Parks, Edd Winfield. SOUTHERN POETS. **SPP**
Parrott, Thomas Marc. ENGLISH POEMS FROM CHAUCER TO KIPLING. **EPC**
——. POETRY OF THE TRANSITION, 1850-1914. **POTT**
Parsley, Cleo M. FATHER. **FAOV**

Parsons, Eugene. FAVORITE SPEAKER, THE. **FS**
Parsons, I. M. MEN WHO MARCH AWAY. **MMA**
Parton, James. HUMOROUS POETRY OF THE ENGLISH LANGUAGE, THE. **HPE**
Parton, Jessie. AMERICAN LYRICS. **AL**
Pasmantier, Jeanne. ANTHOLOGY OF SPANISH LITERATURE IN ENGLISH TRANSLATION, AN. **AnSpL 1-2**
Pater, Alan F. ANTHOLOGY OF MAGAZINE VERSE FOR: 1935, 1936, 1937, & 1938-1942, & YEARBOOKS OF AMERICAN POETRY. **AMV-35, AMV-36, AMV-37, AnMaVe**
Patmore, Coventry. CHILDREN'S GARLAND, THE. **CG**
Pattee, Fred Lewis. CENTURY READINGS FOR A COURSE IN AMERICAN LITERATURE. **CRAL**
Patterson, Elizabeth B. SAINT FRANCIS AND THE POET. **SaFP**
Paul, Harry G. ATLANTIC PROSE AND POETRY. **APP**
———. ENGLISH POEMS. **EhP**
Paulmier, Hilah. ROOSEVELT DAY. **RDAH**
Paxton, Joseph Francis. OKLAHOMA ANTHOLOGY FOR 1929, THE. **OA**
Payne, Robert. WHITE PONY, THE. **WhP**
Paz, Octavio. ANTHOLOGY OF MEXICAN POETRY. **AnMP**
Peacock, W. ENGLISH VERSE. **EV 1-5**
Pearson, Norman Holmes. POETS OF THE ENGLISH LANGUAGE. **PoEL 1-5**
Pearson, Paul M. HUMOROUS SPEAKER, THE. **HSP**
———. SPEAKER, THE. **SPE 1-8**
Peattie, Elia W. POEMS YOU OUGHT TO KNOW. **PYO**
Peck, Richard. MINDSCAPES. **MiP**
Penn Publishing Company, The. EASY ENTERTAINMENTS FOR YOUNG PEOPLE. **EE**
———. EUREKA ENTERTAINMENTS. **EuE**
———. PROSE & POETRY FOR YOUNG PEOPLE. **PPYP**
Pentz, Croft M. SPEAKER'S TREASURY OF 400 QUOTABLE POEMS, THE. **STF**
Percival, M. O. POETRY OF THE NINETIES. **PON**
Perkins, Agnes. NEW COASTS AND STRANGE HARBORS. **NCSH**
Perrine, Laurence. SOUND AND SENSE. **SoSe**
Persons, Eleanor Alice. OUR COUNTRY IN POEM AND PROSE. **OCP**

Pertwee, Ernest. RECITER'S TREASURY OF VERSE, THE. **RTV**
Pertwee, Ernest Guy. RECITER'S TREASURY OF IRISH VERSE & PROSE, THE. **RTI**
——. RECITER'S TREASURY OF SCENES & POEMS, THE. **ReTS**
Peter Pauper Press, The. PATRIOTIC ANTHOLOGY, A. **PaAn**
Peterson, Houston. POET TO POET. **PtP**
Phelps, William Lyon. MOTHERS' ANTHOLOGY, THE. **MotAn**
——. WHAT I LIKE IN POETRY. **WLIP**
Philbrick, Charles H. VARIETY OF POETRY, THE. **VaPo**
Phillips, Robert. MOONSTRUCK. **Moon**
Pierce, Lorne. CANADIAN POETRY IN ENGLISH. **CaP**
——. OUR CANADIAN LITERATURE. **OCL**
Pinto, Vivian de Sola. COMMON MUSE, THE. **CoMu**
——. RESTORATION CARNIVAL. **ReC**
Pitcher, Seymour M. TWO CREATIVE TRADITIONS IN ENGLISH POETRY. **TwCrTr**
Platt, H. G. ONE HUNDRED AND TEN FAVORITE CHILDREN'S POEMS. **OnHT**
Plotz, Helen. AS I WALKED OUT ONE EVENING. **AIW**
——. EARTH IS THE LORD'S, THE. **EaLo**
——. IMAGINATION'S OTHER PLACE. **ImOP**
——. MARVELOUS LIGHT, THE. **ML**
——. UNTUNE THE SKY. **UnS**
Poetry Society of Southern California, The. LOOK TO THIS DAY. **LoDa**
Pool, Phoebe. POEMS OF DEATH. **PoD**
Pooley, Robert C. LITERATURE AND LIFE. **LL 1-4**
Potter, Cora Urquhart. MY RECITATIONS. **MR**
Poulin, A., Jr. CONTEMPORARY AMERICAN POETRY. **CAPP**
Pound, Ezra. CONFUCIUS TO CUMMINGS. **CTC**
Pound, Louise. AMERICAN BALLADS AND SONGS. **ABS**
Pratt, E. J. HEROIC TALES IN VERSE. **HeT**
Prescott, Frederick C. INTRODUCTION TO AMERICAN POETRY, AN. **IAP**
Press, John. GOLDEN TREASURY OF THE BEST SONGS & LYRICS IN THE ENGLISH LANGUAGE, THE. **GTBS-P**
Price, Martin. POETRY: PAST & PRESENT. **PPP**
Priest, Harold Martin. RENAISSANCE AND BAROQUE LYRICS. **RBL**
Procter, Leslie C. SELECTIONS FOR PUBLIC SPEAKING. **SPS**

Pucelli, Rodolfo. ANTHOLOGY OF ITALIAN & ITALO-AMERICAN POETRY. **AnIA**
Pyre, J. F. A. CENTURY READINGS IN ENGLISH LITERATURE. **CRE**
———. GREAT ENGLISH POETS. **GEPC**
Quiller-Couch, Arthur T. ENGLISH SONNETS. **ES** *
———. OXFORD BOOK OF BALLADS, THE. **OBB**
———. OXFORD BOOK OF ENGLISH VERSE, THE. **OBEV**
———. OXFORD BOOK OF VICTORIAN VERSE, THE. **OBVV**
Quintana, Ricardo. ENGLISH POETRY OF THE MID & LATE 18th CENTURY. **EnPE**
———. TWO HUNDRED POEMS. **TwHP**
———. SEVENTEENTH-CENTURY VERSE AND PROSE. **SeCV 1-2**
Quiz Kids. QUIZ KIDS' BOOK, THE. **QKB**
Rabb, Kate Milner. NATIONAL EPICS. **NE**
Rackham, Arthur. MOTHER GOOSE NURSERY RHYMES. **MG**
Rainey, Carol. PSYCHE. **Psy**
Rakow, Edwin. LYRIC VERSE. **LV**
Ramal, Walter, (pseud.) [i.e., Walter de la Mare]. SONGS OF CHILDHOOD. **SOC**
Rand, Theodore H. TREASURY OF CANADIAN VERSE. **TCV**
Randall, Dudley. BLACK POETRY. **BP** *
———. BLACK POETS, THE. **BPo**
Ray, Randolph. 100 GREAT RELIGIOUS POEMS. **OnGR**
Raymond, George L. ORATOR'S MANUAL, THE. **OM**
Read, Bill. MODERN POETS, THE. **OM**
———. TWENTIETH CENTURY POETRY. **TwCP**
Read, Herbert. KNAPSACK, THE. **KN**
———. LONDON BOOK OF ENGLISH VERSE, THE. **LoBV**
———. THIS WAY, DELIGHT. **ThWaDe**
Reed, Gwendolyn. BIRD SONGS. **BiS**
———. LEAN OUT OF THE WINDOW. **LOW**
———. OUT OF THE ARK. **OA** *
Reeves, James. CASSELL BOOK OF ENGLISH POETRY, THE. **CBEP**
———. MODERN POETS' WORLD, THE. **MoPW**
———. NEW CANON OF ENGLISH POETRY, A. **NCEP**
Reid, Jessie. BOOK OF LOVE, THE. **BOL**
Repplier, Agnes. BOOK OF FAMOUS VERSE, A. **BFVR**
Resnick, Seymour. ANTHOLOGY OF SPANISH LITERATURE IN ENGLISH TRANSLATION, AN. **AnSpL 1-2**
Rexroth, Kenneth. NEW BRITISH POETS, THE. **NeBP**

Rexroth, Kenneth (cont.)

———. ONE HUNDRED POEMS FROM THE CHINESE. **OnPC**
———. ONE HUNDRED POEMS FROM THE JAPANESE. **OnPJ**
Reynolds, James J. MODERN POETRY FOR CHILDREN. **MPC 1-14**
Rhodeniza, V. B. CANADIAN POETRY IN ENGLISH. **CaP**
Rhodes, Clara Lawton. VERSE FOR PATRIOTS. **VP**
Rhys, Ernest. CHRISTMAS HOLIDAY BOOK, A. **CHB**
———. GOLDEN TREASURY OF LONGER POEMS, THE. **GoTL**
———. NEW GOLDEN TREASURY OF SONGS & LYRICS, THE. **NT**
Rhys, Grace. CHILDREN'S GARLAND OF VERSE, THE. **CGOV**
Rhys, Keidrych. MODERN WELSH POETRY. **MoWP**
Rice, Frances. HUMBLER POETS, THE, 1885-1910. **HP-2**
Rice, Sara Sigourney. HOLIDAY SELECTIONS FOR READING & RECITATION. **HS**
Rice, Susan Tracy. EASTER. **EOAH**
———. MOTHERS' DAY. **MOAH**
Rice, Wallace. HUMBLER POETS, THE, 1885-1910. **HP-2**
Richards, Alice Lewis. SMILES. **SL** *
———. WINKS. **WN**
Richards, Carmen Nelson. MINNESOTA SKYLINE. **MiSk**
Richards, Mrs. Waldo (Gertrude Moore). HIGH TIDE. **HTR**
———. LOVE'S HIGH WAY. **LHW**
———. MAGIC CARPET, THE. **MCT**
———. MELODY OF EARTH, THE. **ME**
———. STAR-POINTS. **SPT**
Rickert, Edith. AMERICAN LYRICS. **AL**
———. ANCIENT ENGLISH CHRISTMAS CAROLS, MCCCC TO MDCC. **AnEC**
Riddle, George. MODERN READER AND SPEAKER, A. **MRS**
Rideout, Walter B. AMERICAN POETRY. **AP** **
———. COLLEGE BOOK OF MODERN VERSE, A. **CoBMV**
Riley, Elizabeth. LOVE POEMS. **LoP**
Riley, James Whitcomb. BOOK OF JOYOUS CHILDREN. **BJC**
———. CHILD WORLD, A. **CW**
———. COMPLETE POETICAL WORKS. **CPWR**
———. RILEY CHILD RHYMES. **RCR**
Rinaker, Clarissa. TYPES OF POETRY. **TOP**
Rittenhouse, Jesse B. BIRD-LOVERS' ANTHOLOGY, THE. **BLA**
———. LITTLE BOOK OF AMERICAN POETS, THE, 1787-1900. **LBAP**
———. LITTLE BOOK OF MODERN BRITISH VERSE, THE.

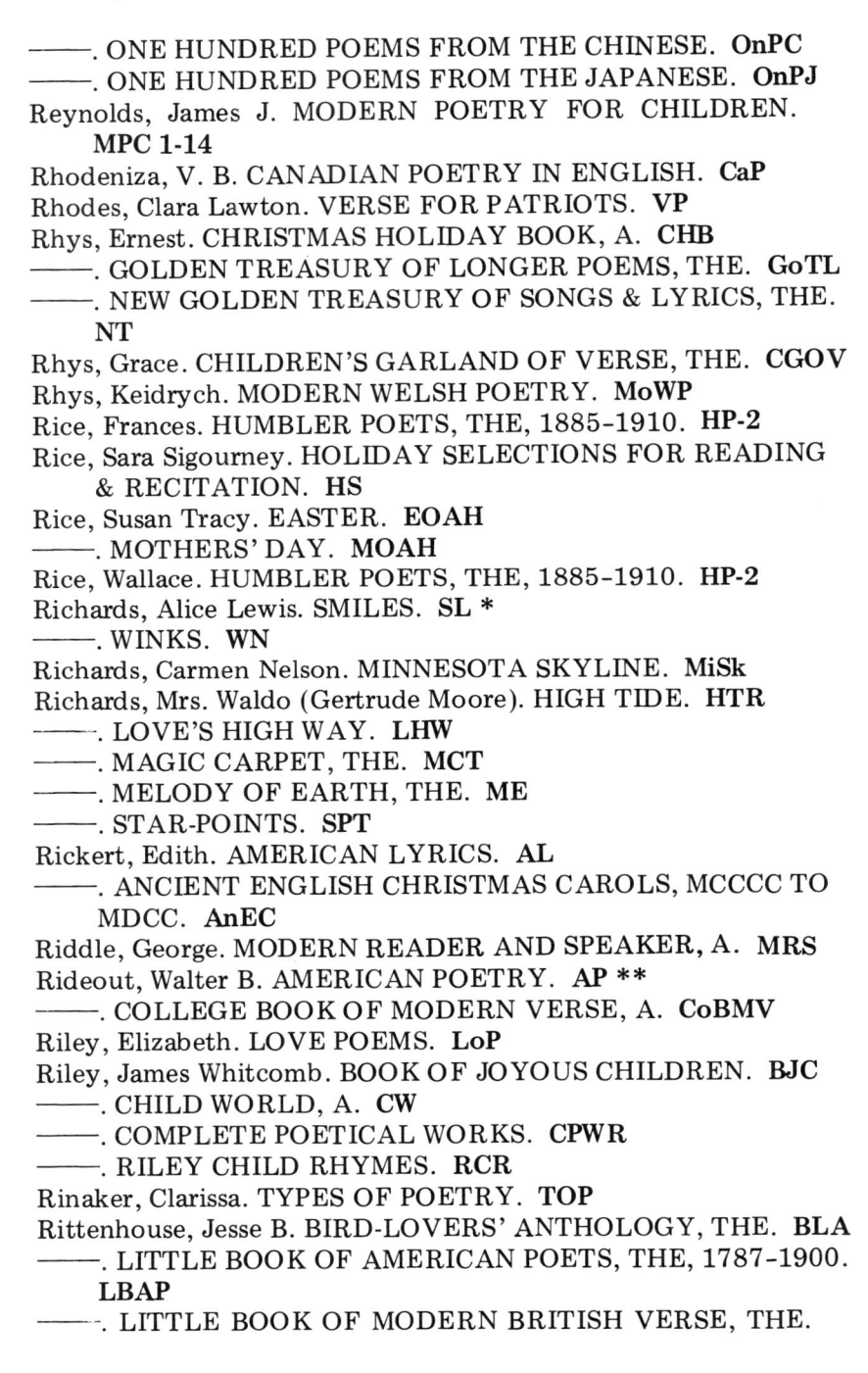

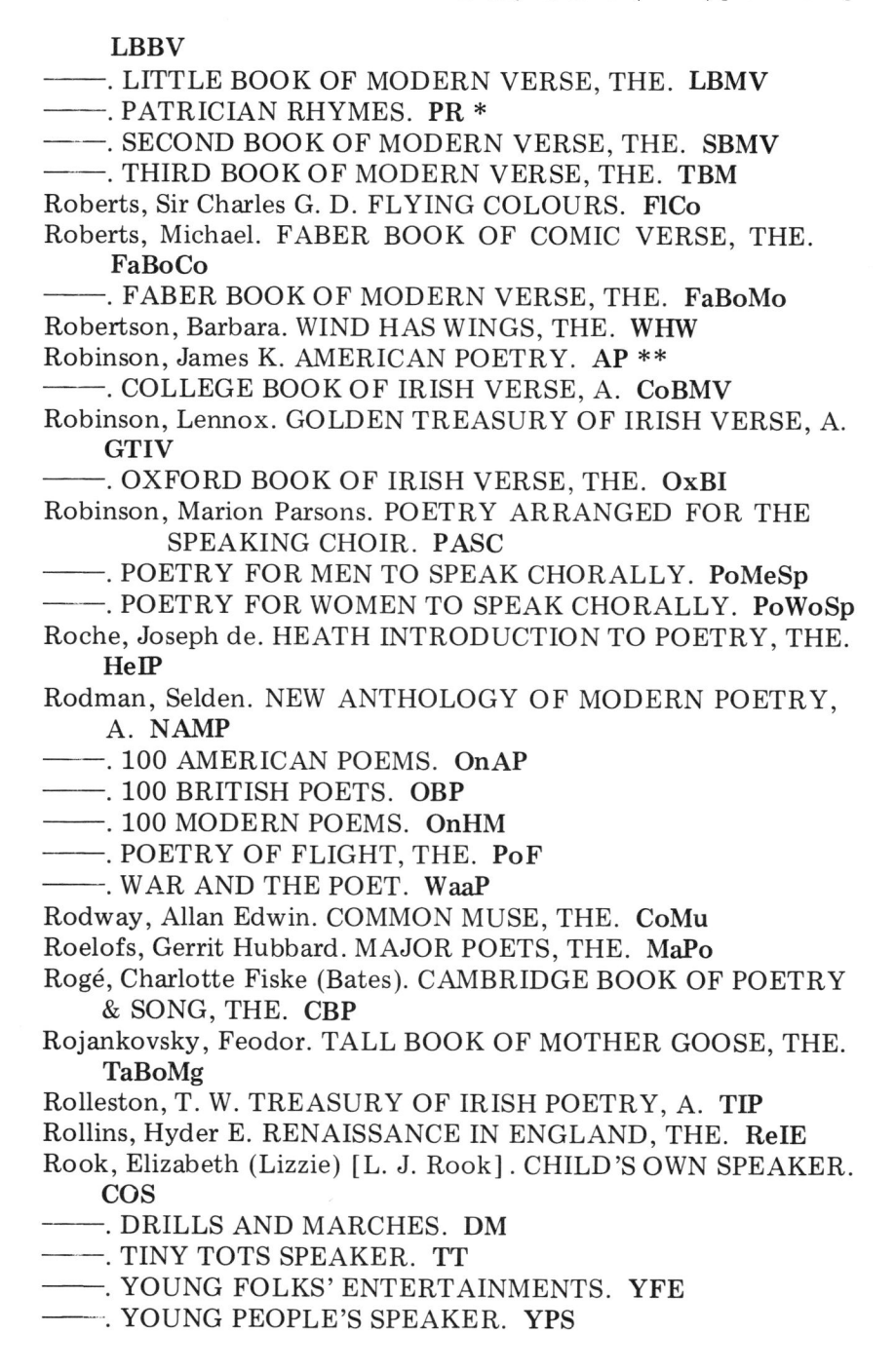

LBBV
———. LITTLE BOOK OF MODERN VERSE, THE. **LBMV**
———. PATRICIAN RHYMES. **PR** *
———. SECOND BOOK OF MODERN VERSE, THE. **SBMV**
———. THIRD BOOK OF MODERN VERSE, THE. **TBM**
Roberts, Sir Charles G. D. FLYING COLOURS. **FlCo**
Roberts, Michael. FABER BOOK OF COMIC VERSE, THE. **FaBoCo**
———. FABER BOOK OF MODERN VERSE, THE. **FaBoMo**
Robertson, Barbara. WIND HAS WINGS, THE. **WHW**
Robinson, James K. AMERICAN POETRY. **AP** **
———. COLLEGE BOOK OF IRISH VERSE, A. **CoBMV**
Robinson, Lennox. GOLDEN TREASURY OF IRISH VERSE, A. **GTIV**
———. OXFORD BOOK OF IRISH VERSE, THE. **OxBI**
Robinson, Marion Parsons. POETRY ARRANGED FOR THE SPEAKING CHOIR. **PASC**
———. POETRY FOR MEN TO SPEAK CHORALLY. **PoMeSp**
———. POETRY FOR WOMEN TO SPEAK CHORALLY. **PoWoSp**
Roche, Joseph de. HEATH INTRODUCTION TO POETRY, THE. **HeIP**
Rodman, Selden. NEW ANTHOLOGY OF MODERN POETRY, A. **NAMP**
———. 100 AMERICAN POEMS. **OnAP**
———. 100 BRITISH POETS. **OBP**
———. 100 MODERN POEMS. **OnHM**
———. POETRY OF FLIGHT, THE. **PoF**
———. WAR AND THE POET. **WaaP**
Rodway, Allan Edwin. COMMON MUSE, THE. **CoMu**
Roelofs, Gerrit Hubbard. MAJOR POETS, THE. **MaPo**
Rogé, Charlotte Fiske (Bates). CAMBRIDGE BOOK OF POETRY & SONG, THE. **CBP**
Rojankovsky, Feodor. TALL BOOK OF MOTHER GOOSE, THE. **TaBoMg**
Rolleston, T. W. TREASURY OF IRISH POETRY, A. **TIP**
Rollins, Hyder E. RENAISSANCE IN ENGLAND, THE. **ReIE**
Rook, Elizabeth (Lizzie) [L. J. Rook]. CHILD'S OWN SPEAKER. **COS**
———. DRILLS AND MARCHES. **DM**
———. TINY TOTS SPEAKER. **TT**
———. YOUNG FOLKS' ENTERTAINMENTS. **YFE**
———. YOUNG PEOPLE'S SPEAKER. **YPS**

Roosevelt, Theodore. DESK DRAWER ANTHOLOGY, THE. **DDA**
Roscoe, Theodora. POEMS BY CONTEMPORARY WOMEN. **PCW**
Rosenthal, M. L. CHIEF MODERN POETS OF ENGLAND & AMERICA. **CMoP**
——. EXPLORING POETRY. **ExPo**
——. NEW MODERN POETRY, THE. **NMP**
——. 100 POSTWAR POEMS. **OPoP**
Ross, David. POET'S GOLD. **PG**
Roualt, Polly. READING OF POETRY, THE. **RePo**
Rowe, Grace. CHORAL SPEAKING ARRANGEMENTS FOR THE LOWER GRADES. **CSL**
Ruby, Kathryn. WE BECOME NEW. **WBN**
Russell, F. A. See Malone, Ted (pseud.)
Sackheim, Eric. BLUES LINES, THE. **BluL**
Salinger, Herman. TWENTIETH-CENTURY GERMAN VERSE. **TwGV**
Sandburg, Carl. AMERICAN SONGBAG, THE. **AS**
——. CHICAGO POEMS. **CPCS**
——. CORNHUSKERS, THE. **CCS**
——. EARLY MOON. **EMS**
——. GOOD MORNING, AMERICA. **GMAS**
——. PEOPLE, YES, THE. **PYS**
——. SMOKE AND STEEL & SLABS OF THE SUNBURNT WEST. **SASS**
Sanders, Gerald D. CHIEF MODERN POETS OF ENGLAND & AMERICA. **CMoP, ChMo, CMP**
——. INTRODUCTION TO AMERICAN POETRY. **IAP**
Sanford, Anne Putnam. ARMISTICE DAY. **AOAH**
——. GRADUATION DAY. **GDAH**
——. MAGIC OF BOOKS, THE. **MOB**
——. NEW PLAYS FOR CHRISTMAS. **NPC**
Sansom, Clive. ENGLISH HEART, THE. **EnH**
Sargent, Epes. STANDARD SPEAKER, THE. **SS** *
Sargent, Helen Child. ENGLISH AND SCOTTISH POPULAR BALLADS. **ESPB**
Sarton, May. POETS SPEAK, THE, 1943. **PoSp**
Sauvain, Alan. BOOK OF LIVELY VERSE, A. **BoLV 1-3**
Schauffler, Robert Haven. ARBOR DAY. **ADAH**
——. ARMISTICE DAY. **AOAH**
——. CHRISTMAS. **COAH**

——. EASTER. **EOAH**
——. FLAG DAY. **FOAH**
——. GRADUATION DAY. **GDAH**
——. HALLOWE'EN. **HOAH**
——. INDEPENDENCE DAY. **IDAH**
——. JUNIOR POETRY CURE. **JPC**
——. LINCOLN'S BIRTHDAY. **LBAH**
——. MAGIC OF BOOKS. **MOB**
——. MEMORIAL DAY. **MDAH**
——. MOTHERS' DAY. **MOAH**
——. POETRY CURE, THE. **PC** *
——. ROOSEVELT DAY. **RDAH**
——. THANKSGIVING. **TOAH**
——. THROUGH ITALY WITH THE POETS. **TIWP**
——. WASHINGTON'S BIRTHDAY. **WOAH**
Schreiber, Ron. 31 NEW AMERICAN POETS. **ThO**
Schwaber, Paul. OF POETRY AND POWER. **OPP**
Scollard, Clinton. BALLADS OF AMERICAN BRAVERY. **BAB**
——. BIRD-LOVERS' ANTHOLOGY, THE. **BLA**
——. PATRICIAN RHYMES. **PR** *
Scott, Tom. OXFORD BOOK OF SCOTTISH VERSE, THE. **OxBS**
Scudder, Horace. AMERICAN POEMS. **AP** *
——. AMERICAN PROSE. **APr**
——. MASTERPIECES OF AMERICAN LITERATURE. **MAL**
——. MASTERPIECES OF BRITISH LITERATURE. **MBL**
Seboyar, Gerald E. READINGS IN ENGLISH AND AMERICAN LITERATURE. **REAL**
——. READINGS IN EUROPEAN LITERATURE. **REL**
Sechrist, Elizabeth Hough. MERRY MEET AGAIN. **MeMeAg**
——. ONE THOUSAND POEMS FOR CHILDREN. **OTPC**
——. POEMS FOR RED LETTER DAYS. **PoRL**
Segnitz, Barbara. PSYCHE. **Psy**
Selden, Elizabeth. BOOK OF FRIENDSHIP, THE. **BoFr**
Service, Robert. COMPLETE POEMS. **CPS**
Seymour-Smith, Martin. NEW CANON OF ENGLISH POETRY, A. **NCEP**
Shafer, Robert. FROM BEOWULF TO THOMAS HARDY. **BTH (1)-2**
Shapcott, Thomas. CONTEMPORARY AMERICAN & AUSTRALIAN POETRY. **CAAP**
Shapiro, David. ANTHOLOGY OF NEW YORK POETS, AN. **ANYP**

Shapiro, Karl. AMERICAN POETRY. **AmP**
———. MODERN AMERICAN & MODERN BRITISH POETRY.
   MoAB
Shawcross, John T. POETRY AND ITS CONVENTIONS. **PAIC**
Shay, Frank. AMERICAN SEA SONGS AND CHANTEYS.
   AmSS
Sheed, F. J. POETRY AND LIFE. **PoLi**
Sheldon, William D. READING OF POETRY, THE. **RePo**
Sherman, Frank Dempster. LITTLE-FOLKS LYRICS. **LFL**
Shields, Sarah Annie (Frost). See Frost, S. A.
Shipley, Joseph T. MODERN FRENCH POETRY. **MFP**
Shipman, Dorothy M. CHRISTMAS RECITATIONS FOR
   YOUNG AND OLD. **CRYO**
———. STARDUST AND HOLLY. **SDH**
Shoemaker, Blanche (Mrs. Blanche [Shoemaker] Wagstaff). CO-
   LONIAL PLAYS FOR THE SCHOOL-ROOM. **CPs**
Shoemaker, Charles C. CHOICE DIALECT. **CD**
———. CHOICE HUMOR. **CHS**
———. HOLIDAY ENTERTAINMENTS. **HE**
———. HUMOROUS DIALOGUES AND DRAMAS. **HD**
———. YOUNG FOLKS' DIALOGUES. **YFD**
Shoemaker, Jacob W. BEST THINGS FROM BEST AUTHORS.
   BTB 1-9
———. PRACTICAL ELOCUTION. **PE**
———. SHOEMAKER'S BEST SELECTIONS. **BS 1-27**
Shoemaker, Rachel W. (Hinkle) [Mrs. J. W. Shoemaker]. AD-
   VANCED ELOCUTION. **AE**
———. BEST THINGS FROM BEST AUTHORS. **BTB 1-9**
———. CHOICE DIALOGUES. **CDS**
———. CLASSIC DIALOGUES AND DRAMAS. **CDD**
———. LITTLE PEOPLE'S SPEAKER. **LPS**
———. SHOEMAKER'S BEST SELECTIONS. **BS 1-27**
———. YOUNG FOLKS' RECITATIONS. **YFR**
Shoup. Grace. POETRY OF TO-DAY. **PT**
Shriner, Sara Venore. SARA SHRINER'S SELECTIONS. **SSS**
Shurter, Edwin Du Bois. MASTERPIECES OF MODERN VERSE.
   MMV
———. NEW POEMS THAT WILL TAKE PRIZES IN SPEAKING
   CONTESTS. **NPSC**
Shute, Katharine Henry. LAND OF SONG, THE. **LOS 1-3**
Siegmeister, Elie. TREASURY OF AMERICAN SONG, A. **TrAS**
Simmons, Clifford. LIVING POETS. **LP**

Simmons, Gary. SINCE FEELING IS FIRST. **SFF**
Simon, Charlie May. LAYS OF THE NEW LAND. **LaNeLa**
Simpson, Louis. INTRODUCTION TO POETRY, AN. **InPS**
———. NEW POETS OF ENGLAND & AMERICA. **NePoEA**
Sisam, Celia. OXFORD BOOK OF MEDIEVAL ENGLISH VERSE, THE. **OxBM**
Sisam, Kenneth. OXFORD BOOK OF MEDIEVAL ENGLISH VERSE, THE. **OxBM**
Sitwell, Edith. ATLANTIC BOOK OF BRITISH & AMERICAN POETRY, THE. **AtBAP**
———. BOOK OF WINTER, A. **BoW**
———. POETS OF OUR TIME. **POTE**
Skelton, Robin. CAVALIER POETS, THE. **CavP**
Skinner, Avery Warner. SELECTIONS FOR MEMORIZING. **SFM**
Skinner, Charles Rufus. ARBOR DAY MANUAL. **AD**
———. BRIGHT SIDE, THE. **BS**
Sloss, Hattie Hecht. CERTAIN POETS OF IMPORTANCE. **CPOI**
Slote, Bernice. DIMENSIONS OF POETRY, THE. **DiPo**
Smeaton, William Henry O. ENGLISH SATIRES. **ESs**
Smith, Arthur James Marshall. BOOK OF CANADIAN POETRY, THE. **BoCaPo**
———. EXPLORING POETRY. **ExPo**
———. MODERN CANADIAN VERSE. **MoCV**
———. 100 POEMS. **OnP**
———. OXFORD BOOK OF CANADIAN VERSE IN ENGLISH & FRENCH, THE. **OBCV**
———. SEVEN CENTURIES OF VERSE, ENGLISH & AMERICAN. **SeCeV**
———. WORDLY MUSE, THE. **WoMu**
Smith, David Nichol. OXFORD BOOK OF EIGHTEENTH CENTURY VERSE, THE. **OBEC**
Smith, E. F. BEECHER'S RECITATIONS & READINGS. **BeR**
Smith, Elva S. BOOK OF LULLABIES, A. **BOL** *
———. CHRISTMAS BOOK OF LEGENDS AND STORIES, THE. **ChrBoLe**
———. CHRISTMAS IN LEGEND AND STORY. **CLS**
———. YEAR AROUND, THE. **YeAR**
Smith, Hallett. RENAISSANCE ENGLAND. **ReEn**
Smith, Janet Adam. FABER BOOK OF CHILDREN'S VERSE, THE. **FaBoCh**
———. FABER BOOK OF COMIC VERSE, THE. **FaBoCo**
———. LOOKING GLASS BOOK OF VERSE, THE. **LoGBV**

Smith, Nora Archibald. GOLDEN NUMBERS. **GN**
———. PINAFORE PALACE. **PPL**
———. POSY RING, THE. **PRWS**
Smith, P. G. SHELDON BOOK OF VERSE, THE. **ShBV 1-4**
Smith, Reed. GOOD READINGS FOR HIGH SCHOOLS. **GR 1-2, GR-a, & Gr-e**
Smith, Stevie. POET'S GARDEN, THE. **PoG**
Smith, William Jay. GOLDEN JOURNEY, THE. **GoJo**
Smith, William Palmer. PROSE AND VERSE FOR SPEAKING & READING. **PVS**
Snell, Ada L. F. WHERE BIRDS SING. **WhBs**
Snow, Royall H. ENGLISH ROMANTIC POETS. **ERP**
———. VICTORIAN AND LATER ENGLISH POETS. **VLEP**
Snow, William Leonard. HIGH SCHOOL PRIZE SPEAKER, THE. **HSPS**
Snyder, Franklyn Bliss. BOOK OF ENGLISH LITERATURE, A. **BEL**
Snyder, Warren. POETICAL FAVORITES—YOURS AND MINE. **PF**
Soper, Henry M. DIALECT READINGS. **SDR**
———. SCRAP-BOOK RECITATIONS. **SR 1-15**
Southwick, Frank Townsend. ELOCUTION AND ACTION. **EA**
———. STEPS TO ORATORY. **SO**
Spacks, Patricia Meyer. EIGHTEENTH-CENTURY POETRY. **EiCP**
———. LATE AUGUSTAN POETRY. **LAuP**
Spann, Marcella. CONFUCIUS TO CUMMINGS. **CTC**
Spaulding, Francis Trow. OPEN GATES. **OG**
Spaulding, Susan Thompson. OPEN GATES. **OG**
Speare, M. E. POCKET BOOK OF VERSE, THE. **PoBoVe**
Spencer, Sylvia. UP FROM THE EARTH. **UFE**
Spender, Stephen. CHOICE OF ENGLISH ROMANTIC POETRY, A. **ChER**
Sprague, Grace E. W. CONTEMPORARY VERSE. **CV**
Squier, Charles L. SONNET, THE. **Sonn**
Srygley, Ola Pauline. HIGH LIGHTS IN AMERICAN LITERATURE. **HiLiAm**
———. HIGH LIGHTS IN ENGLISH LITERATURE. **HiLiEn**
Stafford, Josephine. PATRIOTIC READINGS AND RECITATIONS. **PRR**
Stageberg, Norman C. POETRY AS EXPERIENCE. **PoEx**
Stallworthy, Jon. BOOK OF LOVE POETRY, A. **BoLoP**

Stanford, Ann. WOMEN POETS IN ENGLISH, THE. **WPE**
Strange, G. Robert. VICTORIAN POETRY AND POETICS. **ViPP**
Stanistreet, Grace Marie. GRACE MARIE STANISTREET'S RECITATIONS FOR CHILDREN. **GSRC**
Starkman, Miriam K. 17th CENTURY ENGLISH POETRY. **SCEP 1-2**
Stauffer, Elma. GOOD READINGS FOR HIGH SCHOOLS. **GR 1-2, Gr-a, Gr-e**
Stedman, Edmund Clarence. AMERICAN ANTHOLOGY, AN, 1787-1900. **AA**
———. VICTORIAN ANTHOLOGY, A, 1837-1895. **VA**
Steele, Silax Sexton. STEELE'S EXHIBITION DIALOGUES. **SED**
Stephens, James. ENGLISH ROMANTIC POETS. **ERP**
———. VICTORIAN AND LATER ENGLISH POETS. **VLEP**
Stern, Philip Van Doren. POCKET BOOK OF AMERICA, THE. **PoBoAm**
———. POCKET COMPANION, THE. **PoCo**
———. POCKET READER, THE. **PoRe**
Stevens, David. AMERICAN PATRIOTIC PROSE AND VERSE. **APPV**
Stevens, Ruth Francis (Davis). AMERICAN PATRIOTIC PROSE AND VERSE. **APPV**
Stevenson, Burton Egbert. DAYS AND DEEDS. **DD**
———. GREAT AMERICANS, AS SEEN BY THE POETS. **GA**
———. HOME BOOK OF MODERN VERSE, THE. **HBMV**
———. HOME BOOK OF VERSE, THE. **HBV**
———. HOME BOOK OF VERSE FOR YOUNG FOLKS, THE. **HBVY**
———. MY COUNTRY. **MC ***
———. POEMS OF AMERICAN HISTORY. **PAH**
Stevenson, Robert Louis. CHILD'S GARDEN OF VERSE. **CGV**
Stewart, Douglas. MODERN AUSTRALIAN VERSE (Vol. II of Poetry in Australia). **PoAu-2**
Stewart, Meum. DISTAFF MUSE, THE. **DiM**
Stewart, Randall. AMERICAN POETRY. **AmPo**
———. ENGLISH LYRIC POETRY. **EnLP**
Stewart, Vincent. THREE DIMENSIONS OF POETRY. **TDP**
Stork, Charles Wharton. ANTHOLOGY OF NORWEGIAN LYRICS. **AnNoLy**
———. ANTHOLOGY OF SWEDISH LYRICS, FROM 1750 to 1925. **AnSL**
———. SECOND BOOK OF DANISH VERSE, A. **BoDS**

Stokes, Mrs. Anne (Knott). OPEN DOOR TO POETRY, THE. **ODP**
Stover, Kermit. ON THIS DAY. **OTD**
Strand, Mark. CONTEMPORARY AMERICAN POETS, THE. **CoAP**
Stratton, Clarence. LITERATURE AND LIFE. **LL 1-4**
Strong, Leonard Alfred George. BEST POEMS, THE, OF 1923, 1924, 1926. **BP 3-6**
Stroop, Gladys Trueblood. SELECTIONS FOR PUBLIC SPEAKING. **SPS**
Stryk, Lucien. HEARTLAND II. **HeS**
Sturch, Elizabeth. GATEWAY TO POETRY, A. **GatP**
Suskin, Albert. ROMAN HISTORY IN TRANSLATION. **RoL**
Swallow, Alan. AMERICAN WRITING, 1943. **AmWr**
———. RINEHART BOOK OF VERSE, THE. **RiBV**
Swann, Mona. MANY VOICES. **MV 1-2**
Swett, John. SCHOOL ELOCUTION. **SE**
Sylvester, Richard S. ANCHOR ANTHOLOGY OF SEVENTEENTH CENTURY VERSE, THE, Vol. II. **AnAnS-2**
———. ANCHOR ANTHOLOGY OF SIXTEENTH CENTURY VERSE, THE. **AAS**
Tate, Allen. MODERN VERSE IN ENGLISH, 1900-1950. **MoVe**
———. PRINCETON VERSE BETWEEN TWO WARS. **PriVe**
Taylor, Geoffrey. ENGLISH LOVE POEMS. **EnLoPo**
———. ENGLISH, SCOTTISH, & WELSH LANDSCAPE, 1700-c.1860. **EnSW**
———. IRISH POEMS OF TODAY. **IrP**
———. IRISH POETS OF THE NINETEENTH CENTURY. **IrPN**
Taylor, Henry. POETRY: POINTS OF DEPARTURE. **PPoD**
Taylor, Warren. POETRY IN ENGLISH. **PoIE**
Teasdale, Sara. ANSWERING VOICE, THE. **AV**
———. RAINBOW GOLD. **RG**
Teter, George E. BOOK OF HUMOROUS POEMS, A. **BHP**
———. ONE HUNDRED NARRATIVE POEMS. **OHNP**
Thacher, Lucy W. LISTENING CHILD, THE. **LC**
Thatcher, George. TALKS. **TK**
Thaxter, Celia. STORIES AND POEMS FOR CHILDREN. **SAP**
Therese, Sister M. I SING OF A MAIDEN. **ISi**
Thomas, Charles Swain. ATLANTIC PROSE AND POETRY. **APP**
Thomas, Josephine. OUR HOLIDAYS IN POETRY. **OHIP**
Thomas, Mary Roenah. YOUNG FOLKS' BOOK OF MIRTH, THE. **BOM**
Thomas, Wright. READING POEMS. **ReaPo**
Thompson, Blanche Jennings. MORE SILVER PENNIES. **MoSiPe**

——. SILVER PENNIES. **SP**
——. WITH HARP AND LUTE. **WHL**
Thompson, Slason. HUMBLER POETS, THE (1870-1885). **HP-1**
Thompson, Stith. BRITISH POETS OF THE NINETEENTH CENTURY. **BPN**
——. ENGLISH LITERATURE AND ITS BACKGROUNDS. **EnLi 1-2**
——. OUR HERITAGE OF WORLD LITERATURE. **OuHeWo**
Thorn, Alice G. SINGING WORLDS. **SiWo**
Thorp, Willard. OXFORD ANTHOLOGY OF ENGLISH POETRY, AN. **OAEP**
——. POETRY OF THE TRANSITION. **POTT**
Thurman, Judith. TO SEE THE WORLD AFRESH. **TSWA**
Thurston, Rosetta Lura. POETRY ARRANGED FOR THE SPEAKING CHOIR. **PASC**
——. POETRY FOR MEN TO SPEAK CHORALLY. **PoMeSp**
——. POETRY FOR WOMEN TO SPEAK CHORALLY. **PoWoSp**
Thwing, Walter E. BEST LOVED STORY POEMS. **BeLS**
Tileston, Mary W. (Foote). CHILDREN'S BOOK OF BALLADS, THE. **CBB**
——. CHILD'S HARVEST OF VERSE, THE. **CHV**
——. SUGAR AND SPICE. **SAS**
Tillotson, Geoffrey. EIGHTEENTH CENTURY ENGLISH LITERATURE. **EiCL**
Toaffe, James G. POEMS ON POETRY. **PP**
Tobin, James Edward. COLLEGE BOOK OF ENGLISH LITERATURE. **CoBE**
——. JOYCE KILMER'S ANTHOLOGY OF CATHOLIC POETS. **JKCP**
Tobitt, Janet E. SAUCY SAILOR & OTHER DRAMATIZED BALLADS, THE. **SaSa**
——. SING ME YOUR SONG, O! **SiMeYo**
Todd, James Maclean. VOICES FROM THE PAST. **VoFP**
Todd, Janet Maclean. VOICES FROM THE PAST. **VoFP**
Toliver, Harold F. FORMS OF POETRY. **FosPo**
Townsend, John Rowe. MODERN POETRY. **MPo**
Trapp, Jacob. MODERN RELIGIOUS POEMS. **MoRP**
Trueblood, Thomas Clarkson. CHOICE READINGS. **FTR**
——. STANDARD SELECTIONS. **StS**
Tufte, Virginia. HIGH WEDLOCK THEN BE HONOURED. **HW**
Tupper, James W. NARRATIVE AND LYRIC POETRY. **NAL**

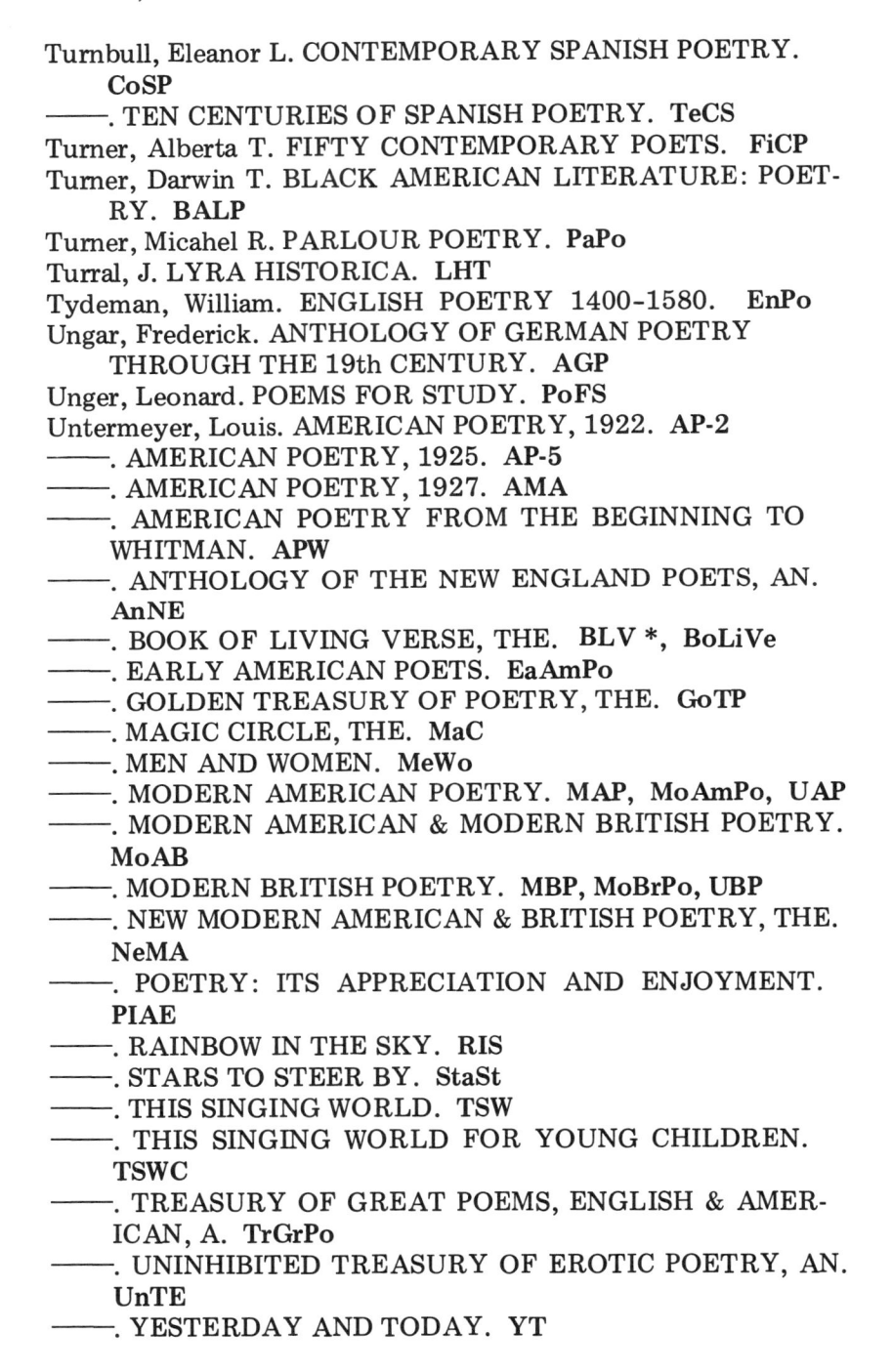

Turnbull, Eleanor L. CONTEMPORARY SPANISH POETRY. CoSP
——. TEN CENTURIES OF SPANISH POETRY. TeCS
Turner, Alberta T. FIFTY CONTEMPORARY POETS. FiCP
Turner, Darwin T. BLACK AMERICAN LITERATURE: POETRY. BALP
Turner, Micahel R. PARLOUR POETRY. PaPo
Turral, J. LYRA HISTORICA. LHT
Tydeman, William. ENGLISH POETRY 1400-1580. EnPo
Ungar, Frederick. ANTHOLOGY OF GERMAN POETRY THROUGH THE 19th CENTURY. AGP
Unger, Leonard. POEMS FOR STUDY. PoFS
Untermeyer, Louis. AMERICAN POETRY, 1922. AP-2
——. AMERICAN POETRY, 1925. AP-5
——. AMERICAN POETRY, 1927. AMA
——. AMERICAN POETRY FROM THE BEGINNING TO WHITMAN. APW
——. ANTHOLOGY OF THE NEW ENGLAND POETS, AN. AnNE
——. BOOK OF LIVING VERSE, THE. BLV *, BoLiVe
——. EARLY AMERICAN POETS. EaAmPo
——. GOLDEN TREASURY OF POETRY, THE. GoTP
——. MAGIC CIRCLE, THE. MaC
——. MEN AND WOMEN. MeWo
——. MODERN AMERICAN POETRY. MAP, MoAmPo, UAP
——. MODERN AMERICAN & MODERN BRITISH POETRY. MoAB
——. MODERN BRITISH POETRY. MBP, MoBrPo, UBP
——. NEW MODERN AMERICAN & BRITISH POETRY, THE. NeMA
——. POETRY: ITS APPRECIATION AND ENJOYMENT. PIAE
——. RAINBOW IN THE SKY. RIS
——. STARS TO STEER BY. StaSt
——. THIS SINGING WORLD. TSW
——. THIS SINGING WORLD FOR YOUNG CHILDREN. TSWC
——. TREASURY OF GREAT POEMS, ENGLISH & AMERICAN, A. TrGrPo
——. UNINHIBITED TREASURY OF EROTIC POETRY, AN. UnTE
——. YESTERDAY AND TODAY. YT

Van Doren, Carl. PATRIOTIC ANTHOLOGY, THE. PaA
Van Doren, Mark. ANTHOLOGY OF WORLD POETRY, AN. AWP
——. INTRODUCTION TO POETRY. InPo
——. JUNIOR ANTHOLOGY OF WORLD POETRY, A. JAWP
——. MASTERPIECES OF AMERICAN POETS. MOAP
——. WORLD'S BEST POEMS, THE. WBP
Van Doren Stern, Philip. See Stern, Philip Van Doren
Van Dyke, Henry. POEMS. PVD
Van Nostrand, Albert D. CONSCIOUS VOICE, THE. CoV
Vance, Bruce. BEING BORN AND GROWING OLDER. BBGO
Vincent, Jean Anne. PATRIOTIC POEMS AMERICA LOVES. PAL
Wagenknecht, Edward. STORY OF JESUS IN THE WORLD'S LITERATURE, THE. StJW
Wagner, Charles A. PRIZE POEMS, 1913-1929. PP *
Wagner, Linda W. INTRODUCING POEMS. IPWM
Wagstaff, Mrs. Blanche. See Shoemaker, Blanche.
Wain, John. ANTHOLOGY OF MODERN POETRY. AnMoPo
Waingrow, Marshall. EIGHTEENTH CENTURY ENGLISH LITERATURE. EiCL
Waite, Harlow O. POETRY FROM LITERATURE OF OUR TIME. PoLFOT
Waley, Arthur. TRANSLATIONS FROM THE CHINESE. TrCh
Walker, F. C. POEMS, CHIEFLY NARRATIVE. PCN
Walker, Jerry L. POP/ROCK SONGS OF THE EARTH. PoRo
Wallace, Robert. POEMS ON POETRY. PP
Wallerstein, Ruth C. SEVENTEENTH-CENTURY VERSE AND PROSE. SeCV 1-2
Wallington, Mrs. Nellie (Urner). AMERICAN HISTORY BY AMERICAN POETS. AH 1-2
Wallis, Charles L. TREASURY OF POEMS FOR WORSHIP AND DEVOTION, A. TrPWD
Walser, Richard Gaither. NORTH CAROLINA POETRY. NoCaPo
——. POETS OF NORTH CAROLINA. PoNC
Walsh, Chad. TODAY'S POETS. ToPo
Walsh, Thomas. CATHOLIC ANTHOLOGY, THE. CAW
Walters, Dorothy. I HEAR MY SISITERS SAYING. IHMS
Walters, L. D'O. ANTHOLOGY OF RECENT POETRY, AN. AnRP
Ward, Alfred Charles. BOOK OF AMERICAN VERSE, A. BAV
Ward, Thomas Humphrey. ENGLISH POETS, THE. EPW 1-5
Warren, Robert Penn. UNDERSTANDING POETRY. UnPo

Waterman, S. D. GRADED MEMORY SELECTIONS. **GMs**
Watkins, Dwight Everett. MASTERPIECES OF MODERN VERSE. **MMV**
——. NEW POEMS THAT WILL TAKE PRIZES IN SPEAKING CONTESTS. **NPSC**
Watson, J. R. VICTORIAN POETRY. **VPC**
Watt, William. ENGLISH LITERATURE AND ITS BACKGROUNDS. **EnLi 1-2**
Wattles, Willard. SUNFLOWERS. **S**
Watts, Charles H., II. CONSCIOUS VOICE, THE. **CoV**
Wavell, A. P. OTHER MEN'S FLOWERS. **OtMeF**
Weatherhead, A. Kingsley. POEM, THE. **PoAn**
Webster, Lawrence. CATCH YOUR BREATH. **CaYB**
Welland, D. S. R. PRE-RAPHAELITES IN LITERATURE AND ART, THE. **PrRL**
Wells, Carolyn. BOOK OF HUMOROUS VERSE, THE. **BOHV**
——. CAT IN VERSE, THE **CIV** *
——. NONSENSE ANTHOLOGY, THE. **NA**
——. PARODY ANTHOLOGY, A. **PA**
——. SATIRE ANTHOLOGY, A. **SAy**
——. VERS DE SOCIETE ANTHOLOGY, A. **VSA**
——. WHIMSEY ANTHOLOGY, A. **WA**
Wells, Henry W. ONE THOUSAND AND ONE POEMS OF MANKIND. **OnPM**
——. WORLD LITERATURE. **WoL**
Were, Mary Winter, (pseud.). POEMS BY CONTEMPORARY WOMEN. **PCW**
Werner, Jane. GOLDEN BOOK OF POETRY, THE. **GoBP**
Werner, Edgar S., & Company. WERNER'S READING AND RECITATIONS. **WRR 1-58**
Westley, George Herbert. FOR LOVE'S SWEET SAKE. **FLS**
Wetherby, Terry. NEW POETS: WOMEN. **NPW**
Whall, A. L. GREEK READER, THE. **GrR**
Wharton, Edith. ETERNAL PASSION IN ENGLISH LITERATURE. **EtPaEn**
Wheeler, Mary. STEAMBOATIN' DAYS. **StDa**
Whimster, D. C. CENTURY OF LYRICS, A, 1550-1650. **CenL**
White, Alice M. G. SAUCY SAILOR AND OTHER DRAMATIZED BALLADS, THE. **SaSa**
White, E. B. SUBTREASURY OF AMERICAN HUMOR, A. **SuAmHu**
White, Helen C. SEVENTEENTH-CENTURY VERSE AND PROSE. **SeCV 1-2**

White, Katharine S. SUBTREASURY OF AMERICAN HUMOR, A. **SuAmHu**
White, Marcus. POETRY FOR SCHOOL READINGS. **PSR**
Whitley, Alvin. ENGLISH POETRY OF THE MID & LATE EIGHTEENTH CENTURY. **EnPE**
Whitlock, Pamela. ALL DAY LONG. **AlDL**
Whitney, Lois. EIGHTEENTH CENTURY POETRY AND PROSE. **EiPP**
Whittier, John Greenleaf. CHILD LIFE. **WCL**
——. SONGS OF THREE CENTURIES. **STC**
Whyte-Edgar, Mrs. C. M. WREATH OF CANADIAN SONG, A. **WCS**
Wiggin, Kate Douglas. GOLDEN NUMBERS. **GN**
——. PINAFORE PALACE. **PPL**
——. POSY RING, THE. **PRWS**
Wilbor, Elsie M. DELSARTE RECITATION BOOK. **DRB**
Wilbur, Richard. MODERN AMERICAN & MODERN BRITISH POETRY. **MoAB**
Wiley, Paul L. BRITISH POETRY 1880-1920. **BrPo**
Wilking, J. F. SHELDON BOOK OF VERSE, THE. **ShBV 1-4**
Wilkinson, Marguerite. CONTEMPORARY POETRY. **CP**
——. GOLDEN SONGS OF THE GOLDEN STATE. **GS**
——. NEW VOICES. **NV** *
——. RADIANT TREE, THE. **RT**
——. YULE FIRE. **YF**
Willard, Ellen M. YULETIDE ENTERTAINMENTS. **YTE**
Williams, A. Dallas. PRAISE OF LINCOLN, THE. **POL** *
Williams, Charles. NEW BOOK OF ENGLISH VERSE, THE. **NBE**
Williams, Gwyn. PRESENTING WELSH POETRY. **PrWP**
Williams, John. ENGLISH RENAISSANCE POETRY. **EnRePo**
Williams, Miller. CONTEMPORARY POETRY IN AMERICA. **CoPAm**
Williams, Oscar. F. T. PALGRAVE'S THE GOLDEN TREASURY OF THE BEST SONGS AND LYRICAL POEMS. **GTBS-W**
——. LITTLE TREASURY OF AMERICAN POETRY, A. **LiTA**
——. LITTLE TREASURY OF BRITISH POETRY, A. **LiTB**
——. LITTLE TREASURY OF GREAT POETRY, A. **LiTG**
——. LITTLE TREASURY OF MODERN POETRY, A, ENGLISH & AMERICAN. **LiTM**
——. MAJOR METAPHYSICAL POETS OF THE 17th CENTURY, THE. **MaMe**

Williams, Oscar (cont.)

———. MASTER POEMS OF THE ENGLISH LANGUAGE. MasP
———. NEW POCKET ANTHOLOGY OF AMERICAN VERSE FROM COLONIAL DAYS TO THE PRESENT, THE. NEPA
———. NEW POEMS, 1942. NePo
———. SILVER TREASURY OF LIGHT VERSE, A. SiTL
———. WAR POETS, THE. WaP
Williard, Rudolph. MEDIEVAL ENGLISH VERSE & PROSE IN MODERNIZED VERSIONS. MeEV
Williams, Sherman. SELECTIONS FOR MEMORIZING. SM
———. WILLIAM'S CHOICE LITERATURE. WCLG 1-2, WCLI 1-2
Williamson, W. M. ETERNAL SEA, THE. EtS
Willy, Margaret. METAPHYSICAL POETS, THE. MetP
Wilson, Bertha M. WILSON'S DRILLS AND MARCHES. WDM
Wilson, Floyd Baker. WILSON'S RECITATIONS AND DIALOGUES. WRD
Wilson, James Southall. ENCHANTED YEARS, THE. EY
Wilson, William Andrew. SELECTED MEMORY GEMS. SMG
Windsor, M. E. LYRA HISTORICA. LHT
Winslow, Ann. TRIAL BALANCE. TB
Winters, Yvor. POETS OF THE PACIFIC: 2d series. PtPa
———. QUEST FOR REALITY. QFR
Withers, Carl. PENGUIN BOOK OF SONNETS, THE. PeBoSo
Withers, Percy. GARLAND OF CHILDHOOD, THE. GC
Wollman, Maurice. HARRAP BOOK OF MODERN VERSE, THE. HaMV
Wood, Henry Firth. GOOD HUMOR. GH
Wood, Ray. FUN IN AMERICAN FOLK RHYMES. FuAF
Woods, George Benjamin. POETRY OF THE VICTORIAN PERIOD. PoVP
Woods, Ralph L. FAMOUS POEMS AND THE LITTLE-KNOWN STORIES BEHIND THEM. FaPL
———. SECOND TREASURY OF THE FAMILIAR, A. TreFT
———. THIRD TREASURY OF THE FAMILIAR, A. TreFT
———. TREASURY OF THE FAMILIAR, A. TreF
Woollcott, Alexander. AS YOU WERE. AsYW
Wright, Blanche Fisher. REAL MOTHER GOOSE, THE. ReMoGo
Wright, David. FABER BOOK OF TWENTIETH CENTURY VERSE, THE. FaBoTw
———. PENGUIN BOOK OF ENGLISH LANGUAGE, THE. PeER
Wright, Judith. BOOK OF AUSTRALIAN VERSE, A. BoAV
———. NEW LAND, NEW LANGUAGE. NeLNL

Wright, Lee. POCKET MYSTERY READER, THE. **PoMyRe**
Yarmolinsky, Avraham. CONTEMPORARY GERMAN POETRY. **CGP**
———. TREASURY OF RUSSIAN VERSE, A. **TrRV**
Yeats, William Butler. OXFORD BOOK OF MODERN VERSE, THE, 1892-1935. **OBMV**
Yoseloff, Thomas. SEVEN POETS IN SEARCH OF AN ANSWER. **SePoSe**
Young, Karl. CENTURY READINGS IN ENGLISH LITERATURE. **CRE**
Zaturenska, Marya. MENTOR BOOK OF RELIGIOUS VERSE, THE. **MeRV**
———. SILVER SWAN, THE. **SiSw**
Zeitlin, Jacob. TYPES OF POETRY. **TOP**
Ziv, Frederic W. VALIANT MUSE, THE. **VM**